Solo Travel

A Wiley Brand

Solo Travel

by Lee Mylne

A Wiley Brand

Solo Travel For Dummies®

Published by: **John Wiley & Sons, Inc.**, 111 River Street, Hoboken, NJ 07030-5774, www.wiley.com

Copyright © 2024 by John Wiley & Sons, Inc., Hoboken, New Jersey

Media and software compilation copyright © 2024 by John Wiley & Sons, Inc. All rights reserved.

Published simultaneously in Canada

For general information on our other products and services, please contact our Customer Care Department within the U.S. at 877-762-2974, outside the U.S. at 317-572-3993, or fax 317-572-4002. For technical support, please visit https://hub.wiley.com/community/support/dummies.

Wiley publishes in a variety of print and electronic formats and by print-on-demand. Some material included with standard print versions of this book may not be included in e-books or in print-on-demand. If this book refers to media such as a CD or DVD that is not included in the version you purchased, you may download this material at http://booksupport.wiley.com. For more information about Wiley products, visit www.wiley.com.

Library of Congress Control Number: 2023951279

ISBN 978-1-394-21816-5 (pbk); ISBN 978-1-394-21817-2 (ebk); ISBN 978-1-394-21818-9 (ebk)

SKY10062806_121523

Contents at a Glance

Introduction... 1

CHAPTER 1: Exploring the World as a Solo Traveler 5

CHAPTER 2: Preparing for Your Solo Adventure................................... 19

CHAPTER 3: Managing the Logistics of Solo Travel 55

CHAPTER 4: You Can't Take It All with You: Packing............................ 81

CHAPTER 5: Don't Leave Home Without Them: Money, ID, and Devices 95

CHAPTER 6: A Room of Your Own 119

CHAPTER 7: Table for One 143

CHAPTER 8: Meeting People and Making New Friends....................... 159

CHAPTER 9: Keeping Healthy.. 181

CHAPTER 10: Ten Tips for Successful Solo Travel............................... 201

CHAPTER 11: Avoiding Ten Common Mistakes Solo Travelers Make.................. 209

CHAPTER 12: Ten Great Destinations for Solo Travelers....................... 215

Index... 227

Table of Contents

INTRODUCTION...1
    About This Book 1
    Foolish Assumptions...2
    Icons Used in This Book..3
    Beyond the Book 3
    Where to Go from Here...4

CHAPTER 1: **Exploring the World as a Solo Traveler** 5
    The Pros and Cons of Going It Alone 6
        Why traveling alone may be the best decision
        you ever make...6
        Knowing it won't all be smooth sailing..............................8
        Why solo travel doesn't have to break the budget...........9
        Things to consider when traveling independently 10
        Is it safe to go it alone?...11
    Choosing Your Destination 12
        Exploring new places...13
        Revisiting favorite destinations 14
    Encountering Others on Your Solo Journey 17

CHAPTER 2: **Preparing for Your Solo Adventure**...........................19
    Where Should You Go — and When? 20
        Choosing the right destination...20
        Picking the best time to travel..21
        Keeping an eye on travel advisories.................................22
        Staying safe in strange places 23
    How to Find the Best Travel Deals 26
        How to get there on a budget 26
        Avoiding the dreaded single supplement.......................29
        Using public transport...31
    Choosing an Adventure Holiday for One....................................35
        Pull on your hiking boots 35
        Sailing into the wild blue yonder......................................38
        Pedal power...42
        Hitting the slopes on skis or snowboard 44
        Giddy-up! Horse-riding holidays 46
        Lending a hand by volunteering 48
        Running away...51

CHAPTER 3: **Managing the Logistics of Solo Travel** 55

Preparing to Make Your Solo Adventure a Reality 56
Doing your homework 56
Checking health requirements 59
Maximizing your travel rewards programs 60
Up, up, and away — getting the most from airlines 61
Making the most of transit time 63
Being Prepared When Things Go Wrong 66
Purchasing travel insurance for one 66
Using your credit card for insurance coverage 69
Making an emergency plan 71
Handling health emergencies 72
When Mother Nature decides to intervene 73
Dealing with lost luggage 74
Self-defense and street smarts 76
Taking Steps to Reassure Your Loved Ones 78

CHAPTER 4: **You Can't Take It All with You: Packing** 81

Enjoying the Benefits of Packing Light 82
Choosing the Right Luggage 83
Packing the Essentials 84
Packing with your destination in mind 85
Reining in the urge to overpack 85
Saving Space When You Pack 87
Useful Items and Gadgets 90
Chargers, adapters, and other tech gadgets 90
Other helpful items and gadgets 92

CHAPTER 5: **Don't Leave Home Without Them:
Money, ID, and Devices** 95

Going International? Passport and Visa Requirements 96
Getting a passport 96
Which visa is right for you? 97
Coping with Customs and taxes 98
Choosing Credit, Cash, or a Combination 100
Credit cards 101
Debit cards 102
Prepaid travel money cards 102
Cash 103
Whatever happened to traveler's checks? 105

Keeping in Touch with Home..106
    Setting up your phone and other devices 106
    Finding internet access anywhere 108
    Facebook (and other forums) can be your friend..................109
    The pitfalls of social media 111
Avoiding Scams..112
    Cheap airline ticket scams 113
    Visa scams...113
    Carry-my-bag scams...114
    Taxi scams..114
    Vehicle hire scams 115
    Wrong change or overcharging................................116
    Card skimming 116
    Fake ticket scams 116
    Friend or relative-in-need scams 117
    What to do if you're the victim of a scam...................118

CHAPTER 6: **A Room of Your Own**..................................119
Choosing the Right Accommodations for You...........................120
    What's your budget?...120
    Location, location, location 121
    Checking things out before you check in...................122
Hosteling at Any Age 123
    What to know about hostels....................................123
    How to find hostels..125
Becoming Part of the Family at a Homestay.........................126
    Knowing where to find homestay options..................127
    B&Bs — A homestay and hotel hybrid 128
Cheap and Cheerful Budget Stays.....................................130
    Airbnb and home-swapping.....................................130
    House-sitting 131
    Couchsurfing 131
    The Y-M-C-A! (and other nonprofit orgs).................132
    University rooms..132
    Pubs..133
    Temple stays...134
    Monastery stays 136
Splashing Out for Some R&R at a Ritzy Resort 136
Package Holidays for One 138
Staying Safe in Your Space 139

CHAPTER 7: **Table for One**...143

    Tackling the Fear of Eating Out Alone.................................144

        Selecting a good spot for a solo meal 145

        Enjoying cheap eats and street food..........................147

    Tips for Coping with Dining Alone.......................................152

    How to Avoid Unwanted Company.......................................156

    Enjoying Culinary Experiences as Entertainment..........157

CHAPTER 8: **Meeting People and Making New Friends**...........159

    Doing Your Cultural Homework 160

        Respecting local laws and traditions 160

        Dress to impress 163

        Learning the local lingo 164

    Socializing When You're Out and About..............................166

        Where to meet fellow travelers.................................167

        How to meet the locals 168

    Sex and the Single Traveler..170

        Dating in a new country 171

        Staying safe: STDs and other pitfalls 174

        Issues for LGBTI+ travelers 176

        Using your intuition 177

        Little white lies to keep you safe...............................179

CHAPTER 9: **Keeping Healthy** 181

    Preparing to Travel in Good Health 182

    Staying Healthy While You're Away.....................................183

        Avoiding "economy class syndrome".......................183

        Beating the dreaded jetlag 184

        Practicing good hygiene..186

        Drinking the water (or not) 187

        Doing your best to avoid gastro bugs and other nasties.......187

        Coping with COVID..188

        Staying away from alcohol and other stimulants 189

        Sexual health 191

        Avoiding accidents 192

        Getting help when you need it 193

    How to Beat the Blues 194

        Combating loneliness...194

        Exercising around the world..196

        Mindfulness and other strategies..............................197

    Dealing with Decision Fatigue..198

CHAPTER 10: **Ten Tips for Successful Solo Travel**...........................201

Research Your Destination..201
Plan Your Budget...202
Choose the Right Accommodation.................................203
Make an Effort to Meet People.......................................203
Make Safety a Priority...204
Take Public Transport..204
Soak Up the Local Culture...205
Be Flexible..206
Do Something You Wouldn't Normally Do.....................206
Embrace the Freedom...208

CHAPTER 11: **Avoiding Ten Common Mistakes Solo Travelers Make**..209

Not Doing Your Research...210
Packing Too Much..210
Sharing Too Much Personal Information with Strangers...........211
Not Listening to the Locals..211
Being Careless or Too Trusting..211
Letting Fear Take Over...212
Being Too Polite...213
Not Keeping Track of Documents....................................213
Getting Tired and Emotional...214
Not Asking for Help When You Need It............................214

CHAPTER 12: **Ten Great Destinations for Solo Travelers**.........215

Australia...216
Austria..217
Finland..217
Ireland..218
Japan..219
New Zealand...220
Scotland...221
Singapore...222
Thailand..223
Vietnam..224

INDEX...227

Introduction

Traveling has long been an important part of my life. The bug bit me hard when I was in my 20s and I've never stopped . . . except for that little blip during 2020, 2021, and 2022, when a pandemic kept most everyone at home. Even then, when border closures kept me within my home state in Australia, I was able to continue to see the parts of it I hadn't seen before.

I was already widely traveled when I swapped my career as a newspaper journalist for the peripatetic life of a travel writer. It seemed a natural continuation of a passion that has grown as the years passed and shows no signs of dimming. I have traveled solo, with friends and partners, with my family, as part of tour groups, and with other travel writers on press trips. Every way of traveling has its own pros and cons, but solo travel brings a different dimension to exploring new places.

For me, solo travel results in the best stories, the ones that are often found when I divert from the day's plan to follow an intriguing road sign or to visit a place that someone's told me about the night before. It's the result of freedom to change direction on a whim or linger for longer in a place that calls for more time.

Traveling solo opens up the world in a way you may not expect. If you're daunted by the thought of going it alone, be assured that the rewards are great. Solo travel will change you and your view of the world. As you leave the comfort of everything you know to see new places and meet new people, cherish every moment — along with every mistake you make — and know that you'll return home with memories and stories to last a lifetime (or at least until the bug bites again).

About This Book

If the idea of solo travel is daunting, you're not alone. It takes a certain amount of confidence to take that first step toward going it alone. Even if you are an experienced traveler, there is a different dimension to traveling alone that might make you hesitate. This book is designed to allay those fears and to show you that with thorough planning, good research, and backup plans, you can cope with anything that the world throws at you.

I've written countless travel articles for publications around the world as well as about a dozen guide books. I've visited 65 countries, lived in 6 of them, and undertaken some big overland adventures in Europe and the Middle East. You'll read about some of my experiences as a solo traveler — and the mistakes I've made — in these pages.

I've taken a global approach to writing this book, knowing that some of you will be reading this in the USA, Canada, the United Kingdom, Australia, or New Zealand. And you'll all be looking to travel in different parts of the world, making your way to every continent as you explore our beautiful planet.

This book aims to give you the tools to set out on your own and confidently go it alone, making friends along the way and returning home — no matter how long or short your journey is — with a new sense of self-reliance. As the Chinese philosopher Laozi said, "A journey of a thousand miles begins with a single step." Reading this book may be the first step you take on your solo travel journey.

Foolish Assumptions

While writing this book I've made the assumption that many of you are either just beginning to consider solo travel as an option or are wondering if it's something you can actually do.

I also assumed that, like me, you already have a deep love of travel but for various reasons you haven't traveled solo before. You certainly don't want to stop traveling, so the other option is to go it alone. But there's some hesitation there — a fear of the unknown, perhaps. That's why you are reading this book — to help you make up your mind.

You may be young and fancy-free, hitting the backpacker trail on an extended trip, or planning to be a digital nomad. You might be an older adventurer but without a travel companion. Or you might simply enjoy being on your own and having the freedom to go where you please. Whatever your circumstances are, I've assumed that you need reassurance that solo travel is something within your ability to tackle — and I hope this book does that!

Icons Used in This Book

Throughout the book, I use a handful of icons to point out various types of information. Here's what they are and what they mean:

As I've traveled, I've found ways to make some aspects of solo travel easier. These tips should help you, too!

This is an important point that's key to solo travel or travel in general. It's a nudge to think about something you probably already know but need reminding of. Sometimes it's just about common sense.

A heads-up about something that might cause an issue, put you in danger, or is worth avoiding if possible.

This icon points out helpful online resources as well as items you can find on the resources page at www.dummies.com/go/solotravelfd.

Beyond the Book

I've put together an online resources page to help you find more information about some of the accommodations and organizations that can tell you more about everything that comes with being a solo traveler. Here's just some of what you'll find:

>> Links to websites with more background info on places mentioned in this book

>> Links to tourism businesses that are solo-friendly

>> Visa, passport, and other important travel info

Simply go to www.dummies.com/go/solotravelfd. Be sure to bookmark the site so you can easily find it later.

Where to Go from Here

Armed with the knowledge you'll glean from this book, you'll soon be ready to hit the road as a solo traveler, so start planning your next trip!

How should you navigate this book? You can start at the beginning and read it straight through if you want. There's lots of info throughout, and even if it's a section you're not sure you need, there might be some tips and tricks in there that might be useful.

If you're just beginning to think about whether you're ready to step out as a solo traveler, start with Chapters 1 through 4. They'll give you lots of reassurance that going solo is well within your grasp, and tips on how to plan and execute your first solo trip.

If you prefer, you can dip in and out of chapters that grab your interest or seem relevant to the travel you're planning. If you're wondering how to meet people on your travels, take a look at Chapter 8. Is dining alone your greatest fear? Turn to Chapter 7. If you're wondering where to stay, you'll find plenty of ideas in Chapter 6. If you're looking for ideas for where to go, turn to Chapter 12.

There's no time like the present to start planning your next trip. Thanks for reading this book first. I wish you safe and happy travels!

Chapter **1**

Exploring the World as a Solo Traveler

G oing out into the world as a solo traveler is something you should do at least once in your life. Even if you have traveled widely, the experience of traveling alone is one that will change you and the way you see the world.

Traveling to places beyond your home base expands your worldview and shows you that despite our differences, people are fundamentally the same the world over. By going it alone, you will open yourself to people and experiences in a way that traveling in the cocoon of companionship prevents. It's a brave step, but one that will change you in ways you can't imagine before you set out.

In this chapter, I discuss how to build your confidence when traveling solo for the first time, how to get the most out of going back to favorite destinations, and give you tips on how to stay safe when you're on the road alone.

FIND ONLINE

Throughout this book, I reference all kinds of online resources to help you plan and enjoy your travels. To find a handy list of links to all these resources, go to www.dummies.com/go/solotravelfd.

The Pros and Cons of Going It Alone

If you're new to solo travel — or just contemplating it for the first time — it might seem daunting. It's no small thing to be out there in the world on your own, with no support system or ready-made friend to share the ups and downs with. It's a worthwhile exercise to weigh up the pros and cons of traveling alone before you decide to abandon the idea — and with luck, you will come to see that the benefits of solo travel do outweigh the downsides.

Like life in general, all travel has its bad days and disappointments, especially if you are on the road for a long time. The hotel room might not be quite what you expected — but oh, how that sunset from the balcony makes up for the tiny bathroom! Then there are the truly awful days when you really just want nothing more than to go home to your own bed . . . but the next day will reveal something wonderful, and you remember why you are on this journey!

REMEMBER

This book is definitely pro–solo travel, but I also guide you through all the realities of a traveling life on your own, not just the good ones. As with all styles of travel, traveling alone can be a roller-coaster that you need to learn to ride. Knowing what the ups and downs might be is the first step towards a smooth ride.

Why traveling alone may be the best decision you ever make

Traveling solo may be the most empowering decision you ever make. No matter your age or gender, learning to be self-sufficient while dealing with everything that travel throws at you will teach you more about yourself than you could ever imagine before you start out.

From the moment you begin to plan your trip, you'll be free of the shackles of traveling with someone else. There's no need to wait for others to confirm their vacation dates or save up enough to travel. By traveling solo, you can start your trip whenever it suits *you* — and you alone! Take advantage of cheap deals, make your bookings instantly, and be spontaneous.

The same applies once you are on the road. Want to stay somewhere an extra day or two, or move on more quickly than you planned? You can do it. There are no compromises or negotiations to be made, no one to consult . . . just the freedom and flexibility to do exactly what you want to.

Solo travel will definitely push you out of your comfort zone, even if you're traveling in your own state or country. Knowing that — *expecting* it — will help you deal with it. You'll face your fears and overcome them (the worst ones will probably never even eventuate).

Making all the decisions, from where and when to go, how to get there, where to stay, how to cope when things go wrong (which they inevitably will sometimes) and meeting new people along the way will give you a new sense of independence. Your confidence will grow and your self-reliance will be stronger every day. You'll learn to deal with people of all kinds and to keep your-self safe in situations that you may not have encountered at home.

Most of all, traveling solo will change your perspective on the world. Without the distraction of a companion, you'll be more aware of your surroundings and more observant of what is around you.

REMEMBER

Solo travel also allows you to learn about yourself. Time on your own inevitably results in self-reflection — "Hey, I did that!" — and time to contemplate what you're seeing as you travel. It may make you appreciate what you have at home and how your life has panned out so far. Then there may be those moments when you give thanks for a life that is far removed from those you are see-ing on your travels. Clean running water — or *hot* water for your daily shower — may suddenly seem not so much a necessity, but a privilege.

If you're traveling to escape a difficult or traumatic situation — a romantic break-up, a job that didn't work out, a bereavement that you need time to adjust to — then traveling alone can be a healing process. Getting away from your everyday life and thinking about challenges you face on the road, or simply soaking up the beauty of the world, can put things in perspective again.

Solo travel gives you the space to be yourself, to take each day as it comes, ditch the pressures of your everyday life, and — even for a short while — become the person you know you really are.

Knowing it won't all be smooth sailing

All travel has its ups and downs, whether you're on your own or not. Solo travel might seem to amplify those highs and lows when you have to cope with them yourself. But knowing from the outset that it won't all be easy is the first step to dealing with problems when they occur.

There are moments when things go wrong when you'll really wish you had a traveling companion. For example, when you're waiting by the luggage carousel in Lisbon while your bag is holidaying in Havana, you're on your own, with no one to borrow clothes or toothpaste from. Or you lose your wallet and cards and there's no travel companion to lend you money to tide you over until the bank can sort things out for you. But you will cope because you always do!

Travel can be exhausting and it's important to look after yourself mentally, emotionally, and physically when you're traveling alone. It's quite natural to go through periods of loneliness or to feel homesick from time to time, and those times are likely to be when you're tired. Sometimes all you want is to have someone along to help you make decisions or to toss ideas around with. Just know that these feelings will pass. Take a day off from everything, curl up with a book, have a cry, and you'll be ready to tackle the world again.

Culture shock is one of the big things that can upset your equilibrium. When nothing is familiar, people don't behave the way they do at home, and you're floundering to make yourself understood, it can feel like you can't cope. But you will.

TIP

Doing your research before you leave home can help you anticipate and deal with culture shock if you are going to a foreign country. If you are well prepared for what you are seeing or experiencing, culture shock can be a great learning experience. Be open to the differences between what you are used to and how other people live. There may be a degree of discomfort, but that will ease as you adjust to new surroundings, new languages, and new sights, sounds, and smells.

Language barriers are one aspect of culture shock that may be hard to deal with; not everyone in the world speaks English, and communication may be difficult in some places. One of the biggest challenges you may face in some parts of the world is that you may not be able to make yourself understood, particularly in a situation where it is important, such as illness or being a victim of crime.

Solo travel will definitely help sharpen your problem-solving skills, and you will learn to be self-reliant very quickly.

Why solo travel doesn't have to break the budget

Travel expenses can be higher when you're a solo traveler, but that doesn't mean you'll have to scrimp to avoid busting your budget.

The most annoying part of solo travel on a budget — any budget — is the single supplement that's imposed by some tour companies and cruise ships. Hotels generally charge by the room rather than the person, so you'd be paying the same amount with a friend or partner, but sharing the cost; while that's not strictly a single supplement, the effect is the same. However, there are ways around it (see Chapter 6 for more details).

While solo travel means you don't have anyone to share the cost of things like accommodations or car rental with, it also means you have complete control over how, when, and how much you spend while you're traveling. Effective planning, knowing how much you have to spend, and pre-booking where you can in order to know what your available funds can stretch to are the keys to sticking to your budget.

TIP

The cost of accommodations can be kept to a minimum by choosing to house-sit, home swap, or stay in a shared room in a hostel (and if you don't fancy that, hostels have private rooms that are often cheaper than a hotel room). See Chapter 6 for more ideas on ways to keep your cost for accommodations down.

Traveling solo means no one is going to insist that you spend up big on a fancy dinner at a Michelin-starred restaurant . . . you can opt for those three-minute noodles in your room if you like. And if you do go to an expensive restaurant, as a solo diner you can order what you like without potentially having to subsidize someone else's menu choices, and you can savor every minute of the experience without distraction.

Look for ways of saving money — you have no one to negotiate with over how you do that — and make the most of free activities you can find in your destination. Many outdoor activities such as hiking or hitting the beach are free, as are many museums, galleries, and festivals.

REMEMBER

Overall, the independence you have as a solo traveler will be a benefit that will outweigh the fact that you have no one to share costs with.

Things to consider when traveling independently

Solo travel doesn't necessarily mean being on your own all the time. Some solo travelers prefer to travel, at least some of the time, as part of an organized group. That option might be something that if you are just starting out on your solo travel journey, you might want to consider — you'll be solo but not alone.

Purists might argue that joining a group tour is not solo travel, but I think it's a very reasonable way of easing yourself into a greater adventure in the future. As a first-time solo traveler, you will be gaining an insight into how you feel about being the solo in a crowd — and learning that you will likely never be the only one! If you are contemplating a trip to a place where you might be worried about security or about making cultural missteps, such as the Middle East or Africa, a group tour will give you reassurance that you'll have guides to lead you through the tricky parts.

Taking care of your health is vital to a successful solo trip. Preparation is important; make sure you have all the necessary vaccinations before leaving home and carry with you everything you'll need to deal with minor ailments or injury (see more in Chapter 9). With no companion to take charge if you get sick, it's important to avoid that happening if you possibly can. And I really can't stress too strongly how important it is to have travel insurance to cover not only any potential medical costs but also every aspect of what can go wrong when you're traveling.

Will you get lonely? The honest answer is yes, probably . . . at least sometimes. Maybe you'll be missing someone's birthday or a family gathering of some kind. Maybe you've just spent too much time on your own lately and need to start reconnecting with other travelers or meeting the locals in a more meaningful way.

When everything around you is unfamiliar, or things don't quite go to plan, it's easy to give in to loneliness. The trick is not to bury yourself in your room, but to get back out there and engage with the world again. Have a good cry, then get on with it.

Recognize that there will always be moments when you wish you had someone to share the experience with, but comfort yourself with the thought that at least *you* are getting to do it (rather than sitting home, dreaming about it).

Is it safe to go it alone?

All travel comes with risks, but that's no reason to stay home. Life is full of risks, and people take them every day without thinking too much about it. As a solo traveler, particularly abroad, you'll need to keep your wits about you and take precautions that you might not bother about at home — but for the most part, you'll be safe as long as you're sensible and maintain an awareness of your surroundings.

Research your destination before you go, even if you're traveling in your own country. Find out which neighborhoods to avoid or if there are particular scams you should know about. Talk to other people who might have visited your chosen destination, or look at social media sites that might have useful information about the area you'll be in.

Basic security measures — like not leaving your drink unattended in a bar, keeping your cash or valuables out of sight (or locked in your hotel room safe), and not walking alone at night — will help lessen your risk of assault or robbery. For women solo travelers, an extra level of vigilance should be applied, particularly about revealing that you are traveling alone or where you are staying. Being friendly is fine, but in some cultures this can be misinterpreted. Again, research is the key.

REMEMBER

Traveling alone is common, and most trips are without any major safety issues for solo travelers. Common sense, knowledge of the place you are visiting, and some basic precautions (outlined in Chapter 3) will help to keep you as safe as possible.

Choosing Your Destination

If you've already taken the plunge into solo travel, you're halfway there when it comes to choosing your next destination. If you're still on the fence and trying to decide where to go for your first foray into the world of solo, I would suggest starting small and close.

What I mean by that is choose a destination in your home country. If you're not sure you'll be comfortable as a solo traveler, test the water by traveling without one of the major stresses of language problems. If you're in your home country, you won't have any trouble being understood or following what's going on around you.

TIP

A weekend away is a good test. If you can do two days away on your own, you can likely do a week. Build your confidence slowly before tackling a longer trip. Take a road trip to a nearby town where there's plenty to see and do, or go and hang out at a resort for a couple of days. There's no rule about what style of trip you need to take. It's all about *knowing* you can do this on your own!

If you just fancy winding down with a cocktail and a good book beside a swimming pool . . . do it! If you want to go hiking in a national park, lace up those boots. The choice is yours, and that's the beauty of solo travel.

Once you've built up that confidence, look at going further away. If you're going abroad on your own for the first time, the same thing applies — choose an English-speaking country, where the culture shock won't be so great. You'll still find plenty of differences, whether you're in the United Kingdom, Ireland, Canada, the USA, Australia, New Zealand, the Pacific, or the Caribbean — but at least the language will be the same.

Step three will be to up the ante again, and book a ticket to somewhere that's completely foreign to you. Do your research, of course, but by now you'll be match-fit for solo travel and ready to handle anything. In Chapter 12, I suggest a few places I have traveled solo that I think you'll enjoy.

Exploring new places

Take the advice of the Dalai Lama: "Once a year, go somewhere you've never been before."

There's a certain thrill attached to the prospect of going somewhere you've never been before. I find this even if it's somewhere in my own country! That expectation and anticipation of what you might find and who you might meet never grows stale.

Of course, you will have done your research before you arrive, but a good way to introduce yourself to a new city is to take a short tour that will give you the lay of the land. Depending on what kind of traveler you are, choose a method that best suits you.

Walking tours are terrific, giving you the chance to talk to the guide or to other people on the tour, picking up some tips for what to see or where to go later on. It's also a brilliant way to counteract jetlag when you've just arrived. Another way of tackling this introduction to a big city is to take a bus tour, such as those hop-on, hop-off tours that cover all the major sights.

If you're in a smaller place, I recommend just pounding the pavement on your own. Work out what you want to see and head out with your phone or a map to guide you. Or just wander and see where you end up (without getting lost, hopefully). Ask at your hotel about what the locals recommend, chat to people in coffee shops or small stores you might visit. The locals will have the best ideas.

The first time I ever stayed in Bangkok's Chinatown district I took a free walking tour offered by my hotel. It ended at what is reputedly Chinatown's oldest coffee shop, founded in 1927 and still owned by the same family. It's a time capsule, with paint peeling off the walls, the clientele mostly elderly men, smoking, gossiping, and drinking strong black coffee. I would never have found it on my own.

Cross off the major sights you want to see, then explore further. Check if there are any events on that interest you and head out to concerts, markets, festivals.

WARNING

Whenever you are exploring a new place, find out which neighborhoods to avoid. Wandering is wonderful, but your safety must be a priority.

If you have a particular interest, or if your destination is known for something special, try to find a tour that fits that. If you're a cook, look for a cooking class or food tour that focuses on the region's specialty or maybe you'd like to learn to play an instrument that is associated with the place you're visiting. I'm not a foodie, but I love art and can happily wander any city looking at the sculptures, statues, and street art. Public art is free, and you never know what's around the next corner.

Taking public transport is another way to take a dive into a city's real life. Not only is it a cheap way of getting around, you'll be traveling alongside the people who live there.

TIP

Even if you're not planning to self-cater, pop in to a supermarket — it's a revelation! I was astounded at the aisles and aisles of vodka on sale alongside groceries in Polish supermarkets, and I love to look at the unfamiliar labels on products in foreign languages and try to guess what they might be. Even if there's a language barrier, usually some sign language with a local will give you the idea.

Nowhere is exactly what you expect. You can do as much research as you like, but the reality will always be just a little bit different and surprising. And that is one of the joys of travel.

Revisiting favorite destinations

If you find somewhere you love, there's nothing to stop you returning again and again. I've been to Thailand eight times and to Vietnam five times. My first overseas trip, as a 19-year-old traveling solo, was to Norfolk Island, a tiny island in the South Pacific, pictured in Figure 1-1. I've been back four times over the years. You can't keep me away from New Zealand, and that's not only because I have family and friends there.

While it might seem strange to return to the same place again and again, when there are so many other places in the world to explore, keep in mind that each country is multifaceted and has many different destinations and experiences to enjoy. On your first visit, you might tick off the must-do sights and experiences, but that's not all that a place has to offer. Scratch the surface of any city or region in a country, and you'll find the differences that make it worthwhile going back again and again. If you really fall in love with a particular destination, you'll want to get to know it as well as you can — and that might mean returning more than once.

FIGURE 1-1: Norfolk Island, a tiny island in the South Pacific.

Take my Vietnam trips as an example. My first visit was aboard a large cruise ship, which sailed from Singapore to Ho Chi Minh City (Saigon). I didn't care for the cruising part very much, but I absolutely fell in love with Vietnam. Among the passengers on the ship were a group of Vietnamese war veterans who were returning to Con Dao Island, which had been used as a prisoner-of-war camp in several eras of Vietnamese history. Our day on the island was an insight into an element of war history that I didn't know, from the Vietnamese perspective, and I learned something of the veterans' history with this place.

On my second trip, I hit the main tourist stops — Ho Chi Minh City, Hue, Hoi An, and Hanoi — ticking them off, seeing more history, and having some cheap clothes made by the skillful tailors who whip up whatever you want the same day. My third trip was to the resort island of Phu Quoq in the south, with a few days in Saigon.

On my fourth visit, I concentrated on the north of Vietnam, heading from Hanoi to beautiful Ha Long Bay, where I spent a night aboard a traditional junk among the limestone outcrops that make it famous (that's more my style of cruising). Then it was on, by overnight sleeper train, to the highlands of Sapa where the highlight was market day, attended by hill tribes in their colorful traditional dress, pictured in Figure 1-2.

Lee Mylne(Author)

FIGURE 1-2: Colorful dress of hill tribes, Sapa, Vietnam.

A few years later, my next visit was split between the beach resort town of Nha Trang and the hill town of Da Lat, where I munched on fried crickets, visited a silkworm factory, and saw the surrounding countryside on a motorbike tour.

Every time I returned, there was something new and different to discover and explore. And I know if I go again, there will be another layer of this fascinating place to peel back.

So if you find somewhere you enjoy but don't have time to see everything, keep it in mind for a return visit. Sometimes short trips with bite-sized exploration is a better way of seeing a place. The worst thing is to try to see *everything* in a short time. You'll be moving so fast, you'll get only a glimpse, a brief impression of what the place is about. Stay put in one city, state, or region and get an in-depth look at what it has to offer.

When you travel far — from one hemisphere or continent to another — it's tempting to try to see it all, but slow travel is going to give you a more authentic look at a destination. That doesn't mean you have to stay a long time, but rather than rushing around, slow your pace and you'll enjoy the experience more.

Encountering Others on Your Solo Journey

You are much more likely to meet new people if you're traveling solo. It's easy to stay in your little bubble with a traveling companion and not branch out and talk to others. Solo, you are much more approachable to other people and you are more open to making those new connections, whether they are fellow travelers, expats, or locals.

If you're staying in hostels, you'll find plenty of chances to meet new friends or even potential travel buddies, for a few days (or longer, if that's what you're looking for). Apart from staying at close quarters in a dorm, many hostels are great at organizing social events, so it's unlikely you'll ever be lonely. If you're on a well-worn tourist path, it's not unusual to run into the same people again later in your trip.

You'll also meet fellow travelers by signing up for tours. Often the best ones are those that involve an activity or adventure component, such as a group hike or a kayaking tour, where you're all in the same boat (so to speak).

Connecting with locals is often more difficult. Learning the language is a good start, even if it's just a smattering of phrases that show you are interested in communicating with them. If you are going abroad, it's definitely a good idea to do some serious research into cultural differences, to ensure that you do not give unintended offense or breach any customs or rules. But with some effort on your part, and goodwill on theirs, you can usually make meaningful connections with people from your host country. Smiles and genuine attempts to communicate go a huge way to breaking down barriers.

REMEMBER

Solo travel will make you a better communicator, whether you are looking for a doorway to understanding another culture, a short-term travel companion, or even a romantic liaison. In Chapter 9, you can discover more about all these aspects of traveling solo.

Chapter **2**

Preparing for Your Solo Adventure

The secret of successful solo travel is all in the planning. Good preparation is going to spare you unnecessary trouble and trauma. And to be honest, being well-organized ensures you'll have more time to soak up all your chosen destination has to offer if you're not wasting it sorting out tangled messes of travel arrangements. Being prepared before you board your plane, train, or ship is going to be well worth the effort.

In this chapter, I share some tips for ensuring that it's all smooth sailing (so to speak). From deciding where to go to planning your itinerary, pre-booking what and where you can, and making sure you have all your essential documents, such as passport or other ID, in order. Then there is the on-the-road advice I've gleaned from my own travels and those of my solo-traveling friends. All of it is designed to reinforce your belief that traveling alone can be as much fun — or more — than you ever expected.

If being a free agent is the traveling style that appeals to you, this chapter can get you started with practical information to prepare for your solo adventure. Whether it's your first, or whether you're a veteran of going it alone, I hope you'll find useful insights into planning a great trip, be it short or long.

Find links to all the web addresses mentioned in this chapter, along with other helpful resources, at www.dummies.com/go/solotravelfd.

Where Should You Go — and When?

The right destination can make — or break — your trip. Part of the thrill of planning your trip is the anticipation of seeing that place you've always longed to visit. Perhaps you've always wanted to come face-to-face with an orangutan in Borneo or dreamed of hiking in the Himalayas. Whatever your ideal vacation is, doing your homework before you set out will be the key to ensuring you're not disappointed.

Choosing the right destination

The secret of successful solo travel is partly about choosing a destination that's welcoming and open to those traveling alone. You want to be comfortable and — unless you're an absolute hermit — you want to engage with people along the way, whether they're locals or fellow travelers. Traveling is as much about the people you meet and the conversations you have as it is about the places you see. It's about learning to be part of the wider world, seeing how other people live, and soaking up the differences and similarities between you all, no matter where or how you live your life.

Also make sure that your desired destination isn't infamous as a hotspot for tourist scams or crime. Use government websites, travel guides, social media, blogs, and news sites to do some research (more on this later in this chapter in the section, "Keeping an eye on travel advisories") and speak to people you know who have visited the destination.

TIP

If you're traveling solo for the first time, you may want to choose somewhere you'll be comfortable with. That may be as simple as staying in your own country but exploring part of it that you've never seen before. Or it may be going to another English-speaking country where language barriers aren't going to add to your nerves about being out there on your own for the first time. Once you become at ease with your own ability to handle the challenges that solo travel brings — and you *will* — then it might be time to push the boundaries a little further.

Picking the best time to travel

When to go is as important as where. Once you have a destination in mind, do some research into the seasons and weather that might impact your vacation. Is it typhoon season? Will it be horribly humid or wet? Is the best time to go when the fall colors are at their most vibrant? Traveling in the high season may mean you have the best weather, but the prices may be sky-high, and the crowds may be daunting. Do you really want to queue for hours for entry to the Louvre in Paris or La Sagrada Familia in Barcelona? Or be surrounded by noisy families during school vacation time?

TIP

Check out what's happening in your destination before you book. Unless you really want to attend that fabulous festival, it might be best to avoid the higher prices and harder-to-find accommodation — not to mention the crowds. At the same time, knowing what's on may increase your interest in the place. And don't forget that if you'll only have a couple of days in one place, you want to be sure that the art museum you so desperately want to visit will be open on those days. Check for public holidays that might impact your travel plans.

Do some research into which are the peak, shoulder and low travel seasons in your chosen destination before making your travel bookings. Your budget may depend on it!

For example, in most of Australia and New Zealand the peak season is from mid-December to the end of January when schools empty for the long summer break. During that time, beaches are crowded and airline seats are in high demand.

REMEMBER

The seasons may be topsy-turvy, depending on where you're going. When it's winter in the northern hemisphere, it's summer in places like Australia and New Zealand in the southern hemisphere, and vice versa.

TIP

Seasonal events can also have an impact on your travel experience. In some countries, religious or cultural holidays, such as Ramadan or Chinese New Year, mean huge numbers of domestic travelers are on the move, which can mean peak demand — and crowds — for transport. The advantage of this is that if you stay in big cities during this time, they're less likely to be crowded. Large festivals, such as cherry blossom time in Japan, should also be factored into your trip planning.

Another factor to consider when planning your trip is the cost of living in your destination. Compare the cost of basic items, including dining out, with what you would expect to pay at home and decide whether your budget will stand it. For example, Scandinavian countries such as Norway, Denmark, and Finland are renowned for being budget-busting places to spend any length of time, as is Iceland. Islands such as the Caymans, Bora Bora, New Caledonia, or Fiji, where everything is imported, are also likely to have higher prices.

In Chapter 12, I share some personal favorite destinations that might whet your appetite for your next vacation.

Keeping an eye on travel advisories

As dull as it may sound, government departments can be your best source of advice when it comes to staying safe while traveling to foreign climes. Government travel advisories are designed to give you up-to-date information that will help you decide whether it's currently safe to travel to a particular country and help you reduce the potential risks or problems associated with traveling there.

Are there protests or political unrest in your country of choice? A natural disaster unfolding? Are terrorist attacks likely? What health risks might you be exposed to?

**FIND
ONLINE**

The governments of the USA, Canada, United Kingdom, and Australia, among others, provide this online advice for their traveling citizens (find links to those countries' pages at www. dummies.com/go/solotravelfd). Advice levels range from a heads-up or telling you to exercise normal levels of caution (as you would at home) to "do not travel" directives.

WARNING

High-risk travel areas could put you at risk of kidnapping, hostage-taking, theft, and other crimes, or serious injury. In such areas, there is often little diplomatic or consular support for travelers and limited assistance if you get into serious trouble.

As well as general advice on a wide range of travel topics, such as local laws, health, and safety, these websites can also tell you what to do when things go wrong and where you can seek help from your embassy or consulate.

Be aware that deciding to travel against the government advice could also impact your ability to file a claim on your travel insurance if things do go horribly wrong.

REMEMBER

It's your own responsibility to be fully informed about the destination(s) you are visiting — even if only in transit — and to keep aware of potentially changing circumstances.

It's also a sensible idea to sign up to the free **Smart Traveler Enrollment Program** (STEP; https://step.state.gov/step/) to receive alerts and updates while traveling and to allow the government — or your family — to locate you in an emergency. When you enroll, you will receive important information about safety conditions in your destination. STEP enrollment also ensures that the nearest US embassy or consulate will be able to contact you if conditions change, so you can change your travel plans if necessary or take advantage of any assistance they can offer you. While this is for American citizens, other countries have similar programs for their citizens. In Australia, this is called **Smart Traveller** (www.smarttraveller.gov.au), while Canada has a **Registration of Canadians Abroad** service (www.travel.gc.ca/travelling/registration). For the United Kingdom, check www.gov.uk/foreign-travel-advice to search for information about countries or territories and sign up for email updates.

Staying safe in strange places

All travel has inherent risks, but minimizing them is the key to a successful holiday. For solo travelers, some of those risks might be increased — and that's certainly the case for solo female travelers, even in relatively "safe" countries. But my advice here should apply to *all* travelers, because we are all somewhat vulnerable when we are out of our comfort zones.

Taking precautions before leaving home is the first step. This includes finding out all you can about the risk of traveling to your chosen destination and registering your trip with your government agency (see "Keeping an eye on travel advisories," earlier in this chapter). Knowledge is power.

Women traveling alone, of course, are more likely to stand out in the crowd and in some places to look and dress differently to local women, making them potential targets for unwanted male attention. Most of the time, this might only be stares or comments but it can be uncomfortable. A few tips to help minimize this discomfort are:

» **Research the local culture and customs before you arrive and do your best to conform to them.**

» **If you're visiting a conservative or religious place, dress appropriately.** No matter how hot it is, cover your shoulders, arms and sometimes legs and head. I always pack a sarong or shawl that can fit into a day bag for unexpected times when it might be needed. This might be while visiting a Buddhist temple in Asia or any place in the Middle East where conservative dress is expected. Loose clothing is not only cooler in many places, but also does not show your curves. *Note:* Men should also be aware that in some places, bare legs are not acceptable, so pack some light long trousers just in case you need them.

» **Buy a wedding ring.** A cheap gold band on your ring finger may help deter amorous suitors. Sadly, in some countries, married women are treated with more respect than single women.

» **Pack flat, comfortable shoes.** It will help if you need to run and makes you look less vulnerable. Imagine sprinting in heels on a cobblestone street? No thanks.

» **Learn some key phrases in the local language.** Saying, "No," or, "Go away," or something similar but more offensive can be very effective if delivered forcefully. You can see the shock of the unexpected on the face of the recipient!

» **Use a free safety app.** Apps like RedZone, MayDay, Tripwhistle, Chirpey and Noonlight allow you to report incidents and areas of danger and to contact police in your location. SafeUP is an app designed to help women and nonbinary people feel safer in unfamiliar surroundings. Available in 38 countries, the app connects a user by voice or video call to nearby trained volunteers who will stay on the line as long as necessary, notify the police, or even show up in person to walk with the app user if requested. You can access it in the USA, Canada, United Kingdom, across Europe and Scandinavia, Australia, New Zealand, Israel, and Iceland, including in places as small as Cyprus, Malta, and Gibraltar.

If you don't fancy the idea of a group tour but would still like company for part of your trip, there are many apps that can match you up with a compatible travel buddy. The women-only Tourlina is one option, where you enter your destination and travel dates to be matched with other verified users who will be in the same place at the same time. This is a good option if you'll be traveling to places where you might prefer not to be alone.

TIP

The safest place in the world for travel in 2023, according to an annual report by travel insurance provider Berkshire Hathaway Travel Protection (BHTP), is the Netherlands, with Switzerland taking the title for solo women travelers.

Other female-focused websites include www.adventurewomen. com, www.blackgirltraveltoo.com, and https://wildwomen expeditions.com. Facebook groups such as **Solo Female Travelers** and **The Solo Female Traveler Network** are also great sources of support and advice.

Solo travelers — of any gender — don't have the advantage of safety in numbers and need to be more aware of potential dangers. While it's unlikely to happen, it's better to be prepared for trouble and to avoid it before it starts. Some tips that you can put into play before you leave home include:

>> **Invest in a sturdy, theft-proof bag to carry.** Choose one that stays closely strapped to your body, such as a crossbody bag or belt bag. Look for one with features such as secure zippers, slash-resistant straps, and strong fabric. If you use a backpack, which is much easier for thieves to access, don't keep anything valuable or important in it.

>> **Make a "secondary" wallet or purse, with some expired credit cards and a small amount of cash in it.** If confronted by a mugger, hand that over while keeping your real wallet, cards, or cash well hidden. By the time the thief realizes their mistake, hopefully they'll have put a safe distance between you.

>> **Consider a self-defense course if you are traveling to a risky place.** Knowing some basic techniques may be useful if you are mugged or inadvertently get involved in an argument, no matter what gender you are.

Personal safety is not the only thing you need to worry about while you're on the road — especially if you're taking a solo road trip. Driving long distances alone can be very tiring, so make sure you have plenty of rest breaks where you actually get out of the car, get some fresh air, and stretch. Fatigue is a number one killer on the roads. If you are driving in a foreign country, be hyper-aware of your surroundings and whether you are driving on the wrong side of the road. While the US, Canada, South America, and Europe drive on the right-hand side, in the UK, Australia, New Zealand, India, Japan, parts of Africa, and some other countries, vehicles stick to the left. Take special care when the traffic is not busy, as that's when you're most likely to make a mistake!

Knowing the road rules, speed limits, and any quirks of motoring where you are traveling is important. Driving while under the influence of alcohol or drugs incurs heavy penalties in most places, so be sure to comply!

How to Find the Best Travel Deals

Solo travel is always going to be more expensive than splitting some of the costs with a companion. Any way of keeping costs down from the get-go is going to help keep your budget in check and give you more to spend on the things that really matter.

How to get there on a budget

When planning your travel, be eagle-eyed in looking for the best deals on getting there. As you may be aware, airfares are sky-high after the COVID pandemic, but shopping around, jumping on deals, and being flexible will help you snag the lowest fares.

If flying, use a price comparison website that will allow you to judge which airlines are offering deals (I suggest a few at www.dummies.com/go/SoloTravelFD). When flying from Australia to New Zealand, I looked at Qantas and Air New Zealand — the two national carriers that were the obvious choices — and then at other major carriers on the route such as Emirates and Etihad. By using Skyscanner (www.skyscanner.net), I came up with a better option, both in departure and arrival times, on China Airlines — a Taiwanese carrier I had never heard of before — for around half the price being offered by the other airlines (and with much more convenient arrival and departure times). So sometimes it's the unexpected options that will work best for you and you may just end up with a new favorite airline.

Look at stopover options when planning your flights. Sometimes it's not the direct flights to your destination that are the cheapest, with the added benefit that you just may be able to add a couple of days at another destination to your itinerary.

Consider flying into a smaller airport, used by smaller airlines for their lower operating costs. For example, if you're headed to Paris, instead of booking to Charles De Gaulle Airport, look at flights to Orly. Similarly, London's Luton, Stansted, City, or Gatwick airports are equally well connected to the city, all still less than an hour by express train. In New York, flying from Long Island MacArthur Airport will mean you pay less than if you booked a flight from JFK or La Guardia. Add in the lower cost of parking at a smaller airport, and you're well ahead.

Flying isn't the only option, of course. Trains and buses may be slower but if you're not constrained by time, they may also be significantly cheaper. Overnight trains have the advantage of saving you a night's accommodation as well as getting you to your destination. And it's much better for the planet!

Bus and train passes can be a great value if you're planning on traveling for more than a week or so. You may still have to book your seat ahead of time, but passes that allow you to hop on and off at various stops can deliver good savings.

TIP

Rome2Rio (www.rome2rio.com) is a fantastic website for checking out the cheapest way to get from one place to another, covering thousands of options for train, bus, ferry, and flight routes across the world. It also gives you rates for hotels and rental cars.

TIP

If your travel dates are flexible, consider traveling in the shoulder or offseason. If you want to travel but don't really mind where you go, look for deals to *anywhere!* Since you're going solo, you don't need to wait to consult anyone else — so grab that deal and book it while you can! Make sure you avoid school holiday times and book flights as far in advance as you can. Choose your day of travel carefully, too. Midweek travel prices are usually lower, and the time of day matters, too. Travel early or late in the day for the best deals. Low-cost budget airlines are bearable for short flights and regularly have cheap deals.

Traveling light can also help your budget if you are flying to your destination. Avoid any baggage fees by traveling with carry-on only (see more in Chapter 4).

If you plan to take to the seas, book as early as you can for the best cruising deals. Last-minute bargains are less likely as demand for cruises grows in the post-pandemic world. Sign up for cruise line newsletters or to their Facebook and Twitter accounts for specials, spot sales, and promotional offers.

Book an "inside" cabin for the best price on a cruise ship. True, there's no window but it's much less expensive than those on the outside of the ship, let alone those with a balcony. You want to be out of your cabin anyway, meeting people and taking advantage of all the facilities offered, don't you? Use the cabin for sleeping only!

If you fancy river cruising more than the high seas, you've made a good choice budget-wise. Most river cruises are all-inclusive, meaning you have a clearer idea of your budget and don't need to spend more on-board for meals, drinks, or shore excursions.

TIP

Booking all your travel through one tour company can often result in savings. As well as your tour, ask about airfares, airport transfers, and pre- and post-tour accommodation in cities you want to explore further. However, this is not always the case, so do the math first.

TIP

Consider using free cash-back apps that share with you some of the commission they earn from your purchases (usually between 1 and 5 percent). Some have links to credit cards or accommodation providers or organizations such as PayPal. Some travel booking sites, such as Booking.com offer discounts to frequent users. However, be aware that sometimes prices are inflated and shop around to ensure you are getting a genuine deal.

On tours that offer add-on half-day or day tours at an extra cost, investigate how easy it would be get there on your own and what it would cost. Often, it's not necessary to be part of the crowd, or there may be something else you'd prefer to spend the time doing. On one of my early solo travels, my room-share companion in Paris broke away from the tour for an afternoon because she wanted to visit the Musee Rodin, which wasn't included on our itinerary. It was a lesson to me, that if you want it enough, insist on some flexibility from your tour operator.

When booking online, make sure to check which currency you're paying in, as the exchange rate might affect your budget. It's always better to pay in your own currency if you can and save those foreign currency transaction fees. See more advice on managing your travel funds in Chapter 5.

Avoiding the dreaded single supplement

Traveling solo sometimes comes at a hefty price, often in the form of the "single supplement." One of the ghastly realities of traveling alone is that you pay for that privilege. Most hotels base their room rates on double or twin occupancy — whether there are two people in the room or just one! The reasoning behind this is that it still costs the same to clean and prepare the room, even if there's only one occupant.

WARNING

As a solo traveler, you may pay the same as two people sharing. Single supplements can range from 10 to 100 percent of the standard double/twin rate. It applies equally to accommodation of other kinds, too, such as a cabin on a cruise ship. In a very few cases, some single supplements are more than a double rate because a solo traveler is considered to spend less on things like food, drinks, and entertainment.

In hotels, there's really no way around this if you're traveling independently, but for those who choose a tour or package deal, it is possible to avoid the dreaded single supplement.

The first thing is to check the company's policy on single supplements. Be aware that some who say "no single supplement" really just mean that they offer the opportunity to share with another solo traveler, but if you *really* want a room of your own you *will* have to pay extra. That said, there are a few companies that don't charge a single supplement but you'll have to hunt them out.

Many tour companies give clients the option of sharing a room with another solo traveler (of the same gender) in order to avoid the single supplement. Most claim to do their best to pair you up with someone of similar age and interests — but there's no guarantee that you'll end up best buddies. However, if you sign up for room/cabin sharing and there are no other solo passengers to match you with, you will get your own room without the single supplement being imposed.

Look for tour companies that specialize in solo travelers. For example, **Two's A Crowd** (https://twosacrowd.com.au) is one that exclusively runs small-group tours (up to 15 people) for solo travelers, offering low single supplements and no sharing. It's Australian-based but has a range of itineraries that includes things like Mississippi River cruises.

Overseas Adventure Travel (OAT; www.oattravel.com) has been including solo travelers in its small group tours since 1978 and in 2023 offered 30,000 single spaces, with only 8 percent incurring a single supplement fee. For those who miss out, they offer a room-mate matching program. OAT also offers a big range of women-only tours. Tours include travel to Egypt, Morocco, Sicily, and the South Pacific as well as small ship cruises (up to 25 passengers) to Antarctica, the Arctic, and South America.

TIP

Other strategies for avoiding paying a single supplement include:

>> Ask! Sometimes it's as easy as asking the tour operator to waive the single supplement or to consider a discount for a solo traveler. Try the subtle art of negotiation or reach out on social media to ask about specific tours — you might just get lucky!

>> Once you have settled on your holiday destination, try a Google search for "no single supplement" or "no solo supplement" and your destination, and see what comes up. It might give you options you haven't yet considered.

>> Travel in low or shoulder season, when companies are more likely to be trying to fill their tours.

>> Look for hotels that charge per room, rather than per person per night, then you know you're not being slugged extra for having that King-size bed all to yourself.

>> Consider alternatives to hotels. Hostels, house-sitting, and Airbnb won't incur extra fees just because you are on your own.

>> Shop around to make sure that trying to avoid a single supplement isn't at the expense of finding a better deal. Paying the supplement on a tour that's cheaper overall might be worth it.

>> Watch for tour companies offering discounted single supplements on selected tours. If you are flexible in your

timing and choice of destination, you may be able to benefit from these deals.

>> Book early or late. The best deals get snapped up quickly, so get in first if you see something that appeals. Booking late can work if the tour is not selling well and last-minute deals are offered.

If you're booking on a group tour and want to pay the single supplement to ensure a room of your own, make sure you check that single rooms are available for every overnight stop to avoid any nasty mid-trip surprises.

TIP

Ask your tour company for a breakdown of travelers who have booked so far. How many couples? How many solo travelers? What is the age range? For privacy reasons they will be limited in what they can tell you, but this information alone should be able to give you an idea of who you'll be traveling with.

Using public transport

I love public transport! Give me a train, tram, or bus any day over a cab or Uber. Here is the whole of humanity going about their business, heading to work, school, or play as they do every day. And not only that — it's cheaper than any other transport option except Shanks's pony. Even a bicycle requires some financial investment!

You don't need to hire a car to get around, especially in cities that have great public transport networks — and they are many! In 2023, *Time Out* magazine surveyed more than 20,000 people in 50 cities around the world to come up with the best for public transport, voted on by local residents who use it regularly. The top ten:

>> **Berlin,** for its comfortable, safe and timely U-Bahn, S-Bahn, buses, and trams. The U-Bahn (underground) is simple to navigate and efficient. Buy a day ticket or a seven-day ticket.

>> **Prague,** where you can ride the tram while gazing out at its picturesque streets or take the metro, with three color-coded lines (green, yellow, and red) covering almost every part of the city. A 24- or 72-hour ticket also lets you ride the funicular to Petrin.

>> **Tokyo,** where the trains are sardine-can packed (best to avoid commuter hours altogether) but brilliantly efficient and easy for non-Japanese speakers to use. I'll vouch for that! The Greater Tokyo Pass gives you five days of unlimited travel on all train and tram lines and some bus lines.

>> **Copenhagen,** for its reliable network of trains, buses and water buses. One ticket covers it all, so buy a Copenhagen Card to zip around the whole of the Danish capital.

>> **Stockholm,** where you get a dose of art and culture with your ticket, with the *tunnelbana* (subway) stations adorned with paintings and mosaics. Your options here also include trams, buses and ferries to the islands.

>> **Singapore,** where the Singapore Tourist Pass takes away the hassle of paying for each fare and the MyTransport.SG app makes planning your trip easy. The buses and MRT lines are easy to use and will take you to all the main attractions.

>> **Hong Kong,** with an extensive network of metro lines, all accessible with an Octopus Card to take care of paying. On this compact island, a metro station is never far away.

>> **Taipei** has a terrific MRT light rail system, with plenty of English-language signage. It's clean, comfortable, and efficient, making it easy to get around Taiwan's fascinating capital. A large range of passes is available (and they make cute souvenirs too).

>> **Shanghai** boasts the world's largest metro system — and one of the most efficient. All forms of transport — trains, buses, ferries, maglevs, and taxis — can be paid for using the Shanghai Public Transportation Card.

>> **Amsterdam** has a great network of trains, trams, ferries, and buses. Buy an I Amsterdam City Card for unlimited use of public transport and free entrance to 38 museums and attractions over 24, 48, or 72 hours.

Also on the list are London (the Underground will get you almost everywhere, as pictured in Figure 2-1), Madrid, Edinburgh, Paris, New York, Montreal, Chicago, Beijing, and Mumbai. To that list, I'm going to add a few personal favorites: Vienna, Bangkok, and Melbourne. Wherever you are heading, check out the passes available, from tourist offers to daily, weekly, or monthly tickets that can save you money.

Lee Mylne(Author)

FIGURE 2-1: Use public transport to and from the airport.

TIP

Multi-day transport passes often include discounted entry to major tourist attractions including museums, galleries, and theme parks.

TIP

Use handy smartphone apps such as Google Maps to help plan your public transport journeys, as well as destination-specific apps such as Japan's Navitime, which searches bus and train timetables in multiple languages. Another good one is Moovit, excellent for the UK, which includes public transport, bikes, Uber, or any other form of transport. Mapway is a popular app for Android phones and covers a host of major cities around the world. Most of these apps are free.

If it's practical, start the way you mean to go on by taking public transport from the airport to your hotel. Check the distance you may have to walk from the bus or train station to the hotel first and consider how much luggage you have (for tips on packing light, see Chapter 4) to drag or carry with you. In most cases, public transport will be much cheaper than taxi or ride-share fares as will airport shuttle services that will take you right to the door, or very close by. Sometimes it's even preferable to take a train part of the way and do a shorter hop with your bags by taxi for the final part of the journey.

Public transport is one of the best ways of familiarizing yourself with a city you've never been to before. And you certainly won't be the only person traveling alone on a bus, tram, or train. Instead of navigating unfamiliar streets, with all the stress of potentially getting lost — whether in a car or on foot — sit back on any form of public transport and watch the world go by. Before you set out, research payment methods for the public transport in your destination. In many major cities, you'll need to buy a travel card with stored value on it, while others will accept a credit card or phone wallet to "tap on" to pay your fare. Some — increasingly fewer — will accept cash paid to the driver (but won't always give you change). Make sure you know which stop you want to get off at, or ask the driver or another passenger if in doubt. Most travelers have over-shot their destination and had to back-track at some stage in their travels.

Always carry a business card from your hotel (or get the receptionist to write the address down for you in the local language) so if you get lost, you can easily ask for directions or show a taxi driver.

Use public transport as a cheap way to see the sights. Find out which tram or bus routes offer the best sightseeing options, as many of them pass major landmarks that the commercial bus tours take in.

If you feel like investing a little in your orientation exercise, book a tour on the open-top buses that ply these routes in all major cities. They're not free, but can be a great way of orienting yourself when you first arrive in a new city.

Many major cities now offer bike-share or electric scooter rentals as an affordable but independent way of getting around. For just a few dollars (but often a "bond" payment as well), you can hire a bike and pedal your way around the city for an hour or a day.

In some places, public transport is limited or difficult to access. Find out what the local ride-share or "taxi" services are, as there may be local versions of Uber. For example, the low-cost motorbike ride app **Gojek** (www.gojek.com) which started in Indonesia in 2010, now offers its services in four countries in southeast Asia — the others are Singapore, Vietnam, and Thailand.

Choosing an Adventure Holiday for One

Adventure holidays for one can combine the advantages of traveling solo with the benefits of group travel. If you want to truly go it alone in every respect, many of the adventures listed here can be done in solitary splendor, with careful planning. But that's the beauty of joining up with a small group tour — all the planning and logistics are taken care of for you. You just have to show up and take part. How much time you spend with your companions on the tour is up to you, to a great extent.

Pull on your hiking boots

The great thing about a walking holiday is that it's something that anyone with a reasonable level of fitness can do. Age is no barrier and with a bit of training, the world is literally at your feet. If you decide to strike out on your own, the chances are you'll soon meet up with like-minded hikers, but if solitary time is what you need, it's easy to keep to yourself.

Some of the world's most famous long walks can be tackled in an organized group, but this still means you can spend time alone along the route. Dipping in and out of companionship is as easy as changing your pace.

Guided walks are also a great way to travel solo, but with a group and have the advantage of having a lot of the organization — and the carrying of luggage — done for you.

One of the most iconic walks in Europe is the **Camino de Santiago** (the Way of St. James), a network of ancient pilgrim routes that come together at Santiago de Compostela in northwest Spain. The main — and most popular route — stretches for nearly 500 miles (780km) from St John-Pied-du-Port, near Biarritz in northern France, to Santiago de Compostela. Pilgrims of all kinds have been walking this trail since the ninth century, many of them alone. Today, 350,000 people each year walk it, more than half of them women.

TIP

Camino de Santiago Planning is a Facebook page which shares tips and information for anyone about to tackle the journey. There are a number of other Facebook pages devoted to this walk, including Camigas, which puts women on the Camino in touch with each other.

Another iconic hiking adventure is the **Inca Trail** in Peru, which takes in the incredible Machu Picchu. The **Inca Trail** begins from the Sacred Valley, travels up through Inti-Punku (Sun Gate), then down to the ruins of Machu Picchu. There are many other Inca footpaths in Peru and the Andes but there is only one "official" Inca Trail that leads directly into Machu Picchu National Park. All other hikes end in the village of Aguas Calientes, where shuttles take tourists to Machu Picchu. As a solo traveler, you cannot go it alone; access to the Inca Trail is controlled by licensed tour operators who employ licensed Peruvian tour guides to accompany hikers.

The Inca Trail can be covered in four or two days, depending on how much of it you want to cover. The trail is 26 miles (43km) long and some of it is steep, so a reasonable level of fitness is required. It is essential that you allow enough time to acclimatize to the high altitude before starting the trek.

TIP

Always check out the requirements for permits and permissions needed if undertaking a solo hike without support from a tour company.

Other great walks to consider when planning your hiking adventure include:

>> The **Pacific Northwest Trail** (www.pnt.org) runs 1,200 miles (1,931km) from the Rocky Mountains of Montana to Cape Alava, Washington, on the shores of the Pacific Ocean. Less well-known than the Appalachian or Pacific Crest trails, it can be tackled in ten sections traversing some of North America's wildest public lands. Sightings of grizzly bears and gray wolves are likely.

>> Canada's **Great Divide Trail** (www.greatdividetrail.com) is described as "one of the most spectacular and challenging" long-distance trails in the world. It traverses the continental divide between Alberta and British Columbia, covering 684 miles (1,100 km). Not for the faint-hearted, some parts of the trail are unmarked.

>> If you're looking for a walk that can take you months, look no further than **Land's End to John O'Groats** (www.landsendjohnogroats.info) in the UK. This is the ultimate self-guided long-distance walk, where there is no definitive way of tackling it; each hiker can choose from a multitude of

possible routes between England's southern-most point, Land's End in Cornwall and John O'Groats at the northern tip of Scotland. The most direct will cover around 1,100 miles (1,770 km) and take around two to three months, depending on your pace and number of rest days.

» The **West Highland Way** (www.westhighlandway.org) in Scotland is 96 miles (154 km) long, running between Milngavie, north of Glasgow, and Fort William in the Scottish Highlands. Starting at the southern end of the route (Milngavie), eases you into the walk with the less strenuous sections. Expect to walk between 9 and 15 miles (14.5 and 24 km) each day, with accommodations along the way at campgrounds, hostels, bunkhouses, pubs, B&Bs, and hotels.

» New Zealand's most famous long walk is the **Milford Track** (www.fiordland.org.nz), in the South Island, which can be tackled independently or with a guide. Over five days, you walk (New Zealanders call it "tramping") 33 miles (53.5km) through the heart of Fiordland National Park to spectacular Milford Sound. Guided walks stay at private lodges, while independent walkers stay in Department of Conservation huts. A booking system operates for independent hikers, which is open only from October to April or May. In logistical terms, the easiest way by far is to book with a guiding company.

» Australia has many multi-day walks, but one of my favorites is the **Overland Track** (https://parks.tas.gov.au/ explore-our-parks/cradle-mountain/overland-track) in Tasmania. Although only 40 miles (65 km), the trek takes six days and bushwalking experience is recommended — unless, like me, you decide to go with a guided group. As a solo traveler, this was an excellent way of ensuring every- thing was taken care of, including accommodation and meals along the track. The scenery is spectacular, as you walk through eucalypt forests, glacial valleys, rainforests; cross golden moors; and gaze at waterfalls and mountains in the Cradle Mountain-Lake St Clair National Park.

» Japan's ancient pilgrimage trails provide some wonderful opportunities for solo self-guided walks. The five-day **Nakasendo Way** (www.nakasendoway.com) takes you through forests, mountains, small towns, and countryside, with the chance to stop off at onsens (bath houses) and stay in local guesthouses. Another is the **Kumano Kodo** trail (https://www.tb-kumano.jp/en/kumano-kodo/) across the Kii Peninsula, one of only two World Heritage listed walks (the other is the Camino de Santiago). A number of tour companies offer packages that will book your accommodation and transfer baggage for you, so all you have to do is walk!

TIP

The Tongariro Crossing (www.tongarirocrossing.com) in New Zealand's North Island is often touted as the world's best one-day walk. Tongariro maunga (mountain) has deep significance for Maori people, but this is not an easy walk. The weather can be unpredictable, and in peak season, up to 3,000 people make the crossing. Planning and booking is essential, especially for solo travelers.

REMEMBER

When hiking solo, it is vital to always make sure someone knows of your plans and when you expect to return.

Many long-distance walks can be tackled in short bursts, ideal if you are building up your fitness for a bigger trip or are short of time. Most have websites that will detail how to access certain parts of the trail and how to manage the logistics.

One-day (or shorter) walks are also available without heading to the wilderness. Check local websites or walking groups to find out what's available and if visitors are welcome. For example, in Britain, walking charity The Ramblers offers free "wellbeing walks" for members, with newcomers or visitors given three free walks before joining. The group runs 50,000 group walks across the country every year, an excellent option for solo travelers wanting to explore off-the-beaten-track places in the company of those who know them well.

As the philosopher Lao Tzu said: "A journey of a thousand miles begins with a single step." Take the step!

Sailing into the wild blue yonder

Sailing or cruising holidays can be one of the most relaxing ways to get away from it all. One of the most idyllic holidays I've ever had was aboard a private yacht sailing part of the tropical Queensland coast in Australia. The trip was to take two weeks; to drive the same distance along the coast would only take five hours, and I wondered how quickly boredom would set in. I need not have worried. Life on the ocean waves turned out to be an unexpected reconnection with nature, as passing dolphins, turtles, manta rays, and seabirds turned up with languid regularity; sunsets and rainbows kept the skies alive; and uninhabited islands provided shore time.

The world takes on a different perspective from the water, whether you choose a river cruise, large ocean liner, expedition ship, charter yacht, or canal barge.

Solo sailors can sign up for any number of adventures; handy crew members are always in demand. Many local sailing clubs are happy to have visitors aboard (usually at certain times of the week) since someone willing to haul on ropes and operate the winch is a valuable asset to any crew. Tall ship voyages — for a day or longer — are a classic way to set sail and quickly bond with others as you work together.

The Caribbean offers wonderful sailing, as do the Mediterranean countries like Turkey, Greece, Italy, and Croatia. All are renowned for their sailing and there are many tour operators running group sailing trips. In Europe sailing is usually from May to September, although the Turkish season extends a month or two longer.

Australia's Whitsunday region has 74 islands off the coast of Queensland, on the Great Barrier Reef. Airlie Beach and Hamilton Island are the centers for all sailing trips and are well-known for their nightlife if you're in the mood to party.

Rubicon 3 Adventure (www.rubicon3adventure.com) is a UK-based sailing company that invites people to hop on and off the yacht at certain points on its journey. No sailing experience is required for some trips and the course of the passage is made up as you go along, depending on the wind, the weather and the group you are sailing with. The custom-built 60-foot expedition yachts accommodate eight people, including the skipper and crew — and many guests are over-50s. You may be sailing in the Caribbean, across the Atlantic, in the Baltic Sea, or off the coast of Scandinavia, England, or Scotland.

If a more relaxing cruise aboard a ship is more your style, there are many options. My preference has always been for expedition ships. These are typically smaller, with lower passenger numbers, allowing everyone to get to know each other and providing a more intimate experience.

Expeditions are ideal for adventurous solo travelers and have the advantage of traveling with like-minded people. Always wanted to swim with sea lions in the Galapagos (yep, my dream!) or marvel at the icy grandeur of the Artic or Antarctica? The chances are your passion is shared by the others on board your ship, most of whom will be knowledgeable and interested in the place you are bound for. You're also unlikely to be the only solo traveler aboard. In some cases, this is enough to form long and lasting friendships.

Cruise prices are usually based on double occupancy and solo travelers pay a single supplement.

Joining an expedition ship also means that — like other cruise ships — everything is taken care of from the moment you arrive at your embarkation point. Many expedition cruise companies send a representative to meet you at the airport and escort you to the ship.

For some people, larger cruise ships — those that offer everything and anything, from rollercoasters and nightly entertainment to on-board spas, libraries, shops, and multitudes of restaurants, along with thousands of passengers — are the way to go.

Whichever style of cruise you choose, find out what pre- and post-voyage extensions are offered by your cruise company; these often provide a great way to see more in a place you may not get back to again, such as Alaska's Denali National Park or the Nabatean tombs of Petra in Jordan. Of course, you may never want to leave the ship, and that's an option, too!

Mealtimes for solo travelers (see Chapter 7) are also made easier on cruises as you have plenty to talk about with fellow travelers after a day's on-shore excursion. Check with the cruise company on their seating policy — is it open seating where you can choose a new table every night or sit with the new buddies you've made every night, a rotational system where you meet someone new each night, or a set seating plan. On some ships, it's possible to dine alone if you choose to.

Some ships have a limited number of single cabins for those who like total privacy, while on others you can take the more affordable option of sharing with another solo traveler of the same gender. This might result in a friendship, but my experience of this — while not unbearable — did not team me up with a kindred spirit. And beware of snorers!

Each cruise company and each ship has a different level of availability for single or shared cabins, so make sure you enquire and book early.

If you're feeling really intrepid, have plenty of time, and aren't too concerned about levels of luxury, consider getting to your overseas destination by cargo ship or freighter. Some ships have limited numbers of cabins for usually a total of between 4 and 12 passengers (you'll almost certainly have to share with someone). It won't be the most glamorous cruise you've ever taken — but I guarantee it will be memorable! I traveled solo aboard a supply ship (pictured in Figure 2-2) from Mangareva in the Gambier Islands, 1,000 miles southeast of Tahiti in French Polynesia, to Pitcairn Island, one of the most remote places in the world, in the South Pacific. Pitcairn has no airport, so ship is the only way to get there, and apart from a few cruise ships that anchor offshore from time to time, the regular way of getting there (and staying for more than a day) is on the supply ship. It took four days, during which time we saw little land, and it was one of the most interesting trips I have ever made, with long conversations with a well-traveled and interesting crew and a few other passengers.

Lee Mylne(Author)

FIGURE 2-2: Cargo ship awaiting passengers at Mangareva.

TIP

Pack seasick pills. Your ship may be in the high seas, and rough weather can be an issue. With luck, anti-motion sickness pills will help stave off the dreaded *mal de mer.*

Cargo ship travel can be booked through specialist companies and can be expensive (depending on your destination). Be prepared to be flexible, as departure days are not set in stone. Some companies that facilitate these journeys are **Cargo Ship Voyages** (www.cargoshipvoyages.com), **SlowTravel** (www.langsamreisen.de/en/freightertravel), and **Freighter Trips** (www.freightertrips.com). Be prepared to (probably) share a cabin, eat simple but hearty meals with the crew, and have almost no entertainment — apart from books, movies, and conversation.

WARNING

If you opt for freighter or cargo ship travel, check that your travel insurance will cover you.

Pedal power

Two-wheeled adventures have a lot going for them. Not only are you reducing your carbon footprint, you're also getting out into the real world with nothing between you and what's happening around you. Free-wheeling through country lanes or rice paddies can open up a whole new world and as a solo traveler can put you in touch with the locals in a way that no bus tour can hope to achieve.

If you're an intrepid and experienced cyclist, you may want to go it alone or take part in a hardcore multi-day or weeks-long ride, but there are plenty of options for those who are occasional bike riders. Specialist cycling tours are a safe and easy way of exploring by bike, with the advantage of having bike and all gear provided, an itinerary that includes your accommodation along the way, and support if you need it (oh no, a puncture!).

TIP

It might seem obvious, but prepare for a cycling holiday by getting some practice at home before you leave! Head out on the weekends and explore your local area so you're fit for the long haul.

In many major cities, bike share schemes allow you to hire two wheels for an hour, a day, or more. Hundreds of cities across the United States and around the world have these schemes — some also including electric scooters — along with dedicated bike lanes or paths to take the stress out of dodging traffic and making it easy to incorporate pedal power into any style of holiday.

TIP

Check out the reviews for your cycling tour to make sure that the equipment provided will be up to standard.

When choosing to make cycling part of your holiday, consider places where cycling is an integral part of life. China, the

Netherlands or Vietnam, pictured in Figure 2-3, spring to mind. Whether on a multiday or single-day cycling trip, you will be able to get to places a car cannot go and have something in common with the locals.

Lee Mylne(Author)

FIGURE 2-3: Cycling through rice paddies in Vietnam.

Think out of the box. A guided cycling day tour in Thailand was never on my radar but — despite the sweaty heat and some wobbly moments across narrow bridges — it revealed a side of Bangkok I would never have seen otherwise. The bike allowed me to get away from the heaving traffic and revealed hidden neighborhoods, small temples, river estuaries, and more green space than I had imagined. My tour was with **Grasshopper Adventures** (www. grasshopperadventures.com/destinations/bicycle-tours-in-thailand), but there are other reputable companies that offer similar tours, including evening bike tours.

TIP

Worried you aren't fit enough? Electric bikes are an enormous boost to those who aren't match-fit for a cycling holiday, and most cycling vacation specialists offer them as an option.

In eastern Europe, the **Trans Dinarica** (www.transdinarica. com) is a 2,090 miles (3,364km) cross-border cycling route, to be completed in 2024. At the time of writing, it connects Slovenia,

Croatia, and Bosnia and Herzegovina but will ultimately traverse eight countries (the others are Montenegro, Albania, Kosovo, Serbia, and Macedonia) enabling cyclists to pedal through many UNESCO heritage sites, villages, and national parks.

Australia and New Zealand are renowned for their rail trails, disused railway tracks that have been repurposed as cycling routes. The advantage is that they are mostly on flat terrain.

For the super-athletic and experienced riders, mountain bike holidays are another way to experience the great outdoors beyond paved roads and traffic at any level. As always, if you're on unfamiliar terrain, it's best to head out with local experts on a guided or group tour. Some great destinations to look at for inspiration include Canada, Iceland, New Zealand, and Australia.

Hitting the slopes on skis or snowboard

Whether you've never set a ski boot on the slopes before, are ready to move from green runs to blue, or you're aching to hit those double black diamonds, ski resorts are great places for solo travelers. Skiing and snowboarding are naturally inclusive sports where a shared love of the crisp clear mountain air and pure white slopes is a natural ice-breaker. It's not unusual to be standing in a lift line with a stranger in the afternoon and find yourself having drinks or dinner with them that night — perhaps because they are also traveling solo! If your friends or family members aren't snow bunnies, heading to the slopes alone is no hardship. Many others are in the same situation, and are open and ready to meet others. Après-ski is the perfect time to cement new friendships.

TIP

Eat at the bar. Restaurants in ski resort towns usually have a bar menu similar to what you'll be offered at a table but at much lower prices. The other great advantage is that you're much more likely to strike up a conversation with another solo diner. If not, the bartender will not fail to keep you entertained and informed about what's going on.

If you're a beginner or novice, take group lessons. You'll find yourself instantly bonding with others who are also nervous and wobbly, and there'll be plenty to talk about when you retire to the café or bar later. You might even find a ski buddy for the rest of your stay.

Ski improvement camps for intermediate to advanced skiers can be found just about anywhere you plan to strap on your skis, including a number that are designed for — and run by — women. Camps usually run for four or five days.

If you're experienced, think about taking a mountaineering or survival course to ramp up your skills on the mountain.

If you are skiing solo, make sure you do so within the ski resort's boundaries so there will always be someone close by if you need help, direction, or have an accident that requires medical assistance. However, if you're going off-piste or backcountry skiing, it's essential to do so with a group of experienced skiers.

Where to go? The possibilities are endless. Choose a destination that will offer you the chance to explore more than just the snow towns. If you only have time to ski, you'll still be soaking up the atmosphere and culture of somewhere that's foreign to you. Australians love to ski in Japan, not only because time zones and distance mean there's no real jetlag involved, but also because the Japanese culture is never far away. Similarly, if you live in the UK, a ski trip to France, Italy, Austria, or Switzerland will have you picking up those language skills. Colorado provided my first two ski adventures, and how I loved the feel of the American West evoked by just walking down Lincoln Avenue in Steamboat Springs. The USA and Canada are bristling with opportunities for skiers and snowboarders, and don't forget the mountains of Chile and Argentina as well. If you want to go as far as you can, try Queenstown, New Zealand — but don't forget there are also ski resorts on New Zealand's North Island, too.

When choosing a resort for a solo ski holiday, consider the size and style of the resort, distance from the airport, and connections to other resorts.

Gay skiers, put **Aspen Gay Ski Week** (www.gayskiweek.com) on your calendar. Now in its 46th year, every January this huge event is the oldest and largest gay ski event in the USA, with around 3,000 people attending. There are tours of all four Aspen Snowmass ski areas, daily après-ski gatherings at local bars, and nightly "friendship dinners" at restaurants, as well as ticketed dance parties and pool parties.

In Vermont, the annual five-day **Winter Rendezvous** (www. winterrendezvous.com), Stowe's LGBTQ+ pride celebration every January, is a great place to meet people at one of the many activities and events.

TIP

While it's better to ski with a buddy, in case of accident, if you are skiing alone check for a single lift line, which means you can skip the long lines for the chairlifts.

In short, wherever you decide to go, as a solo traveler, you'll find a ski town is full of people just like you, looking for friends with whom to share the joy of the slopes. All you have to do is say hello or ask a question and you'll be on your way to a great conversation and potentially a lasting friendship. Even the resort workers are often on their own, maybe just for a season, and are open to meeting new people.

TIP

Ask about single rooms when booking, as some ski resorts have an allocation that is free of the dreaded single supplement. **Club Med** (www.clubmed.com) offers all-inclusive skiing at more than 20 locations around the world, including France, Italy, Switzerland, Japan, and China. Watch out for selected dates and resorts when there is no single supplement for solo travelers.

Giddy-up! Horse-riding holidays

Channel your inner cowboy (or girl) for the ride of your life on an equestrian holiday in any number of countries around the world. Passionate riders will find horse treks and safaris from a diverse — and sometimes surprising — range of places where you can saddle up to explore new territory.

Wherever you live or travel, you are probably not too far from a dude ranch or horse-riding holiday of some kind.

When choosing a ranch or other type of horse holiday, ask yourself these questions:

>> Where do you want to go? Keep in mind the distance you want to travel and the proximity of the nearest airport.

>> What time of year do you want to ride? In Canada and the northern states of the USA, the busiest time is summer; in southern states, you'll still have warm enough weather to ride in spring, fall, and winter.

>> What kind of ranch are you looking for? Dude ranches range from luxury to rustic, with an equally diverse range of facilities, including hot tubs, Wi-Fi, and spa treatments; others offer a chance to live like a cowboy with few frills.

>> How big is the ranch? Some cater for 100-plus guests, while others are more boutique for only 8 or 10 people. Solo travelers who want to meet others are probably better to choose one where there'll be plenty of company at drinks or dinner.

Within the USA, one of the oldest ranches catering to tourists is **Paradise Guest Ranch** (www.paradiseranch.com), established in 1907 outside Buffalo, Wyoming. With a herd of 185 horses, there's one to suit your ability, and the wranglers will find the perfect match for you. Rides through the meadows of Bighorn National Forest can last from two hours to half- or full-day rides through breathtaking mountain scenery. Other activities include team penning, as you learn to separate steers from a larger group and work them into a pen or barrel and poles courses. Lessons are also available if you want to improve your horsemanship.

TIP

For a list of guest ranches to consider, check out the **Dude Ranchers Association** (www.duderanch.org), which has more than 90 members in the western United States and Canada. Most offer a range of other activities as well as horseback-riding, including fishing, hiking, rodeos, rafting, and more.

In South America, the land of the gaucho welcomes visitors who want to saddle up for a taste of life on a ranch. **Estancia Los Potreros** (www.estancialospotreros.com) in Argentina is one of the best (so my riding friends tell me). As a working ranch, you'll get the chance to ride with the gauchos to round up cattle, move the herd, or help with other tasks. Trail rides are tailored to suit riders' abilities, opening up new landscapes.

An African safari by horseback may not be the first thing you think of when looking at a riding holiday, but the **Classic Safari Company** (www.classicsafaricompany.com.au) offers equestrian adventures in Botswana's Okavango Delta. Working with experienced, long-established local tour operators, the tours usually run with a minimum of two riders, but you will have to pay a single supplement for accommodation unless you are willing to share.

Okavango Horse Safaris (www.okavangohorse.com), founded in 1986, has more than 60 horses and accepts only experienced riders. Groups are a maximum of eight and you'll spend four to six hours in the saddle each day, getting close to the delta's wildlife — giraffes, zebra, lions, elephants, hyenas, hippopotamus, and migratory birds. Game drives are also offered.

Another company offering multiday horse-riding experiences in the Okavango Delta is **African Horseback Safaris** (www.africanhorsesafaris.com), running since 1995 and based at a safari camp for up to 14 guests.

For another horse holiday with a difference, Iceland (www.visiticeland.com) offers a range of tours through the volcanic landscapes and lava fields that make this such a popular destination. Here, your steed with be an Icelandic horse, a breed known for its small stature and reliability. These are the original Viking horses, brought from Norway a thousand years ago and considered one of the purest breeds in the world.

TIP

Summer is the best time to ride in Iceland (although some places do offer winter tours), with many tours available near the capital, Reykjavik.

To ride with purpose, join **Relief Riders International** (www.relief ridersinternational.com), a humanitarian-based, adventure travel company that has been leading horseback journeys through remote areas in Asia providing humanitarian aid to rural communities since 2004. Riders deliver free medical, educational, sanitation, and food supplies to people in remote parts of India, Ecuador, Turkey, and Mongolia.

Lending a hand by volunteering

In the isolated village of Quelqanqa in the Cusco region of Peru, my name is scratched into the concrete foundations of a footbridge built to enable children to cross swollen rivers in safety on their way between home and school. As one of 16 international volunteers in a Community Project Travel group with adventure travel company **World Expeditions** (www.worldexpeditions.com), I combined the chance to trek and see village life in Peru with the opportunity to support a community in a practical way. After a three-day trek through the remote Urubamba mountains, our traveling party joined the villagers in two groups to build the bridge and install a water pipeline to bring clean water to some of the houses in the village that had been without it. Our work was overseen by a qualified engineer to ensure it was carried out with the villagers' safety in mind. Years later, this remains one of the best travel experiences of my life.

Voluntourism is a popular way of combining your vacation with the chance to give back to countries or communities that have opened their doors to you. And as a solo traveler, you can become part of a team helping those less fortunate than yourself. Many tour companies now offer experiences such as the one I had in Peru, where after our work in the village, we trekked back out of the mountains and traveled to Machu Picchu for a few days of relaxation and sightseeing.

WARNING

Some aspects of volunteering can be controversial. Ensure you think about your ability to contribute in a meaningful and ethical way before signing up for a tour that includes working with people or animals.

Make sure you do your research before signing up to be a volunteer. Look at the website of the organization you plan to volunteer with. Are they reputable or a registered charity? Where is the money you are paying likely to end up? How much of that money will stay in the community? How will the community you are volunteering in benefit from the presence of foreign tourists?

TIP

Try to match your own skills and experience with the volunteer role you are fulfilling. For example, if you have no experience in construction, building houses or a school may have unintended consequences if the work is not to a professional standard.

Around the world, there are many companies doing wonderful things in developing communities and it is possible for travelers to help out. While a thoughtful approach should be adopted when considered a volunteering stint, it's still possible to help out in ways that do not negatively impact the recipients of your well-intended generosity.

Consider becoming a citizen scientist. There are many opportunities to help scientists in the field with basic research. Conservation projects abound, from cleaning up beaches to counting turtle hatchlings or planting trees. There are endless opportunities world-wide to combine the great outdoors with a chance to assist in important work from Costa Rica to Croatia, India to Indonesia, Australia to Africa.

Biosphere Expeditions (www.biosphere-expeditions.org) runs citizen-scientist trips to some of the world's most fragile eco-systems. The UN-recognized not-for-profit will get you involved in wildlife surveys and data collection which can influence conservation outcomes. From monitoring brown bears in Swedish woodlands to diving studies of coral reefs and whale sharks in the Maldives, each trip has conservation at its core.

Earth Watch (www.earthwatch.org) is another science-based organization that offers the chance to join researchers around the world. You might be monitoring the health of bee populations in Utah or birdlife in Cuba, helping protect penguins in South Africa, or tracking sharks and rays in Florida.

The European Nature Trust (www.theeuropeannaturetrust. com/travel) has wildlife experiences where volunteers work alongside conservation experts. All trips include a donation to the local projects to support their work in restoring habitats, monitoring populations, anti-poaching initiatives, and dealing with human-wildlife conflict. Projects might include tracking lynx in Spain's Andalucia region or wolves in the Apennines in Italy. Each itinerary also includes plenty of chances to feast on local delicacies, explore palaces and churches, and see other wildlife.

Domino Volunteers (www.dominovolunteers.com) in Colombia matches volunteers' skills to the needs of local charities, working with around 35 social enterprises and foundations throughout Cartagena. Volunteers stay with local host families, meet other volunteers, and take part in community events. Projects might include teaching English, working in an a care home for people who are aged, working in sports programs (surfing, soccer, scuba diving, or more), or promoting recycling programs. Foodies might prefer to help out on a sustainable food project. Placements range from one day to one month.

WARNING

"Orphanage tourism" should be avoided. In some countries orphanages are associated with child trafficking and exploitation. Save the Children estimates that of the 8 million children in orphanages worldwide, up to 90 percent are not orphans at all.

Running away

If getting your adrenaline and your muscles pumping is your idea of a vacation, then signing up for the challenge of a long-distance race may be just the way to explore new terrain.

Big-name events such as the New York, Boston, Chicago, Berlin, or London marathons are bucket-list items for runners. And if you need any incentive other than the bragging rights, there's a medal for runners who finish all five and for age-group runners.

Each marathon has its own atmosphere and thrills, from the sight of the Eiffel Tower as you run through the streets of Paris, to the party atmosphere of New York, or the spectacular landscapes of Patagonia. Every continent has its own special marathon, half-marathon, or ultra-marathon events. Runners are spoiled for choice, and solo travelers will find themselves caught up in the shared passion of fellow runners.

TIP

Look for travel agents who specialize in holidays for runners. One is **Travelling Fit** (www.travellingfit.com); the travel consultants are marathon runners themselves and the business can help you with logistics for more than 30 marathons, including being the official agent for the London, Great Wall (China), and Boston marathons, among others.

In Asia, the **Bangkok marathon** (www.bkkmarathon.com) is one with a difference, starting at 1 a.m. or 2 a.m. to avoid the heat of the day and the city's crazy traffic. At that hour of night, there are few spectators! More popular is the China's **Great Wall Marathon** (www.greatwallmarathon.com), a steep and difficult run — although there is also a "fun run" of just over 5 miles (8.6 km) for those who are working up to the full event. Likewise, the **Luang Prabang Half Marathon** (www.luangprabanghalfmarathon.com) in Laos, which raises money for a children's hospital, is a great one to ease yourself into it.

REMEMBER

For some charity runs, you will have to commit to raising a certain amount of money to gain entry.

In Australia, the **3 Marathons in 3 Days** (www.3marathonsin3days.com) event in Cairns is run by a local club. It's small but popular — with the added bonus of the Great Barrier Reef being just offshore for some post-running relaxation. Competitors can opt to compete in only one or two of the marathons, but the Grand Slam medal goes only to those who complete all three. Another iconic event Down Under is the **Australian Outback Marathon** (www.australianoutbackmarathon.com), a desert run with the sacred monolith Uluru as its backdrop.

At the other end of the spectrum, check out the cool climate courses of the **Antarctic Ice Marathon** (www.icemarathon.com), the **Everest Base Camp Marathon** (www.everestmarathon.com) in Nepal, and the **Polar Circle Marathon** (www.polar-circle-marathon.com) in Greenland.

TIP

All the marathons have smaller or sideline running events — half marathon, fun runs, or walks — to appeal to runners working up to something more challenging and making the events inclusive for all abilities.

It's expensive, but the chance to run through the African savannah with nothing between you and the "big five" game animals who live there is irresistible for some runners. Like some other marathon events, entry to **The Big Five Marathon** (www.big-five-marathon.com) in South Africa is only available in combination with an official tour package.

Another African event is the **Serengeti Girls Run**, a charity run organized by safari company Singita (www.singita.com/conservation/projects/serengeti-girls-run/) in partnership with the Grumeti Fund, which supports the education and empowerment of girls in rural areas. Suitable for runners of all levels, this near-40-mile (63 km) women-only run is held over three days on a private 350,000-acre concession in Tanzania. Runners are accompanied by scouts from the Grumeti Fund Anti-Poaching Unit and a support vehicle to ensure their safety. Participants also have the opportunity to visit the Anti-Poaching Canine Unit and take a tour of the center for Research and Innovation in the Serengeti Ecosystem (RISE). The luxury Singita Sabora Tented Camp is the base for runners, offering evening game drives and massages at the end of the day.

REMEMBER

Some big events have 50,000 runners or more. Although it is more expensive to use a travel agent, they will ensure you are registered correctly and will organize the logistics of getting to your start area (which can sometimes take hours).

There are many events for women runners only, such as the **Thelma and Louise Marathon** (www.madmooseevents.com) in Utah and the **Leading Ladies Marathon** (www.leadingladies marathon.com) in the Black Hills of Dakota. Check on the **Race for Life Marathon** (www.raceforlife.cancerresearchuk.org), raising money for cancer research, held at 150 locations across the UK; the **Osaka International Women's Marathon** (https://www.osaka-marathon.jp/english/index.html) in Japan; or the **All Women's Run** (www.womensfitness.asia/awr-2024/) in the Philippines.

Chapter **3**

Managing the Logistics of Solo Travel

S o . . . you've made the big decision about where to go, and when! You've got your passport and visa(s), if needed, found the best deals, and booked your ticket. In all the excitement — and perhaps a few nerves, if it's your first solo adventure — it's easy to get carried away and forget the fine detail that will help your trip go smoothly.

In this chapter, I make sure that you tick all the boxes you need to ensure that even if something doesn't quite go to plan, you're prepared. That means some pesky little details like having the right insurance, making sure you can deal with disasters minor and major, and keeping in touch with family and friends.

FIND ONLINE

Be sure to check out www.dummies.com/go/solotravelfd for links to all kinds of online resources, including the web addresses mentioned in this chapter.

Preparing to Make Your Solo Adventure a Reality

The practical details of planning a solo trip are often the least exciting — but definitely the most important. As a solo traveler, you need to rely on yourself to ensure everything runs smoothly and you are well-equipped to handle any dramas that might occur along the way. Being well organized and ready for any eventuality can help ensure that your solo adventure dream doesn't become a nightmare.

Doing your homework

Doing as much homework on your destination(s) as you can before you set out will lay the foundation for a stress-free trip. Knowledge is power, after all, and it will enrich the time you spend in a new and unfamiliar place. This will be the case if you're traveling in your own country, but even more so if you're in foreign climes.

FIND ONLINE

A good place to start is to browse government websites. The governments of the USA, Canada, United Kingdom, and Australia, among others, provide online advice for their traveling citizens (find links to those countries' pages at www.dummies.com/go/solotravelfd) that includes information on local laws, potential health issues, places to avoid, and legal issues you might encounter. These websites can also tell you what to do if things go wrong and where you can seek help from your embassy or consulate. Guidebooks and official tourism websites for the country you are visiting can also be good sources of advice and information.

Viewing visa regulations

If you're traveling overseas, these websites will also be able to tell you about visa regulations — and it also pays to check with the official site of the country you intend to visit. Some countries won't require you to have a visa, depending on your citizenship, while others may charge you a fee. Check whether you need to obtain a visa before you leave home or if you can obtain one on arrival (and if so, how to pay for it). For more detail on this, see Chapter 5.

Having the correct visa is essential to a trouble-free arrival. The last thing you want is to be turned around at the immigration desk and put on the next plane home because you have the wrong visa — or worse, no visa at all! And if the next flight isn't that day, you could spend time in detention before you get sent on your way.

Checking your budget and exchange rates

Budgeting for your trip is also important; traveling solo means you have no one else to rely on if you suddenly find yourself short of money. Check out exchange rates where you're going to make sure your budget stretches to accommodate your plans when you get there.

Use an online calculator such as xe.com for up-to-the-minute currency conversions.

TIP

Familiarizing yourself with local customs

Part of your research should also be to find out about local customs. When you are traveling abroad, very different laws and customs may apply. Being a good-mannered visitor means having respect for the laws of the land, which is essential if your vacation is not to be marred by tangling with the strong arm of the law.

Sometimes it's as simple as how you're dressed. Do you need to cover your head, arms, or legs? If you're visiting a conservative or religious place, make sure you dress appropriately. No matter how hot it is, women should always cover shoulders, arms, cleavage/chest, legs, and sometimes heads. Loose clothing is not only cooler in many places, but it also doesn't show the shape of your body. I always take a sarong or shawl that can fit into a day bag for unexpected times when it might be needed. This is something you need to consider if visiting the Middle East or Asia, where conservative dress is expected. Men should also be aware that, in some places, bare legs and torsos are not acceptable. Pack some light long trousers just in case you need them, and always wear a shirt unless you're at the beach or pool.

Every country will have its own customs and standards of polite behavior, and knowing how to interact with people of other cultures will ensure you get the best experience possible while traveling. What traps for the unwary are there to avoid when meeting someone for the first time? In some cultures, it is impolite to look someone in the eye or to shake hands. How should you behave when you're invited to a private home? Should you take off your shoes before entering the house? Is it okay to smoke?

Find out if it's expected that small gifts will be exchanged with hosts. In some cultures, a small token gift that represents your home country in some way will be greeted with delight. In others, tipping is considered an insult.

Religious holidays such as Ramadan in Muslim countries may mean there are restrictions on food and drink, so think about the timing of your trip before you book. In many places, including non-Muslim countries, alcohol and meat are not usually available on religious holidays. Drinking, eating, or smoking in public on these days is culturally insensitive. If you're going to be visiting during these times, make sure you check on what is acceptable or not.

Learning a bit of the local language

Learning the local language, even if it's just a few basic words and phrases, is a clear way to indicate respect for another country or culture. While you might not have time to become conversational before you arrive, showing that you've made an effort will bring smiles to those you attempt to talk to, as they recognize that you've shown an interest in their culture. If your unpracticed attempts to speak the language result in laughter, see it as an ice breaker and battle onward. Translation apps are useful, but don't provide the same kind of connection with others that learning the language does.

TIP

Take time to learn greetings and some basic phrases to help you get by: "How are you?"; "Thank you"; "No"; "How much is that?"; "What is that?"; "Excuse me"; "My name is . . ."; and, "May I take a photo?" It's all you need to start with.

If you're planning to be in a country for a reasonable amount of time, consider taking a short course in conversational language before you go. You might go along to a class in your hometown, but if that's not a viable option, there are plenty available online and as apps or podcasts, where you can practice in private!

Checking health requirements

For every country you visit, it's important to check the health requirements that might be needed before you're allowed past immigration control. Although this has always been the case, restrictions were tightened during the COVID pandemic, and although some have relaxed again since then, it's not worth the drama of potentially being turned away at the border.

For example, if you've traveled via South America, some countries will require you to have current yellow fever vaccinations. Yellow fever is a viral disease that's transmitted by the bite of infected mosquitoes. It causes fever and jaundice and damages the liver and kidneys. It's prevalent in Africa, the Caribbean, and Central and South America.

Every country will be different, so make sure you know the rules and have prepared well ahead of time. Other necessary vaccinations might include rabies, cholera, hepatitis A and B, Japanese encephalitis, measles, meningococcal disease, tetanus, typhoid, and tuberculosis. Some of these come in the form of several booster shots over a period of time, so make sure you allow time to schedule them — at least six to eight weeks if possible. This also applies to anti-malaria tablets, which need to be taken *before* you arrive at your destination (and after you leave). And ensure you have all the documentation you'll need to prove you've had them, such as vaccination certificates.

Depending on your health and destination, there may be other diseases you may need to vaccinate against, so the best advice is to talk to your doctor.

REMEMBER

Some countries require foreign visitors to carry an *International Certificate of Vaccination,* also known as a Yellow Card, or other proof that they have had certain inoculations or medical tests before entering or transiting the country. Before you travel, check your government's official website for information about the country you are heading to — including those you may only be transiting — or contact the foreign embassy of your destination for current entry requirements.

For other health-related information, see Chapter 9.

Maximizing your travel rewards programs

Frequent travelers know this already, but there are so many benefits to joining travel rewards programs that you'd be crazy not to — even if you're an infrequent traveler. And of course, flying isn't the only way to earn points. Hotel stays, car hire, credit card use, even your everyday shopping can help notch up points that can go toward your next vacation.

As well as flights, you can also use your rewards to get priority check-in with airlines, access to airport lounges, late checkouts with hotels, and better deals.

The first thing to consider when choosing a rewards program is how you're most likely to be traveling. If you plan on traveling mostly within your own country, the best program for you will likely be different than if you're planning to go abroad. Choose an airline that services your home airport as well as flying to your likely destinations.

Most major airlines belong to alliances, which mean you can earn points on any of the group's member airlines. **Star Alliance** (www.staralliance.com) is the largest of these, with 26 member airlines, including United Airlines, Air Canada, Air New Zealand, Scandinavian Airlines, Singapore Airlines, South African Airways, and more, traveling to more than 1,200 destinations worldwide. **SkyTeam** (www.skyteam.com) serves 1,088 destinations in 184 countries through its 19-strong membership, which includes Delta Air Lines, Virgin Atlantic, Aero Mexico, Aerolineas Argentinas, Air France, and China Airlines. The **oneworld** alliance (www.oneworld.com) is made up of 13 airlines, including American Airlines, British Airways, Qantas, Alaska Airlines, Cathay Pacific, Finnair, and more. Between them, they serve more than 900 destinations.

TIP

Check if a reward program offers transferable points, which can be used as airline miles, hotel points, or even be used for cash back rewards. Transferable rewards are not tied to a particular airline or hotel until you transfer them to redeem them. These are usually offered by banks or credit card companies, such as American Express or Chase.

One of the best ways to kick-start your points earning is to get a credit card that offers travel rewards points; often, you'll get bonus points just for signing up and spending a minimum amount during a set amount of time.

Points on some programs will expire after a certain time, usually a couple of years at minimum. Check the life of your points — and keep an eye on it so you use them first!

Don't forget that it's not only airlines that offer travel rewards. Hotels, railways, travel agencies, and cruise lines all have their own versions.

Cruise lines might offer benefits like free cabin upgrades, priority disembarkation, VIP seating at dinners, invitations to exclusive parties onboard, and more.

It's also worth noting that you don't need to spend your travel rewards points on travel. When the pandemic hit, and it looked like my air points would expire without ever being used, I went online and spent them all on other things! Most airlines also offer the chance to buy things like travel gadgets, bags, movie tickets, and so on — so you don't need to accumulate enough points to fly to reap some rewards. You can also put your points toward car rental or hotel bookings — even in your own town!

Up, up, and away — getting the most from airlines

Booking your ticket is the first step toward making your solo adventure a reality. Your airfare is also likely to be the most expensive component of your travel plans, so it's important that you get the most out of your chosen airline as you can. It's one area of your travel plans where it may be hard to economize.

Shopping around for the best deals on airfares, whether domestic or international, is essential. Whether you choose to fly business class or economy, getting the biggest bang for your buck will leave you more money to spend on the ground at your destination. Look at some of the comparison websites such as **Kayak** (www. kayak.com), **Google Flights** (www.google.com/travel/flights), **Momondo** (momondo.com), **Skyscanner** (www.skyscanner.net), and **Expedia** (www.expedia.com). These sites — and there are more — offer hundreds of choices across the world (and can also be used to compare hotel and rental car prices).

You should also be aware of when you want to travel and how that will impact the price of your ticket (and your whole holiday). One of the joys of solo travel is that you don't have to consider anyone else, so flexibility to travel when you want to is easier. Traveling in low or shoulder season can offer significant savings, and remember that Monday mornings and Friday afternoons are crowded with business travelers. In North America, sign up to apps like **Hopper** (www.hopper.com) which analyzes the cheapest travel dates and great deals on flights, accommodations, and rental cars.

There are two points of view on when to book. Some say book as far ahead as you can — at least two or three months for an international flight and about one month for a domestic flight. For others, it's better to wait until the last minute, in the hope that you'll snap up a cheap deal if the flight isn't filling up — but these days, that's unlikely. As a solo traveler, your advantage is that you only need one seat, so you'll likely have an easier time finding something when you make the decision to head off on your next adventure.

As well as using online travel agencies, check the airline website itself, as sometimes you'll find a cheaper deal by booking direct.

TIP

If there's very little price difference between the airline's fare and that offered by a travel agency, book with the airline. If there's a cancelation or delay, the rebooking process will be easier than dealing with a third party.

Your choice of airline and the aircraft flying that route will definitely affect your levels of comfort. If you're making a short trip within your own country, you may be able to tolerate some level of discomfort, but if you're tall or traveling long-distance, leg room will be high on your agenda when booking a seat. Unless you're flying first or business class (don't we all wish?), checking out the legroom on your flight might make a difference to your trip.

Research company **Skytrax** has a huge amount of information about international airlines at www.airlinequality.com. As well as an outline of average seat pitches, it also has reviews of airlines, their lounges, and airports around the world, including images, awards, and ratings. You can read what other travelers have to say on other forums such as **TripAdvisor** (www.tripadvisor.com) or **FlyerTalk** (www.flyertalk.com) as well.

Another great resource is **Seat Guru** (www.seatguru.com), which, as well as listing seat pitch and width, gives you all sorts of other information about your seat, such as whether it has a video screen, Wi-Fi, and power for your laptop.

Emergency exit seats and bulkhead seats usually have the most legroom, although you may have to pay extra to grab one of those for a long flight.

If the flight is not full, you might be lucky enough to have empty seats around you. Middle seats are usually booked last, so book an aisle seat or a window and you might have some elbow room; with real luck you might score a whole row to yourself.

TIP

Fly when no one else wants to — like Christmas Day or Thanksgiving! Not only is your flight likely to be less crowded, the fare may just be cheaper, too. And it might be fun as airline staff get into the holiday mood.

If you're hoping to sleep on a long flight in economy class, avoid the last row of any section or the row in front of an emergency exit, as these seats are the least likely to recline. Stay away from seats near high-traffic areas, such as near the toilets or the galley. On some planes, seats in the back are narrower than the rest. Window seats are good for resting your head but have the disadvantage that you must clamber over other passengers when you need to get out of your seat. But of course, some people love the view from the window seat, like this one in Figure 3-1.

Find out what offers your chosen airline might have available. For example, can you bid for an upgrade in the days before your flight, snagging it for much less than if you had bought a more expensive ticket outright. Is there any option for a free upgrade (sadly, they are much less common than they used to be).

TIP

Sign up for airline e-newsletters to be alerted to sales, discounts, and special offers.

Making the most of transit time

Layovers can be a real drag. You're eager to reach your destination and start enjoying yourself, but instead you're stuck in an airport waiting for the next leg of your flight. Fortunately, you can turn this time into something more productive and enjoyable.

Lee Mylne(Author)

FIGURE 3-1: A seat with a view!

Taking advantage of airline lounges or airport amenities

If you have a long layover between flights (more than five or six hours), consider buying a day pass to your airline's lounge if you don't already have access through your credit card or frequent flier membership. Some day passes are relatively cheap and open the door to showers, unlimited free snacks and drinks, and free Wi-Fi. It may make all the difference to your onward flight, as you'll be refreshed and relaxed.

Another option is to check out the airport amenities; some include spas where you can chill out for an hour or so with a relaxing massage or pedicure. Then there are art galleries, museums, gardens, restaurants, gyms, yoga rooms, and, of course, shopping! One of the best airports for entertainment is Paris-Charles de Gaulle Airport, where the Espace Musees exhibits works of art from the city's best museums as well as concerts, sculpture exhibitions, and games.

If you're stuck at the airport longer than you expect because of delays, bad weather, missed connections, or other situations out of your control, an airport lounge is a great option for catching up on some sleep or just relaxing in comfort. If your delay means an overnight stay and you're not accommodated by the airline, you might be lucky enough to find a 24-hour lounge. However, many of them close at night, and sleeping in the airport itself is an uncomfortable — if not impossible — choice. Domestic airports often close at night.

TIP A comprehensive source of information on airport facilities — and sleeping options — is www.sleepinginairports.net.

Catching up on your sleep in an airport hotel room

Depending on the timing of your layover, consider booking a hotel room so you can sleep. Some major airports have air-side hotels, so you don't even have to go through any security to leave the airport. Some years ago, with a 16-hour layover, I stayed at Dubai International Hotel at Dubai Airport — and it was surreal to open the curtains and look down on the main concourse with travelers bustling off to their flights. This airport also offers very cheap **Sleep Lounges** (www.sleep-n-fly.com) that have sleep pods and single "cabins" suitable for solo travelers, which you can rent for anything from one hour to 24-hours.

Tokyo's Narita Airport has a capsule hotel called Nine Hours, which is useful if you're on an early morning flight or in transit, and it also offers shower rooms and "nap rooms" on a first-come, first served basis.

Turning your layover into a little side trip

If you have a lot of time to kill (and there are no visa issues to consider), it may be worthwhile leaving the airport and exploring the city. Usually, depending on the destination, you'll need at least five or six hours or more to make this feasible.

TIP One easy and stress-free way to do this is to take a "transit tour" offered by the airport. This means you don't need to worry that you'll be back in time for your next flight. Some airports, including Seoul's Incheon Airport in South Korea and **Singapore's Changi Airport** (www.changiairport.com) — regularly voted the best airport in the world — offer free (or very cheap) city tours. At Changi, there are four to choose from, including a City Sights tour that stops for you to admire the astounding Supertrees at Gardens by the Bay, pictured in Figure 3-2. Other airports that offer transit tours include Abu Dhabi, Istanbul, and Doha's Hamad International Airport in Qatar.

FIGURE 3-2: Supertrees at Singapore's Gardens by the Bay.

REMEMBER

A little research into your stopover destination may surprise you with what's on offer.

Being Prepared When Things Go Wrong

Taking simple steps to cope with the unexpected, if it happens, will go a long way toward your own — and your family's — peace of mind. Making sure you have good insurance coverage and having an emergency plan in place will all help to take the panic out of the situation if things do *go* wrong. As a solo traveler, you need to be self-sufficient and rely on your own good sense and forward thinking to cope with the unexpected.

Purchasing travel insurance for one

The old saying goes that if you can't afford travel insurance, you can't afford to travel. And I agree whole-heartedly. On my very first solo international trip, I landed in the hospital within the first week or so, having an emergency appendectomy. Without travel insurance — which I had taken out reluctantly, bemoaning the cost — I would have had no choice but to turn around and go home again, with all my hard-earned travel funds spent on hospital bills. As it was, I was able to recover quickly and continue with my trip, as the insurance company took care of paying for everything. Phew! It was a lesson well learned, and I've never traveled without insurance again.

Insurance companies, especially those who specialize in travel insurance, have any number of horror stories that would convince you to take advantage of their services. Some claims can skyrocket into the hundreds of thousands of dollars and without insurance, meaning you could be counting the cost of that holiday for years to come.

Buying travel insurance is something of a minefield, as you have to determine what the policy offers and whether you will take it all. Prices vary too, so make sure you compare the policies and fees offered by a range of companies. All travel insurance plans are different, and coverage will vary, depending on what's happened, your country of residence, the plan you choose, and any options or upgrades you buy. Don't forget to read the policy wording carefully and don't assume you're covered for every situation, as exclusions or conditions may apply.

Being aware of what kind of coverage you're buying

Think about what you want to be covered for — medical care is probably top of the list, but also consider covering your luggage, cancelation (either by you or your airline), and loss or damage to anything valuable you might be taking with you. What happens if there's an emergency at home — a death in the family, for example? Will your insurance cover the cost of any changes to your flights or money lost on canceled accommodations?

The cost of travel insurance varies widely, depending on where you are going, the length of your trip, your age and health, and the type of trip you're taking (lying on a beach in the Bahamas is less risky than hiking to Everest Base Camp). You can get estimates from various insurance providers through comparison sites like InsureMyTrip.com. Enter your trip cost and dates, your age, citizenship, and where you live, for prices from more than a dozen major insurance companies.

WARNING

There is sometimes a difference between travel insurance and travel medical insurance. Travel insurance typically covers things like lost baggage and canceled flights — but not necessarily medical expenses. Check the policy carefully before buying.

Health insurance

WARNING

Some countries require proof of insurance (especially health insurance) as a condition of entry and countries under United Nations embargo may be excluded by insurance companies. For American citizens, taking out the required insurance for Cuba is more difficult and may need to be obtained from an insurance company outside the USA.

Most national health plans (such as Medicare and Medicaid) do not provide coverage while you are traveling abroad, and the ones that do often require you to pay for services upfront and reimburse you only when you return home. Travel medical insurance is a great safety net to have, particularly if you're traveling to remote or high-risk areas where emergency evacuation might be necessary. Check with your country's national health plan to find out the extent of their coverage and if they have reciprocal agreements with other countries.

REMEMBER

If you get ill or are injured and need medical treatment while traveling, keep all your receipts and documents for any future claims you might need to make on your travel insurance.

Insurance for expensive equipment and tech gadgets

If you're carrying expensive equipment like cameras or laptops, you might have to insure them as extras; if you're planning on undertaking any risk or potentially life-threatening activities — such as sky-diving, skiing, or motorcycling — that will cost extra for coverage, too. Check the fine print to see if you are covered for the cost of being airlifted home in the case of serious illness or injury.

Claims for tech items are also usually subject to limits. So while your travel insurance policy might have a $15,000 overall baggage limit, for example, your smartphone might only be covered for up to $1,000, and your camera and laptop may only be covered up to $3,000. If you want higher coverage for them, you'll need to itemize them on the policy, and it will likely cost you an extra premium. Check if portable items like your laptop are covered by your home owner's insurance, if you have it, and whether it will be covered if you leave the state or the country.

If your camera, laptop, or anything else is stolen, you'll need a copy of a local police report for your insurance company when making a claim. Similarly, if your checked-in luggage goes missing — even temporarily — you'll need a notice from the airline to that effect in order to claim for any essential replacements you need to buy.

Some warnings and additional considerations

Most large travel agencies offer their own insurance and will likely try to sell you their package when you book a holiday. Make sure you read the fine print before you sign up, and shop around to ensure the deal you're being offered is competitive.

Trip-cancelation insurance will help you recoup your money if you have to cancel a trip or change flights to return early or if your travel operator goes bankrupt, and it covers events, such as illness; natural disasters, such as earthquakes, floods, wildfires, or hurricanes; and government advisories.

You also need to keep an eye out for exclusions — items in checked luggage often aren't covered and nor are things that you've left in your hotel room or car. Don't leave anything unattended — sometimes a tricky thing when you're traveling solo. Travel insurance might not cover an unattended bag — even if it's only for a minute — and reject your claim if it's stolen.

If you are planning to travel for an extended period of time, make sure your policy covers you for that time. Most have a limit of one, three, or six months. Frequent travelers should consider an annual policy, which will usually be much more economical than taking out a policy every time you travel.

Take a copy of your travel insurance documents with you when you go away, including the best way to contact your insurer (usually a 24-hour emergency helpline).

Using your credit card for insurance coverage

If you already have a credit card, the free travel insurance on your card can save you money. If you don't have a credit card already, it's worth considering if you intend to travel abroad at least once every year or two.

One of the benefits of credit card insurance is that, unlike stand-alone travel insurance, it isn't location-specific. This means you can continent-hop to your heart's content, from Toronto to Mumbai to Cape Town to Paris to without taking out separate policies and without paying higher premiums for longer around-the-world adventures.

Many credit card companies include travel insurance — but there are sometimes disadvantages that should be considered. For a start, the card may be one that attracts high annual fees or high interest rates. Consider if the fees are less than the stand-alone insurance premiums — it's possible you might come out ahead. But if you're looking at a premium credit card because it offers "free" travel insurance, make sure that what you're getting is really the best deal for your trip. If it isn't, you might be better off buying a standalone multi-trip or single-trip policy.

There may be strings attached to this "free" insurance. You may need to use the card to book your airfares and accommodations, and there are often threshold amounts that you need to spend in order to activate the coverage. Some policies only activate if you book a return ticket, and some banks require you to notify them in order to get full coverage for each trip. Check whether you need to do anything to activate any extra features. While basic coverage will still give you emergency medical treatment, you might not get coverage for property damage or luggage delays.

WARNING

Some credit cards will give you insurance coverage if you use rewards points to buy your tickets, while others won't. Make sure you check the product disclosure statement (PDS) on the policy.

If you have a pre-existing medical condition, be especially careful about checking the PDS. Some credit card insurance doesn't automatically cover pre-existing conditions and have no provision for them even with an extra premium. Those that will usually have a list of them in the PDS.

You also need to think about those interest rates if you are booking everything up on the card and can't pay it off in time to avoid them.

While credit card insurance can offer coverage that's comparable to standalone policies — and sometimes higher for baggage loss and damage — it also usually demands a higher excess, so make sure you compare. If you do have to make a claim, the higher excess charges might end up costing you more than if you'd taken out a standalone policy. And you may not be able to successfully claim unless you pay for any related purchases (such as emergency items after a baggage delay) with the same credit card.

REMEMBER

Credit card insurance doesn't usually apply to domestic travel, although some cards will compensate you for expenses if your flight is delayed and/or you have missed a connection.

Cards that include travel insurance usually also come with other benefits, such as rewards points. If these are a draw for you already, then travel insurance is an added bonus.

If you're an older solo traveler, check whether the credit card you're using (or considering) has an age limit and look for one that doesn't.

REMEMBER

Before you apply for a credit card, always read the fine print to make sure it offers the right insurance coverage for you. Do the math to see if you'll save money and don't ignore the potential to run up debt.

Making an emergency plan

In most cases, you'll never face a medical issue, have an accident, or be the victim of a robbery or violent crime while traveling. But it's always best to be prepared for the worst, so you can deal with it in the unlikely event that it happens.

That's when having an emergency plan in place is vital, and the best time to sit down and make sure you have all eventualities covered is before you leave home. Make this an essential part of your trip planning.

The most important things for you to safeguard are your passport and travel documents. Make sure you've made two copies of them — take one lot with you (and keep it separate to your originals) and leave the other at home with a family member or friend. An additional backup is to scan them and upload to a cloud service such as Google Drive. If the worst happens and they're lost or destroyed, you'll at least have the relevant information to give to your embassy or consulate or airline or other travel provider to get replacements.

While you're making these copies, also keep a list of contact numbers for your bank, credit card company, and any other financial institution that you may need to contact in a fiscal emergency (if you get mugged or lose your cards), as well as your travel agent, airline, or hotel contacts.

These contacts are also essential to have if your phone is lost or stolen while traveling abroad. If this happens, use a backup device (iPad or laptop) to safeguard your data by logging in to any cloud accounts you have; put a stop on your cards, change your passwords, and erase the data from your phone. Contact your bank, credit card company, insurance company, and phone provider to alert them to the loss or theft. Keep the location tracker turned on while you're traveling will also make it easier to find if it's simply lost (and you should not turn this off remotely using the other device).

Prevention is always better than a cure, so make sure you visit your doctor or travel clinic in time to ensure you have the right vaccinations for your destination and to take care of any other medical needs you may have while traveling. Pack any prescription drugs you may need (and a copy of your prescription), face masks, hand sanitizer, and any other items you might need. Research your destination well and learn emergency phrases in the local language so you can ask for help if you need it.

Handling health emergencies

If you find yourself seriously ill or injured, seek help immediately. As a solo traveler, you're particularly vulnerable if you're ill or incapacitated, and it's important to have help as early as possible. You don't want to find yourself so ill that you're unable to call for help. Let your friends and family know where you are and that you're not well, and then look for a doctor or hospital.

Finding an English-speaking doctor may not always be easy, but there are people who can help you. These include your travel insurance company, your hotel, and your embassy or consulate.

Travel insurance companies usually have a 24-hour hotline and should be able to provide you with the name of a reliable doctor nearby. Make sure you always have the number of your country's overseas representative among your paperwork or saved in the contacts on your phone. If there is no embassy representative in the country you're visiting, try another English-speaking embassy to find the name of a doctor.

If you are staying in budget accommodations, consider splurging on a more upmarket hotel until you are feeling better. Most good hotels will call a doctor for you (I had very good service when falling ill in France, with the three-star hotel I was staying at calling in an English-speaking doctor very quickly). It's worth upgrading your hotel, even if the cost means using your credit card. This also has the advantage of being able to order room service if you are too ill to go out for meals.

See a doctor immediately if you have a high fever or one that lasts more than 48 hours. Fever with no obvious sign of infection may indicate serious illness, such as malaria.

Make sure you have a first aid kit on hand for dealing with minor injuries or illness.

When Mother Nature decides to intervene

Cyclones, hurricanes, floods, earthquakes, volcanic eruptions, and other natural disasters can play havoc with your travel plans. Even if you are not directly in the line of the tempest, whatever it may be, the flow-on effects of major disasters can have an impact through delayed flights, closed airports, and other disruptions.

The first thing to realize is that you have no control over events like these — and neither does anyone else. Keep calm and don't take out your frustrations on airline reservation staff, airport workers, or those at your hotel. In almost all cases, they will be doing their best to keep you safe and get you to where you need to go as soon as possible.

Insurance companies will also be trying to deal with a barrage of enquiries and complaints and may take time to respond to you. Your first step is to check if your insurance policy covers you for such events — sometimes they explicitly exclude "acts of God."

TIP

Always keep your passport in a plastic zippered bag. If there's a flood, it will prevent water damage to your most valuable travel possession and save you endless problems trying to get a new one.

The best defense against natural disasters is to do your homework before you plan your travel. Knowing what you might be going to will help you deal with it — if it happens! For example, if you are traveling to a place that experiences severe winters, it might be better to travel in a shoulder season when the extremes might not be so bad. Earthquakes and volcanic eruptions are also easy to research; make an informed decision about whether to travel to places that are known for them.

Wildfires are becoming increasingly common around the world. Even Greek islands and Hawaii are not immune to them anymore. The USA, Canada, and Australia are known for them, depending on where on those vast continents you are visiting. In the heart of Los Angeles or Sydney you are probably safe, but outside urban areas not so much.

If you find yourself caught in a sudden natural disaster, gather as much information from local sources as you can and be prepared to move or act as soon as it's safe or necessary. Usually, there is some warning of an impending weather event such as a cyclone, tornado, or even (sometimes) a volcanic eruption. Talk to your hotel management, tour guide, or local authorities about the best course of action and find out where nearby emergency shelters are located. Talk to local people as well, as they will likely have experienced it before and have good advice. Follow any instructions from local authorities — they'll know the lay of the land and the best course of action. In these scenarios, you'll need to know about potential road and airport closures and be prepared to make necessary arrangements for evacuation if necessary.

Dealing with lost luggage

Is there anything worse than seeing the luggage carousel turn and turn, everyone else claiming their bags and heading for the door of the airport terminal . . . and there's no sign of yours? Most travelers have been there at some time or another! In most cases, there's a delay of some kind, your bag is on the next flight, and all is (eventually) well. Hours without your luggage may be manageable, but few people want to spend days in the same gear — or may be heading to another destination before their luggage is likely to turn up. And for solo travelers, there's no one to borrow a clean shirt from!

Inconvenience can be annoying, and lack of action from your airline can be frustrating, but there *are* actions you can take to make the process more bearable.

The first thing to do when you're sure all the luggage has been unloaded and yours isn't among it, is to head to the baggage claim office in the airport. You can lodge a report with the airline you've just arrived on (even if you've had multiple stops and changed airlines on your journey). They will ask for a description of your bag, your flight information, and details of where you're staying (and for how long). You'll be given a reference number/code that will enable you to check the status of your bag. Remember to keep the paperwork for any insurance claim you might need to make.

REMEMBER

It doesn't cost anything to be kind. Treat the airport staff who are helping to find your lost luggage (or any other unwelcome minor dramas) with kindness and respect. It's not their fault, and they're just doing their jobs. They will be more inclined to do their utmost for you if you accept the situation with good humor and patience.

TIP

Always take a photo of your luggage before you leave home, clearly showing any identifying marks. You know how many black suitcases are out there, all looking the same! The brand and anything you can do to make it stand out will help if it goes MIA. Make sure your name and phone number are clearly marked on a luggage tag.

You may be entitled to a cash payment to cover essentials such as basic clothing and toiletries until your bag arrives. Make sure you keep receipts for everything you buy. If your travel is delayed while you wait for your bag, compensation might extend to transport and accommodations. Airlines don't always offer this, so be sure to ask when you report your bags missing. Lost checked baggage is only treated as delayed — for up to 21 days. After those long three weeks, you will be entitled to compensation, which could be up to several thousand dollars, depending on the rules in the country you're in.

Two international conventions govern how much compensation you may be eligible for if your bags are lost. Under the Warsaw Convention (1929) and the Montreal Convention (1999), you could receive payments for both checked and carry-on bags. Most countries you are likely to travel to are signatories to these conventions.

Some airlines might offer you an amount of money for each day your bags are delayed, to a maximum amount. This is likely to be less than you are entitled to under the conventions, so make sure you don't accept it at face value!

If you want to claim for compensation, you must do so, in writing, within 21 days. You must detail exactly what you are claiming for and include copies of receipts.

If you're really worried about your bags going missing, invest in a tracking device to attach to them.

When your bags do turn up — and in most cases they will — the airline is responsible for delivering them to your door.

If your luggage includes anything of significant value, make sure you have properly insured it. The most sensible thing to do is to carry these items — such as jewelry — in your carry-on.

It's important to note that the Montreal Convention and Warsaw Convention only apply to international travel. If you're traveling on a domestic flight within your own country, or within any other country, they cannot help you.

Self-defense and street smarts

When traveling alone, you sometimes need to rely on your wits and your instinct to avoid trouble. Staying safe should be your number one priority, while still being relaxed enough to enjoy yourself and soak up everything that traveling has to offer. Unfamiliar surroundings are exciting, but they can also leave you open to the unscrupulous individuals who will take advantage of solo travelers. However, being street-smart can help avoid many of the situations that might be sent to challenge you.

Here are a few tips to help you be prepared:

>> **At the airport, keep all valuables close to you.** Don't pack your cell phone, camera, passport, and other travel documents, iPad, Kindle, credit cards, or money in your checked luggage or in a bag that might be in a luggage hold in a train or bus. Keep them where you can always have access to them.

- **Research your destination's safest neighborhoods and try to stay in one of them.** Learn the safest forms of public transport and the best routes to take.

- **When booking your hotel, opt for a room above the ground floor and not too far away from the lobby.** Keep your door locked with the security chain fastened when in the room, and don't open the door if you are not expecting hotel staff or visitors. In cheaper hotels, make sure the room's locks work and if they don't, ask for another room. Pack a rubber doorstop to wedge under the door to keep it closed tight.

- **When checking in, ask the hotel receptionist to write down your room number instead of telling you verbally.** This limits the possibility of anyone overhearing.

- **Learn the lay of the land.** Study walking routes and public transport options before you head out into the street and get advice from hotel staff or fellow travelers about "no go" areas. Taking a guided tour — walking tours are my preferred option — when you first arrive can be a great way of orienting yourself in a new city and picking up some local intelligence from a local guide. If lost, adopt a confident look and pretend you know where you're going until you can find help in a safe place.

- **Carry as few items of value as you need to while out sightseeing or dining.** Make use of your hotel safe or lock valuables, such as your passport and extra cash or cards, in your luggage. Don't flash your cash — or credit card — around and keep jewelry to a minimum, especially in high crime areas.

- **Reduce the risk of pickpocketing** by putting valuables in pockets that are hard to access and staying alert in areas where pickpocketing is common. In crowded areas, thieves may jostle you or create a diversion to distract you. Carry a tamper-proof backpack or handbag.

- **Be cautious about sharing too much information about yourself with waiters, cab drivers, or tour guides.** Don't tell them you are traveling alone or where you are staying.

- **Take an Uber or ride-share service instead of a taxi.** Not only are they usually cheaper, but your vehicle is tracked; this is not so in a taxi.

>> **Stay alert.** Podcasts may be great while you're on a long bus trip, but on the streets, you need to be able to hear as well as see what's happening around you.

>> **Stay sober.** Don't overindulge in alcohol or drugs. Your alertness, reactions and reflexes will be dulled and you'll be even more vulnerable than before. Don't accept drinks from strangers, and never leave your drink (alcoholic or not) unattended. (See more in Chapter 9.)

Taking Steps to Reassure Your Loved Ones

You'll be fine. You know that, but your family and friends are sometimes harder to convince, especially when you're heading out into the world solo. And it's important to reassure them that everything will be okay, you're grown up, and able to take care of yourself, and that you're taking all the precautions necessary to ensure that if and when disaster strikes, you know how to cope.

Sharing your travel plans is really important. Start the reassurance process before you even leave home. Plan an itinerary and leave a hard copy or email detailing where you'll be, and when, with your nearest and dearest. Make sure your itinerary includes your hotel reservations and details of specific planned activities (hiking, mountain climbing, skiing) on particular days. Give them as much detail as you can.

That's a great start to giving them peace of mind; if they need to reach you, they know where you are. If you're in a country that suddenly hits the news for all the wrong reasons — earthquakes, volcanic eruptions, wars and riots, and so on — they have a good idea of the geography and can work out quickly if you're likely to be in a danger zone. Tell them you've registered with your embassy, so they know they have a place to start looking if they can't get in touch with you.

The Smart Traveler Enrollment Program (STEP) is a free service that allows US citizens traveling and living abroad to register their trip with the nearest US embassy or consulate. STEP enrollment ensures you will receive important information from the embassy about safety conditions at your destination country so you can make informed decisions about your travel plans. The STEP service also helps the U.S. embassy know more about your whereabouts and how to contact you in an emergency, and helps family and friends get in touch with you, if necessary. Other countries have similar schemes to aid their citizens: **Canada has a Registration of Canadians Abroad** service (www.travel.gc.ca/travelling/registration), in the United Kingdom check www.gov.uk/foreign-travel-advice to search for information about countries or territories and sign up for email updates, and Australia has its own version of **Smart Traveller** (www.smarttraveller.gov.au).

Technology allows you to stay connected with friends and family during your solo travels, even if you don't do so every day. Using your smartphone to check in on a regular basis will be a great comfort to those who care about you. And of course, if you're posting about your travels on social media, they'll be following along; if there's a significant pause in your posts, they may have cause to worry, so make sure you let them know if you're planning to be offline for any reason or likely to be without internet or phone reception (desert island, anyone?).

If you do get caught in an emergency situation or natural disaster, do your best to contact your family and friends. It's likely they will have heard about it on the news, and they'll be worried. Use social media to mark yourself safe to friends, so they don't need to keep contacting you to ask. In major disasters, travel insurance companies and embassies may have established 24-hour emergency numbers you can call from overseas to register.

IN THIS CHAPTER

» Becoming a believer in packing light

» Considering the best luggage for a solo traveler

» Sorting out the essentials

» Checking out cubes, cells, and other space-savers

» Thinking about tech gadgets and other useful items

Chapter **4**

You Can't Take It All with You: Packing

Your departure date is looming, and it's time to start thinking about what to take with you on your trip. If you're road-tripping, packing is not such a challenge with all that room in the car to carry whatever you fancy — what's that saying about everything except the kitchen sink? If you're flying, however, it's a different story. Realistically, you probably can't take everything with you that you'd like to. Air travel is definitely a case when the adage of "less is more" applies!

In this chapter, I share some tips and tricks for traveling light — or at least within the bounds of your airline's luggage allowances. It's not as difficult as you might imagine, and the more you travel, the better you'll be at deciding what's essential, what's a luxury, and what should definitely be left behind. There are many benefits to traveling light, and as you sort out the best things to take, I also outline some tips for packing so you can fit everything into your bag easily, without feeling deprived.

Can't go without technology? This chapter also looks at ways to stay connected, but still keep the gadgets and tools you'll need to a minimum.

REMEMBER

Carry-on only might be the ideal for many people, but what you take will depend on your own style of travel and your destination. Take a deep breath and prepare to pack.

FIND ONLINE

You can find links to all the web addresses in this chapter, along with additional online resources, at www.dummies.com/go/solotravelfd.

Enjoying the Benefits of Packing Light

As a solo traveler, you'll find many benefits to learning to travel light. Of course, every traveler's needs are different, depending on the length of your trip, your destination, the type of trip you are planning, and how important having a wardrobe selection with you is!

If traveling by plane, the ideal for many people is to travel with carry-on luggage only. If you can manage this, you'll be doing yourself a big favor. The benefits are obvious:

» You can avoid baggage fees.

» You save time waiting around for checked luggage to be unloaded.

» You never have to worry about lost luggage.

» You're able to move more quickly and easily if you're not burdened down by bags. This is true whether you're traveling by plane, train, or bus.

Any place you have to carry your own bag any distance, having a carry-on-sized bag only will be something you'll be grateful for. As a solo traveler, there's no one to share the load with!

REMEMBER

Always check your airline's latest carry-on rules for weight and dimensions, which are subject to change and will vary from airline to airline. It's a good idea to keep your bag under the advertised dimensions as not all baggage cages at the airport match the online dimensions — and the cage is what matters! Your bag must also fit in an overhead compartment or under the seat in front of you.

TIP

There's another great reason to pack light. Doing so — especially if you are traveling by air — is good for the planet. The heavier your luggage is, the more fuel is needed for the plane to reach its destination. Every piece of luggage that you can avoid taking will help reduce the weight of the aircraft, meaning it will pump less carbon dioxide into the atmosphere.

Choosing the Right Luggage

Your choice of luggage will depend on your style of travel and can be as important as what you pack into it. Are you planning to travel solo through South America for a few months, going on a packaged holiday to the Bahamas, or making a quick business trip to Vancouver? If the luggage you already have is not suitable for your next solo adventure, you'll need to find something that is. A smart suitcase on wheels might not be quite the thing for a hiking trip to the Himalayas.

Choosing the right luggage for the occasion will help you decide what to pack. Do you need a backpack, a duffel bag, a traditional suitcase, or a carry-on? Will your carry-on be a briefcase, laptop bag or something slightly bigger that you can pack a lot into? Do you want soft-sided luggage or the sturdiest suitcase you can possibly find? Wheels or no wheels? Where is the handle placed? Are you after something that's made sustainably, from recycled materials?

It might seem daunting, but rest assured that whatever you need, you'll be able to find it from the huge range of luggage choices available. While some travelers are adamant about sticking with a certain type of luggage, I have a wide range of different bags, some of which are pictured in Figure 4-1, that suit different styles of travel. I then make the decision on what to take based on what kind of trip I'm doing.

TIP

If you're trying to stick to a budget, consider buying pre-loved bags. Either check out your local second-hand store (that's where I found my latest suitcase) or go online. One great option is **Worn Wear** (wornwear.patagonia.com), a program that allows you to trade in or buy used Patagonia brand products, including packs, duffle bags, totes, and other gear at cheaper prices than you'd pay for new. Buy online or check the website for store events in the USA where you can take your gear in or go along to buy. You can buy online from anywhere in the world, but returns are not accepted from outside mainland USA.

Lee Mylne(Author)

FIGURE 4-1: Just some of the styles of bags I travel with.

Packing the Essentials

The "essentials" will be different for every traveler. It depends, of course, on what kind of traveler you are. If you're traveling for business, what you consider essential will be different to when you're heading off on holiday to an island resort. If you have special needs or are a traveler with a disability, it's essential that you contact your airline or other transport operator when booking to ensure that any equipment or aids you have can be carried.

Whatever your mode of travel, there are some basic tips that will help you to decide what's truly necessary to take and what can be safely left behind without regret.

Packing with your destination in mind

Start with the basics that you think you'll need. Think carefully about the weather at your destination, the activities you'll be taking part in that might need special gear, and how long you'll be traveling for. Will you have access to a laundry? For a trip to the snow, remember thermals; for business trips, plan your wardrobe to work for your meetings and networking functions. A beach or resort holiday is probably the easiest to pack for, as you'll need very little!

TIP

When packing clothes, layers are the key to coping with any and all weather eventualities. Pack items that you can wear in layers, putting them on or taking them off as needed. Rather than one bulky sweater, pack a short-sleeve shirt and a long-sleeve top that can go over it with a lighter sweater as well. In cold climates, add a lightweight foldable jacket. Try them on before you leave home to make sure the layers fit easily over each other and to see how each piece of clothing works with others.

Reining in the urge to overpack

It can be tempting to overpack because you think you "might" need something or like to have options. Fight this urge and keep it basic. Your future self will thank you.

As a rough guide, depending on your travel plans, packing for a week-long trip should include the following essentials, although you may be able to trim it back if you can't fit it all in your bag. Some smaller items can go in your "handbag" rather than your main carry-on bag, and don't forget that you'll be wearing some items.

>> Seven pairs of underwear and socks

>> Four tops/shirts/t-shirts

>> Three trousers/jeans or shorts

>> One smart outfit for a special dinner (if really necessary)

>> One lightweight foldable jacket or rain jacket

- Three pairs of shoes — walking shoes/hiking boots, flip-flops, and something a bit dressier (women should lean towards stylish sneakers rather than heels)
- Sleepwear
- Swimsuit (even if you're not heading for the beach or a resort, a few laps in your hotel pool is a great way to wind down)
- Spare plastic bag for your wet swimsuit
- Toiletries, medication, and small first-aid kit including sunscreen
- Glasses/sunglasses
- One tote bag or small backpack
- Notebook and pen/s
- A plastic or cloth bag to keep dirty laundry separate from your clean clothes
- Reusable water bottle
- Camera (unless you'll be using your phone)
- A good book (my *very* essential item) or well-loaded e-reader to help pass the time during delays or on the plane

Keep your toiletries and makeup to a minimum. Not only does this take up space, but you may need to check your bag if you're carrying too many liquids. Keep liquid or cream beauty items, perfume, and sunscreen away from clothes, and if you are traveling by plane, remember that altitude and air pressure changes can cause products to expand or leak. Keep them contained in a plastic bag to prevent them making a mess of the rest of the contents of your bag. The last thing you want to being doing on arrival at your destination is a load of laundry!

REMEMBER

If you do decide to check a bag, be sure to keep these essentials with you in your carry-on bag in case your luggage gets delayed or lost:

- Passport or other ID
- Money and cards
- Glasses
- Medication

- ❯❯ Spare underwear
- ❯❯ Hairbrush
- ❯❯ Toothbrush

TIP

Never pack anything fragile in your checked baggage. Wrap it well and take it with you in your carry-on.

Saving Space When You Pack

Space is the deciding factor when planning your packing. In order to fit everything into your chosen bag, think carefully about what items can be reused or re-worn during the course of your trip. Doing double-duty can help save space. For example, if you take a foldable lightweight but sturdy backpack as your carry-on bag, you can also use it as your day pack for sightseeing. (Make sure it has well-padded straps, plenty of storage pockets, and a spot for your water bottle.)

A tote bag that packs flat in your luggage and takes up no room is another essential reusable item. Use it as a shopping bag, take it to the beach, or to keep items such as dirty clothes separate in your bag. My go-to is a handwoven string *bilum* I bought in Papua New Guinea, which takes up no room but expands to carry almost anything and is so strong it's almost indestructible. In fact, the local women often use a bilum for carrying their babies, as shown in Figure 4-2.

Packing techniques are also important when saving space in your bag. Are you a roller or a folder? I'm the latter. Most people adhere to either one or the other, but I don't really think it matters too much. Do whatever works best for you.

Seasoned travelers swear by packing cubes or cells to keep your items organized. This will not only save you time looking for the clean clothes among the dirty ones but will also maximize the space in your bag. Cubes and cells come in different shapes and sizes and are most useful if you are packing a large suitcase. Semi-transparent cells are a good idea, so you can easily find what you're looking for, but some also come in different colors for easy identification. Compression cubes, which can be vacuum pressed to extract the air from them after they are packed, are also useful. I've used them when taking bulky coats and jackets to a European winter, but the hitch is that once you have opened them you need a vacuum pump in order to repack for your homeward journey.

Lee Mylne(Author)

FIGURE 4-2: A string bilum from Papua New Guinea, strong enough to carry a baby.

TIP

My best tips for space–saving are:

>> Wear your bulkiest items of clothing on the plane. This is usually shoes, such as hiking boots, which take up a lot of space in your bag but might also be something like a heavy coat or jacket.

>> Remember to put smaller items inside others, such as stuffing your shoes with socks or other small things.

>> Leave belts flat; a rolled belt takes up more space.

>> Color-coordinate your clothes to minimize the amount you'll need to take. It's easier for men than for women, of course, but mix and match is the name of the game. Wear neutral shades — black, white, gray, beige or navy, for

example — and if you really need a splash of color in your travel wardrobe throw in some scarves.

>> Choose items for their versatility, so you can wear them in different situations.

>> Save space by leaving jewelry and valuables at home. They are safer there, and you are less likely to be a target for muggers and thieves.

>> Use a zippered plastic bag instead of a bulky toiletries bag. Buy travel-sized toothpaste and makeup. Think about what you may be able to buy when you arrive (soap, shampoo, and so on). In some cases, your hotel may provide these things, so there's no need to take your own.

When you're traveling, nobody is going to know or notice you've worn the same clothing again and again!

Saving space when packing has the added benefit that perhaps you'll find something that you just can't resist buying on your travels — and by being economical in what you've taken with you on your trip, you have extra space to squeeze it in to take home. For years, I bypassed too many treasures that lingered in my memory long after I had left them behind for lack of space. On my first day of a three-week trip through eastern Canada, I fell in love with a Celtic cross that now hangs on my balcony wall. But I agonized because it was large and heavy and *it was the first day!* Did I really want to lug it around Canada and across the world to home? Yes, I did. And the proof is in Figure 4-3.

Another option to consider is shipping your souvenirs home. In many cases, reputable stores will arrange shipping for you at an extra cost. If they don't, and you think you'll want to buy up big on Moroccan pottery or African baskets, check carriers and costs before leaving home.

Pack your items in the order you'll be using them — the things you want to use first should be packed on top. For example, if you're arriving at your destination late at night and plan on falling straight into bed, pack your pajamas last.

FIGURE 4-3: If you really want that souvenir, you'll make it fit somehow.

Useful Items and Gadgets

While a digital detox might sound appealing, the reality is that few people travel without at least some technology, whether it's a way of keeping in touch with home, sharing your travels with the world at large via social media, or just making traveling a bit easier. Not all the useful items I carry on my travels are high tech, but they're all a key part of making each trip more comfortable and enjoyable.

Chargers, adapters, and other tech gadgets

In these days of keeping connected, there's no doubt that electronic gear is something that takes up a huge amount of space in your luggage. Think carefully about what you need to take. Laptop? Maybe only if you're traveling on business; for most people a smartphone will do the trick for social media posts and emails. Large DSL camera and lenses? If you're going on safari or on a birdwatching tour, maybe . . . if not, perhaps your phone camera is all you need for holiday memories.

Pack a small storage device for downloading or backing up your photos or upload them to a cloud-based server. You'll save a whole lot of space without either of those items, along with the assorted chargers and accessories that are needed for them.

Generally, if you're traveling with spare batteries for your phone, laptop, or camera, for aircraft safety reasons, they need to go in your carry-on luggage only — not your checked bags.

A wireless portable charger is also handy to have for those times when you're out and about all day without access to chargers or for when you just plain forget to charge up overnight.

Your mobile phone can act as camera, flashlight, and alarm clock . . . so you can leave all those at home!

If you're traveling abroad, you'll also need an electrical adapter that fits the power plugs in the country you are visiting. Buy a "universal" adapter so you only have to buy one, no matter how many different countries you visit (on this trip and in the future). That said, don't assume a set of adapter plugs or a universal adapter will cover you everywhere — double-check that it has the specific plug that works where you're going. Some adapters now have fast-charging capability, which can be handy if you run short of time to charge your devices. Make sure your adapter has a surge protector, and has USB ports built in, which will be handy if you are trying to charge multiple devices at once, especially if you are somewhere where there are limited power outlets. The other thing to look for is the voltage input on your devices (it will be on the cord, plug or on the device itself) and make sure you have the correct voltage conversion accessory if necessary.

Keep all your chargers and cords in a pouch or bag together, so you always know where they are. I always pack mine in my carry-on luggage in case my checked bag goes missing.

To research the plug(s) you need for any destination worldwide, check out the **International Electrotechnical Commission's** world plugs list (www.iec.ch/world-plugs), which allows you to search by country and has handy diagrams of plugs' prong fitting and voltages in each country. Some countries have multiple plug types, so seek advice from your travel company or hotel accommodations on what type you will need there or get adapter plugs for all the listed plug types for that country.

Buy adapter plugs, such as those in my collection in Figure 4-4, before you leave home. It's much easier than trying to find one when you get to your destination (which will often only sell them for other destinations anyway). If you forget, international airports are a good place to find them.

Lee Mylne(Author)

FIGURE 4-4: Adapter plugs for other countries should be purchased before you travel.

Once you have your technology needs sorted and down to a minimum, there are a few other things that will be handy to have with you, especially if you are flying.

Other helpful items and gadgets

If you're prone to overpacking, invest in an electric handheld luggage scale. This will enable you to weigh your bags at home before you get to the airport and find your checked luggage is over the limit. It's a simple and easy way to avoid excess baggage fees and to save the embarrassment of opening up your suitcase on the floor of the terminal and discarding or rearranging things before you have to high-tail it to the departure gate in a fluster.

For inflight comfort, invest in noise-canceling headphones, which can be a boon on noisy flights. Make sure you choose a set that actually do shut out the noise and that have good quality sound. Remember to also ask about the battery life, especially if you're on a long-haul international flight.

Pack an inflatable neck pillow in your carry-on bag for long flights or night flights (especially if you are in economy class). Look for an adjustable one, rather than the traditional u-shaped pillow, for greater comfort. Add to that a good eye mask and ear plugs if you don't have noise-canceling headphones.

No matter what type of trip you are taking — road, rail, or air — a reusable water bottle should be at the top of everyone's packing list. It's more convenient (and cheaper) than having to find and buy bottled water, and you'll be helping save the planet, too! On flights, stretch your legs with a walk to the galley and ask the cabin crew to fill it up for you. And don't forget you'll use it every day while you're sightseeing. While there are plenty of plastic reusable bottles available, I really like a stainless steel one, which keeps the water cooler for longer, is sturdier, and doesn't risk leaching synthetic particles into the water. If you like to drink with a straw, take a stainless-steel straw as well.

TIP

I never travel without a sarong. It's a useful multi-purpose item, even if you don't want to wear it as a beach or pool cover-up. I've used it as a curtain or privacy screen, sheet, tablecloth, picnic blanket, and towel (not very effective but better than nothing). I've also wrapped it around fragile things in my packing. And it takes up no room at all in your bag.

If you're planning on staying in hostels, look for a decent padlock to take with you for locking up your valuables. Some padlocks are now designed to be opened with your fingerprint, which saves trying to remember your combination! And of course, you can always use it on your luggage, too.

TIP

Keeping your personal information safe should be a top priority while traveling, and an easy way to do that is with an RFID-blocking wallet, which prevents skimmers from stealing your credit card info just by walking by you.

While I'm a bibliophile who never travels without a real book, a tablet or e-reader loaded with books and maps can also save weight and space. If you're like me and prefer a physical book, take one that you won't mind leaving behind; that way, you can exchange or donate it along the way and pick up a new one.

IN THIS CHAPTER

» Carrying cash, credit cards, or both

» Knowing your passport and visa requirements

» Keeping in touch with friends and family

Chapter **5**

Don't Leave Home Without Them: Money, ID, and Devices

Whether you are planning to travel in your own country or take the big step and head to foreign lands, making sure you have ticked all the boxes before you leave home is vital to a stress-free takeoff.

In this chapter, I lead you through the essential steps for ensuring you've got everything you need for a smooth getaway and a trouble-free trip, from applying for a passport and visa if you need one to the best ways to keep in touch with your loved ones and avoid scams. You'll also find some handy tips for making the most of your travel budget and handling your money while you're away.

FIND ONLINE

If you find the online resources provided in this chapter helpful, be sure to check out www.dummies.com/go/solotravelfd for handy links to these resources and more.

Going International? Passport and Visa Requirements

If you have braved a few solo trips at home, it might be time to look further afield to new countries, cultures, and experiences. There's nothing quite like the feel of a brand-new passport in your hand (I'm on number six and the thrill never wears off). It doesn't matter where you're going, international travel means you must have a passport and possibly a visa, depending on your destination. Turning up at the airport without one or both can result in being unable to board your flight, so don't overlook this most important step in your plans.

Luckily, getting a passport is relatively easy. However, it can take time, so ensure that you plan ahead, know when you'll be traveling and allow time for the process.

Your passport will be the most important document you ever hold, apart from your birth certificate. Take good care of it.

WARNING

Some countries require your passport to still have at least six months' validity on it when you arrive. If you do not have this you may be refused boarding your plane at the airport when you depart from home.

Getting a passport

The first step in applying for your passport will be to contact your government's passport office. It will outline the steps you need to follow, which will include providing other identification. Make sure you begin this process several months before you want to travel because it can take some time.

Applying for your first passport will mean you need to have a personal interview, provide recent passport photos (check the dimensions and other requirements carefully or you will be rejected), government-issued photo ID, such as a driver's license, and other identification that proves your citizenship, which will usually be your birth certificate or certificate of naturalization. The cost of your passport will also vary according to where you live and this will be detailed on the government website.

If you are renewing your passport, this is an easier process and can be done online or by mail.

Which visa is right for you?

Whether you need a visa depends on your citizenship and the destination you are traveling to. Many countries have reciprocal arrangements that determine if you need a visa and how much it will cost. Contact the embassy, consulate, or high commission to check the forms of payment they accept.

TIP

For an up-to-date, country-by-country listing of passport requirements around the world, go to the "Foreign Entry Requirement" website of the U.S. State Department at http://travel. state.gov.

Many countries will now issue an electronic visa that takes the place of a stamp in your passport. If you're a tourist, short-term visitor, or business traveler, this is usually a relatively simple process that usually only takes a few minutes online. Some countries, however, require that you send your passport to their embassy or consulate for processing, along with passport photographs and other details, and sometimes this can be a drawn-out process with lots of form-filling and a nervous wait for the outcome. Make sure you allow plenty of time, especially if the country you are traveling to is prone to bureaucracy (I'm looking at you, India) or is not a developed nation. There is nothing worse than being down to the wire before departure day and still not having your passport and visa in hand. Check websites to find out the particular process needed for the destination you are traveling to.

WARNING

When applying for a visa, ensure you do so through the official government website. There are many websites that will offer to process a visa application for you — usually for a substantial fee that you do not have to pay to an official site. While they may not always be scams and will provide the visa, some of them are best avoided (just in case).

Coping with Customs and taxes

Every country you visit will have its own laws regarding what you can and can't bring into the country or take out of it. Making sure you observe these laws and pay any taxes due is vital. Heavy penalties are imposed on travelers who break the laws. There are also restrictions on how much money you can take in and out of most countries.

Most countries have strict regulations around importing plants and animals and any organic matter that might introduce diseases that will harm livestock or agriculture. Check your bags for leftover fruit or other food before you get off the plane.

Some countries are signatories to the Convention on International Trade in Endangered Species. This means they ban the importation of products made from protected wildlife. Banned items include ivory, tortoiseshell, rhinoceros or tiger products, and sturgeon caviar. Be aware that this will apply to products you might bring from home or souvenirs you have picked up on your travels, and they will be confiscated.

Those cute sniffer dogs at airports that run around your bags or across the baggage carousel are there to detect not only illegal drugs such as cocaine, but also plant and animal matter.

Customs checks can be a time-consuming and tedious process. Typically, you will stand in a slow-moving line waiting for your turn to have your passport and declaration documents checked, bags scanned, and potentially a hand-search of your luggage by Customs officers. Keep your cool. Unless you have something to hide this is a formality and most Customs officers are polite and friendly. They will certainly take your appearance and attitude into account when assessing the likelihood of you having something to hide.

TIP

If you have any doubts about what you have in your luggage, err on the side of caution and declare it. I always declare my hiking boots, pictured in Figure 5-1, when coming in or out of Australia or New Zealand, where it's a very serious matter if there is soil attached to the soles (result: very clean boots courtesy of Customs who take them away for a once-over). If you fail to declare something that is later found in your bag during a search, you may find yourself with a hefty fine or at the very least a stern telling-off.

FIGURE 5-1: Boots should always be declared at Customs.

Medications should be labeled clearly, and ideally you should carry a letter from your doctor or a prescription with you (with translations if appropriate).

Where you've been on your travels will also have an impact on your passage through Customs. If you've been in southeast Asia or South America, you're more likely to be thoroughly searched for drugs. You may also need to declare which countries you've traveled in or through because of health risks. For example, if you've traveled via South America, some countries will require you to have current yellow fever vaccinations — and to prove it. For years I've carried a vaccination booklet, as in Figure 5-2, just in case I'm asked for it. For more on health requirements and vaccinations, refer to Chapter 3.

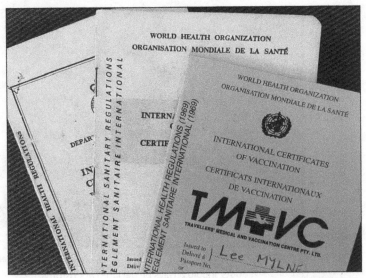

FIGURE 5-2: Vaccination record for yellow fever.

Choosing Credit, Cash, or a Combination

When planning your trip, you always need to think about accessing money once you get there, and this is especially the case if you are traveling overseas. For most people, the best is a combination of cash or cards, but each has its benefits and drawbacks. In the post-COVID world, plastic is king, with credit, debit, or prepaid travel money cards each having their place. I always like to take a little cash with me because there are always times when you need it.

If heading overseas, it is a good idea to open a separate credit or debit card account as your traveling fund, to insulate your everyday accounts from any potential dangers from scammers or unscrupulous traders. Prepaid travel money cards are also useful.

The advantage of using credit and debit cards is that transactions can be disputed if things go wrong. A credit card is a better option in those circumstances, as it offers better protections and it is the card issuer who will deal with the fight to reverse the transaction and get your money back. With a debit card, *you* are the one that has to fight to get it back — and who wants to be dealing with that nightmare while on vacation?

TIP

If your hotel requires a "bond" against any charges you may not pay for before you leave, make sure you know how much it will be. It can vary from one dollar to hundreds, and can sometimes take weeks to be refunded. In some best-case-scenario cases, the money is not actually taken but the card is used as the "bond." Use your credit card, rather than your debit card, to pay for this so your cash flow is not affected. This can be particularly annoying if you're staying at a new hotel every few days, as the amount can be significant over a week or more.

TIP

If your travel plans include hiring a car, you'll probably need a credit card, as some car-hire agencies won't accept a debit card as security. Check with them when you book.

Credit cards

Credit cards are a popular and safe way to carry money, with the advantage of providing a record of all your travel expenses. Look for a credit card that is fee-free, with no foreign exchange fees or annual fees, and that offers a relatively good exchange rate.

WARNING

While it's handy to be able to withdraw cash advances at banks or ATMs using your credit card, remember that this convenience comes at a cost, with high fees attached. You'll pay interest on a cash advance from the moment of your withdrawal, even if you pay your monthly bills on time, as well as a transaction fee on all charges you incur while traveling internationally, whether you're using your own currency or that of the place you are visiting. For overseas cash withdrawals, you should use a travel debit card or travel money card instead.

Some credit cards also give you free travel insurance, but this often has age limits and exclusions for pre-existing medical conditions. You should always check that coverage for COVID-19 is included. Travel insurance that comes with credit cards may need to be "activated," or it may require you to book airfares and/or accommodations using the card — up to a threshold amount — before it is activated. Read more about these logistics in Chapter 3.

Debit cards

Most debit cards are accepted by retailers and ATMs in major cities throughout the world and are an easy way to withdraw money while traveling. While using a debit card rather than a credit card means you are not paying interest, you will be charged a fee by the bank whose ATM you are using (unless it happens to be linked to your own bank, which is unlikely if you're traveling abroad). The fee is based on the amount you are withdrawing, so reducing the number of times you need to withdraw by taking a larger sum out isn't a way of avoiding it. If you think you'll need cash, take some with you and avoid the ATMs.

Look for a low-fee or no-fee debit card that doesn't charge a currency conversion fee and has a reasonable exchange rate and compare its offering with those from travel money cards.

In these days of tap-and-go, using a debit card for restaurants, hotels and other purchases can save you withdrawing cash at all. Just be careful about fees and exchange rates. Major banks usually apply a currency conversion fee for foreign transactions, whether they are purchases or ATM withdrawals.

REMEMBER

Always advise your bank you are traveling overseas, so you don't get stranded if they block your card because of suspicious transactions in a foreign country.

Prepaid travel money cards

Travel money cards are offered by banks, airlines, and money exchange companies like Travelex. Before leaving, you pay money into the card account and use it for purchases and cash withdrawals, just as you would with a debit or credit card. You can choose and lock in a foreign exchange rate when you load money onto the card, so you'll always know exactly what rate you are spending at.

Unlike credit or debit cards, there is no annual fee or interest to pay, but there may be other fees or costs to watch out for. These can include fees to load (or re-load) the card, ATM withdrawal fees, and exchange rate margins when you load and/or close the card. Make sure you check all these before buying a pre-paid card and make sure you know any limits on daily withdrawals. Always read the small print and make comparisons with the costs of using your credit or debit card.

Cash

If you're going to a location where you have less or no access to ATMs or when paying with a card may not be an option, you will need to carry cash. Get some foreign currency before you leave home, either at a bank or — more likely — at an airport exchange bureau, so you have some when you arrive at your destination and can avoid lines at airport arrival hall ATMs.

You should order foreign currency at least a week before your departure date — sometimes more, depending on your destination. Less frequently requested currencies may be harder for your provider to obtain. And remember that exchange rates can change between your order being placed and having the cash in your hand.

I always find cash is handy for very small purchases or for places like markets. It's very rare that cash will be refused, so carrying a little with you is always a good idea. It's also a good idea to thoroughly research your destination's attitude to cash before you go, as some small or remote places will operate on a cash-only economy. And don't forget that you'll always need cash for tips!

Just make sure you take the usual safety precautions. Don't carry large amounts, don't flash it around, and keep it in a safe place. Small notes are always best.

TIP

What to do with those pesky leftover foreign coins or low-value notes, like my stash in Figure 5-3? Money exchange operators usually won't accept coins, but most airports and airlines have boxes or envelopes where you can donate unwanted cash to charity. Otherwise, keep them for your next trip, give them to family and friends traveling to that destination, or just keep them as a souvenir!

Finding the best rate for your dollar

Exchange rates fluctuate on a daily — sometimes hourly — basis, so how do you know you're getting the best rate for your holiday dollar?

The best way is to shop around before you leave home, although this is also likely to only save you a few dollars. Ask your bank for the best deal they can offer and compare it with that being offered by major airport exchange booths.

Lee Mylne(Author)

FIGURE 5-3: Donate leftover foreign cash to charity.

Buying ahead of departure is a good idea because if you wait until you get to the airport, you'll probably pay more in fees and margins. Some airport exchange booths give better rates if you order in advance, but you can still pick it up when you arrive at the airport.

REMEMBER

Websites such as Xe (www.xe.com) and OANDA (www.oanda.com/currency-converter) will give you up-to-the-minute currency conversions.

Sometimes a hotel, restaurant, or shop will give you the option of using your card to pay in either the local currency or in your home currency. Which to choose? It's usually best to stick with the local currency, as you will avoid any inflated exchange rates, coupled with a potential profit margin for the trader. The exchange rate is unlikely to be as good as the one your bank or credit card company would apply.

Using ATMs in strange currencies

There's nothing more unsettling than standing in front of the ATM trying to work out which currency to choose, what the exchange rate is, and whether you're withdrawing $5 or $5,000.

As the people waiting in the line behind you get impatient, the fluster you are in only intensifies.

While an ATM is the easiest way to get cash when you're away from home, it's best to be prepared *before* you start punching buttons on the keypad. Have an idea of how much you want to withdraw and what the equivalent is in the local currency.

REMEMBER

Make sure you know your daily withdrawal limit before you leave home, and change it if necessary. Ensure you know how to do this online in case you need to change it again while you're traveling.

Whether you are at home or abroad, some banks impose a fee every time you use a card at another bank's ATM, and that fee can be higher for international transactions than for domestic ones. In addition, the bank from which you withdraw cash may charge its own fee. Find out the international withdrawal fees before you start your trip.

When possible, stick to official ATMs located at banks, and avoid ATMs in convenience stores and other shops — they are likely to be less secure, with a higher risk of having card readers, cameras, or other devices that can capture your details.

Whatever happened to traveler's checks?

Traveler's checks may almost sound like something from the dinosaur days, but they do still exist. That said, the number of banks that offer them and the number of places that accept them are few and far between. And to be honest, it would only make sense to use them if there was no other option in your chosen destination.

Some people like to carry traveler's checks as a backup since, unlike cash, they can be replaced if lost or stolen. However, because of this added security, there may be fees and commissions involved that make it more cost-effective to take cash or rely on your cards. You may also have to pay fees to an overseas bank or currency exchange when you cash the check. Make sure you find out before you buy them if you'll be able to easily cash them in your destination.

REMEMBER

Be sure to keep a separate record of the check serial numbers so you know them if the checks are lost or stolen.

Keeping in Touch with Home

There's no place like home and while I love to travel, I love to keep in touch with my family and friends I've left behind. Technology has made that so much easier that sometimes it's almost as if you're just down the road. And of course, there's an element of safety for a solo traveler; someone knows where you are or where you should be.

I never leave home without my smartphone and my laptop (and an untidy tangle of cords, chargers, and other related tech stuff). But getting everything set up to run smoothly in a different country is not always easy. In this section, I share some of the tricks and tips for unraveling the messy business of communicating while on the road and for keeping your data safe in strange places.

Setting up your phone and other devices

Some preparation before you head overseas can save you a lot of heartache and frustration — not to mention money — if things go wrong while you're traveling. While you may have tossed your daily cares to the wind, your lightness of being may create the window that a scammer or hacker is looking for in order to swoop in.

Some simple steps before you travel can help protect you from the most common dangers, including loss, theft, or hacking. First, make sure you update and prepare your phone, laptop, and/or tablet before you head off. Consider setting your devices to auto-update so you don't have to worry about it while you're on the road.

Before you travel, set up the "find-my-device" feature on your laptop, phone, and/or tablet, so that if you lose one of them, it will help you locate it. If it looks unlikely you will get your device back, you can remotely erase your data to avoid that being stolen, too.

Set up cloud storage for your devices as well. Apart from the need for storage space for the gazillions of images you're going to be taking on your travels, this is also a good backup if your device is stolen or lost. Google Drive, Google Photos, Apple iCloud, Microsoft OneDrive, and Dropbox are all options for backing up important data.

WARNING

Make sure your cloud backup is only set to connect to Wi-Fi, to avoid a shocking mobile phone bill later.

Use an authenticator app such as Google Authenticator or LastPass Authenticator to set up two-factor authentication for your important accounts — email, banking, and social media — before you leave. SMS two-step verification is another option but is a less secure option and will only work if you have mobile roaming enabled, which will cost you more.

It's best to turn off your phone's data roaming, as it can be frighteningly easy to end up with a horrifyingly large bill if you leave it enabled. The horror stories from travelers who have been caught by this are many. The way to ensure you're not using data inadvertently is to disable your smartphone's roaming (find that in your phone's settings), so that apps are not running in the background.

Use your settings to disable auto-connecting to Wi-Fi, so you don't accidentally connect to a suspicious network. Turn off location services, which can be used to track or attack your devices. You can still use these features, but make it a conscious decision rather than allowing your phone to do it automatically.

If you don't already have login security, make sure access to your phone requires a passcode or facial recognition.

While you're safeguarding your devices, it's a good idea to back up all your data (if you don't do so regularly). If you lose your phone or other device, at least you haven't lost everything that's saved on it (including all those previous travel photos!).

It's also worth considering a small investment in a VPN (virtual private network) before you leave home, which creates a secure connection between your device and the internet. It is a small price to pay to make public Wi-Fi safer to use. Avoid using free VPN services, as many are not reliable or safe.

If you want to use your phone while you're abroad, invest in a local SIM card. You can often buy these on arrival at an airport or online before you leave home. If you have a very new smartphone, you might find it has a feature called an eSIM, which you can use in other countries instead of a local SIM card. This is embedded in your phone (you can't remove it) and is a smaller version of a normal SIM card. To use it, you need to be with a carrier that offers it, but that includes more than 120 worldwide and most major US carriers. Ask your phone provider if you're unsure if you have it or not.

Before you leave home, put together a kit of all the tech gadgets you'll need to keep in touch with the rest of your world. This should include your own chargers, cords and a portable power bank, as well as the right power adapter for the destination if you are traveling internationally. Some hotels will have spares, but don't count on it. I always take a portable hard drive, too, to back up my photos and reduce the risk of losing them if my camera's memory card fails or is damaged (it's happened!). Make sure it's an SSD (solid state drive), which is more stable and able to handle the rigors of the road. My other "must" is a powerboard, so I can charge multiple devices at once, without having to hunt down outlets all over the hotel room (and for those that are stingy with them) or take multiple power adapters if I am overseas.

Download city maps on maps.me or a similar app. Choose one that uses GPS to provide offline directions.

Finding internet access anywhere

Almost every hotel, hostel, resort, airport, cafe, and many retailers now offer free Wi-Fi hotspots. Public Wi-Fi is also usually available around city streets. While this is wonderfully convenient, all of these should still be treated with extreme caution as it's possible unsecured Wi-Fi networks can be used by hackers to steal your login details or personal information. While less dangerous, be aware that your hotel will also be gathering information about you when you use the guest Wi-Fi. Caution should be used at all times when using any kind of public Wi-Fi.

The danger of cybersecurity threats can be heightened during travel from exposure via public Wi-Fi to "shoulder surfing," when all someone needs to do is glance sideways at your screen to pick up some of your sensitive information.

WiFi Map (www.wifimap.io) claims to hold the world's largest directory of public wireless hotspots.

If you are traveling within your own country, where phone bills are not going to be astronomical, you can always use your own mobile tethering system as a safe option.

Make sure your phone isn't set to automatically connect to unfamiliar Wi-Fi networks.

Some digital security comes from paying attention to your surroundings. Keep your devices with you or leave them in your hotel room safe. Do your internet banking in the privacy of your room, not in public places, unless you are sure no one is sitting behind you looking over your shoulder.

When you are not using your phone, keep it locked, and log out of apps when you have finished using them.

Most public libraries around the world offer free internet and computer access to everyone, even though some may impose time limits.

Avoid using public USB charging stations, as they can be hacked to steal your data or inject malware. If you think you might need to use them, take a charge-only cable that can't transfer data, or use your own portable power bank or your own wall charger. Similarly, don't be tempted to use charging points in rideshare cars, even if you are using your own cord, as this will potentially connect your phone to the vehicle's system.

Facebook (and other forums) can be your friend

First, a confession: I love social media. I especially love Facebook and Instagram, and I use them a lot to share my traveling life. It makes me feel connected to my friends and family, as they respond with comments and likes or share their own experiences of a place I'm visiting. It's fun.

Of course, your motivation might be to make your friends at home green with envy with your fabulous images of the exotic places you're visiting. That's certainly one of the benefits of signing up to Facebook, Instagram, or X (formerly known as Twitter). Forget about old-fashioned postcards (although I admit I'm a big fan)!

From that very first clichéd post of your passport and boarding pass or the shot from the window of the plane as you wing your way to somewhere fabulous, you'll be counting the "likes" and knowing that at least some of your friends are wishing they were coming with you. How many will ask, "Can I carry your bags?"

WARNING

Posting a photo of your paper boarding pass might seem like fun, but should be approached with caution. Not only is your full name, seat number, and destination there for the world to see, but the bar code carries even more sensitive information — such as your contact information and passport details. Don't risk that information getting into the hands of skilled hackers who can use it for identity fraud. Frame your photo carefully, so you don't show that information, as I've done in Figure 5-4.

Lee Mylne(Author)

FIGURE 5-4: Hide sensitive information when photographing your boarding pass.

Solo travel can be lonely at times, so social media is a great way of feeling connected to your friends and family, even if they're not with you. It's a great way to keep in touch on longer trips when you might not have the opportunity to keep in touch in other ways. With social media, you can easily post photos and updates so that your loved ones can follow along and feel like they're right there with you.

TIP

But there are other advantages, too. You can use social media platforms to connect with other travelers and locals. Join Facebook groups for travelers in the destination you are visiting, an excellent way of finding out where to eat or what to do. Do this before you leave home, and you may find some real connections for when you arrive.

Facebook groups such as Solo Female Travelers and The Solo Female Traveler Network are also great sources of support and advice and you might also connect with groups that share your special area of interest in the place you are traveling to, whether it is in your own country or overseas. For example, there are a number of Facebook pages devoted to travelers wanting to walk the Camino de Santiago in Spain, including Camigas, which puts women on the Camino in touch with each other. Check local community pages to find events at which visitors are welcome, such as sailing days or park runs.

Instagram can be used in a similar way, to find people with similar interests in your destination.

But remember that while social media can be a great way to stay connected with friends and family, meet new people, and document your travels, it should not take over your life. Make sure you take some time off it, or you will miss the best part of travel — being there!

The pitfalls of social media

Social media can be addictive. And the time when you least want that to happen is when you are traveling or on vacation. The biggest pitfall of all is to get so obsessed with your social media posts and your followers' reactions to them — so that you miss out on being in the moment and enjoying the best of the place you're in. Always be sure to temper your enthusiasm for social media with a reality check!

It's very easy to decide to post a quick selfie of your travels and then get sucked into the vortex of looking at what everyone else is posting and before you know it, you've spent a good hour (or more) with your nose in your phone, missing out on what's going on around you. Travel is such a privilege that it's almost a sin to waste any opportunities to soak up everything you can.

While I love using social media, and I do spend time using it when I travel, I try to leave it until the end of the day, when I'm back at my accommodation and have some quiet time to reflect on the day. Part of that might be posting my images, or answering messages from friends and family. But it might also be writing notes from the day; journals are a great idea if you like to record and write about your experiences. That said, looking back on your social media posts can also be a great way to reflect.

But if you're always focused on taking photos or checking your phone, you might miss some of the best parts of the day. Like that whale or dolphin breaching the water, the burst of fireworks, the fleeting glimpse of a shy platypus in a rippling stream. Sometimes it is better to put your phone or camera down and savor the moment. Over decades of traveling, I've learned that the most memorable experiences are sometimes those when the unexpected happens, and if you're not watching and listening you may miss them.

Take my advice and try to cut back on your social media while traveling. It will enhance your experience.

Avoiding Scams

Point me to someone, of any age, gender, or background, who hasn't fallen — or nearly fallen, anyway — for a scam while traveling abroad. I'll be amazed. Sometimes you can be lucky and that gut instinct of *something's not quite right here* will kick in and you'll walk away before the worst happens. But scams and cons of all kinds are getting more sophisticated by the day and when traveling solo, you're at your most vulnerable.

It's a good idea to talk to people who've been to that destination you're heading for and ask them what to be wary of. There are steps you can take to minimize your risk, but there are still traps for the trusting or unwary.

While you'll be most alert to scams when you are on the road, be aware that travel scams can start even before you leave home. Here are some of the most common scams and ways you can try to avoid becoming a victim.

Cheap airline ticket scams

If it sounds too good to be true, it probably is. Be wary of deals on airline tickets offering deal-of-a-lifetime prices. Airline ticket fraud is rife, according to Interpol. And the end result is that you could end up with no ticket and the money has gone to fund criminals in their next scam.

How does it work? Interpol warns that criminals offer tickets bought using stolen or hacked credit cards for sale at bargain prices using sophisticated fake websites or social networking accounts. Sometimes they pose as branches of well-known travel agents and ask for immediate payment to seal the deal. They will send you a flight booking confirmation, but your ticket may never be honored.

If the owner of the credit card, which was used fraudulently, reports it before your flight, the airline will cancel the ticket, and you'll be unable to travel. A worse scenario is that you make your flight overseas without drama, but the return ticket is canceled and you are stranded in other country. Then there is the expensive business of buying a new ticket — and you will have little chance of getting your initial outlay back.

Be suspicious if the ticket price is significantly cheaper than anywhere else and if the departure date is within a few days of it being advertised. Do some research into the travel agency, including calling a number you have sourced from somewhere other than the website offering the cheap deal. Fake websites are sometimes so well done it's difficult to tell the difference from the real thing.

Visa scams

If you need a visa for your dream destination, make sure you buy it direct from the country's consulate or embassy. Visa scams are set up to trick travelers into buying visas that are not needed, overpriced, or illegal. While there are some legitimate third-party websites that will charge a fee to submit a visa application for you, some of these are scammers.

Make sure you are buying direct from the embassy or consulate or at very least from an organization recommended by them. Read the government travel advice on entry and exit requirements.

If you travel on a fake visa, you may be arrested, deported, or jailed on arrival at your destination.

Carry-my-bag scams

Never agree to carry a bag, or something in your own bag, across an international border for anyone else either on a flight or other method of transport. It's not uncommon for a stranger or casual acquaintance — someone you've chummed up with on your travels — to ask for this harmless-sounding favor. They may offer to pay you or give you a sob-story about a family need. The package or bag is likely to look innocuous but could contain hidden drugs or other contraband items.

Even if the person is someone you know and trust, be wary. Make sure you see what is inside it and are confident that all is as it seems. Even if the parcel is gift-wrapped, insist on seeing the contents. Never carry a bag or package for anyone you've just met.

Even if it isn't drugs, make sure you check to be sure it's not a restricted or prohibited item at your next destination (see the section, "Coping with Customs and taxes," earlier in this chapter).

Taxi scams

From your arrival at an unfamiliar airport to the taxi taking you for your departing flight, taxis are a familiar scam. Jetlagged, you stagger off the plane after a long flight, intent only on getting to your hotel. You are a prime target for unscrupulous taxi drivers. And there are many, in all parts of the world. Unlicensed, unmetered drivers often operate from airport arrivals halls and major tourist destinations. These drivers offer flat-rate fees to tourists. In many cases, the fees are much higher than metered fares. This happened to me, in Paris, but a passing local overheard my negotiation with the driver and intervened to give him a dressing-down and put me on the right track to a fair fare.

Check that the meter is turned on. Don't fall for the old ruse that it's not working. Insist on a metered ride — find another taxi, if necessary. In most countries it is illegal for licenced taxi drivers not to use the meter.

TIP

If you have doubts about the route taken or the fare, take a note of the taxi number, company name, and if possible, the driver's name, which should be displayed inside the vehicle.

Unlicensed taxi drivers at airports will likely be lurking inside the terminal, waiting for new arrivals and will follow and harass you to convince you to accept their offer. Although there are signs in many airports banning this practice, it is still rife. Licensed taxi drivers will be outside the terminal in their vehicle at the official taxi rank. Head there and you should be safe.

Another way to avoid this scenario is to use another form of transport to get to your accommodation. Major airports usually have excellent train or bus services to the city center, or use a shuttle bus that will drop you at the door of your hotel. As a solo traveler with no one to share the cost of a taxi with, this is also usually a much more economical option.

WARNING

Beware of friendly taxi drivers who offer you cheap tours. They will take you to shops where they receive a commission, where you are likely to be heavily pressured to buy, to be overcharged, or will be sold dodgy goods.

Vehicle hire scams

Car hire scams are rife in some countries. The most common is being falsely accused of damaging a vehicle. Ensure that you inspect the vehicle closely (and take photos) before you drive away. Some car hire places have demanded thousands of dollars in damages for alleged damage and will threaten and harass unwitting customers.

Never hand your passport over as collateral when hiring a vehicle of any kind, including a motorcycle or jet ski. The car hire operator will keep it until you pay for the supposed damage.

Before you hire a vehicle, read online reviews of local travel companies, and check that your insurance covers you for the type of vehicle you are driving or riding.

Wrong change or overcharging

Those funny, unfamiliar banknotes and coins can be a trap for the unwary. So, too, can exchange rates, and it is these two things that can make it easy for sly traders and taxi drivers to overcharge you or — more commonly — short-change you. For example, you give them a $50 note and they give you change for $5. The original note has been quickly slipped out of sight, so even if you argue, they can pull out a lower denomination note and say, "No, this is the one you gave me." Yes, it has happened to me. But sometimes, if you challenge it and stand your ground, they will know the jig is up and hand over the rest of the change.

TIP

In a bar or restaurant, if there is no written menu or no prices on the menu, ensure you negotiate the price before the food starts arriving on your table.

The best protection in a case like this is to be confident. Before you travel, familiarize yourself with the local currency, get a sense of how much things should cost, and what the exchange rate is, and take your time in checking your change when it is handed over.

Card skimming

Card skimming is unfortunately not uncommon. *Skimming* refers to copying the information off the magnetic strip on your credit or debit card.

Be vigilant and don't let the person you are paying move the card out of your sight below the counter or in a back room or office. Sometimes they will pretend the card machine is not working and have to move to another one. If this happens, demand your card back immediately and leave, or pay with cash.

Fake ticket scams

One of the joys of travel is often the chance to see your favorite musicians in concert or a big musical or theatre show. Tickets are often hard to come by for the most popular events, and it's tempting to try all avenues to get your hands on them. It's a scammer's dream.

Always buy a ticket from a reputable online outlet. Scammers can set up fake websites that look genuine but you may never see your ticket once you have paid the money (and they will have your card details). If a deal looks too good to be true, it just might be.

Remember, as a solo traveler, your chances of getting just one ticket are probably higher than for anyone wanting two or more!

If you are staying in a big hotel, see if your hotel concierge can obtain a ticket for you. Hotels often have special arrangements with theatres to get tickets for their guests. There are legal ticket resellers, but make sure you check that they are genuine. Your accommodation may also be able to advise you on this.

WARNING

In some countries, it may be against the law to buy from unlicensed ticket sellers.

Scalpers sell tickets outside of venues, but this is also banned in some places, where the transaction must be made a certain distance from the event. And you will likely be paying a very inflated price.

Friend or relative-in-need scams

This scam is more likely to impact your family than it is you, but it is worth being alert to it. Scammers may phone, email, or message your friends and family — sometimes by hacking your social media accounts while you're traveling and pretending to be you. A desperate message will arrive from "you," detailing a terrible emergency and asking for money. They may lie and say something like you have been robbed and are stranded without any funds or that you have been in an accident and need urgent medical care to be paid for.

Make sure you are keeping in regular touch with your family or close friends so they know you are safe. Warn them of this possibility before you travel, so they are alert to it. If they are contacted in this way, tell them to ask a question that only you will know the answer to. The scammer will often go quiet and disappear when they know they've been rumbled.

What to do if you're the victim of a scam

If you're overseas and have been the victim of a scam, the first step is to report it to local police and make sure that you get a police report. You can also seek assistance from consular officers at your country's embassy or consulate, who may be able to give you advice or information. However, embassies will not lend you money or give legal advice.

Contact your bank or credit card company immediately, as they may be able to close your account or reverse a fraudulent transaction on your card.

The next step is to speak to your travel insurance provider. Most have a 24-hour emergency number you can call from overseas, and they will be able to advise you on whether your insurance policy will cover you for any financial losses.

Chapter **6**

A Room of Your Own

ll I want is a room somewhere, far away from the cold night air . . . so sang Eliza Doolittle (Audrey Hepburn) in the classic musical *My Fair Lady*. And sometimes when I am traveling, with no room booked at the end of a long day on the road, that's the song that plays in my head.

If you're like me, a room of your own at the end of the day is a wonderful refuge from the hurly-burly of traveling or sight-seeing. Whatever has happened during the day, that welcoming room, with clean sheets and a hot shower is all that's needed to put the world right again.

In this chapter, I show you all the options for that safe haven at the end of the day. Whether you're looking for luxury, budget, or something a little different to the norm, it's out there, with the welcome mat waiting for you — or other lovely messages, sometimes spelt out artistically on your bed, as in Figure 6-1.

FIND ONLINE

Head to www.dummies.com/go/solotravelfd for links to all the web addresses provided in this chapter, as well as additional online resources.

FIGURE 6-1: A "good night" message on a hotel bed in Sri Lanka.

Choosing the Right Accommodations for You

Everyone's needs are different, but choosing the right accommodations is essential if you are to be settled.

WARNING

The first night in a new destination is *not* the best time to go looking for somewhere to stay — and I say this from experience. There's nothing worse than trawling from place to place finding that "no vacancy" sign out everywhere. If you're on foot, it's even worse. Plan ahead and book a stay for your first night or two at least.

What's your budget?

Your budget will be a key factor in your choice of accommodation, but even with a modest budget it's possible to find some quirky and often lovely accommodation. That said, it can work the other way, too; price isn't always an indication of quality.

If a standard hotel is what you're looking for, there are ways to get the best room rates possible. Try an online bidding site, where you make an offer for a hotel room. If a hotel's occupancy is low at the time you want to stay, they may accept an offer lower than the standard rate. Your offer will be accepted or rejected instantly, and it's free to bid, so you've got nothing to lose. Before you bid, check out the usual booking websites like Expedia and Booking. com to see the going rate for the hotel you want to stay at.

REMEMBER

Whatever method of booking you use, always take the booking confirmation with you, either printed out or on your mobile device.

Location, location, location

Location is everything when booking your accommodations. First, decide whether you want to be in the heart of the action or prefer a more tranquil setting. Most travelers want to be close to major attractions to avoid transport costs and hassles.

Try to find accommodations in a well-serviced central location; somewhere near public transport or if you are a business traveler, somewhere close to where you need to be — especially on your first day.

TIP

If you're traveling for work, keep in mind that a hotel near a business center isn't always the best choice. An area that's bustling with office workers during the day may be desolate at night.

In many ways, you get what you pay for. The more central your accommodations are, the more expensive it's likely to be. However, weigh up the advantages of being close to the places you want to see and the cost or ease of getting around. If public transport is excellent, staying a little further out of town might be feasible. Use maps to locate your preferred hotel and work out the logistics of getting from there to the places you'll want to visit during your stay.

TIP

Always pack an eye mask and earplugs if you're a light sleeper. They take up no space in your luggage and can be the two things that ensure a good night's sleep.

If you are planning to stay in a hostel (see the section "Hosteling at Any Age," later in this chapter), be aware that some are located in less-desirable areas. Do your research! When you check in, ask staff if there are any nearby streets or areas to be avoided. Party hostels tend to be close to the nightlife, which means you can expect noise, so if that's not your scene, make sure you book a hostel with a quieter vibe.

Always try to arrive at your accommodations in daylight. There's nothing worse than not knowing exactly where you are going and having to find it in the dark. And it's much safer.

Find a local landmark — church spire, town hall clock, minaret, billboard — to help you find your way back to your hotel. Take a photo of it to show to locals if you get lost and need directions. Or just look up for it and follow your nose.

There's nothing worse than getting to your room and finding that there's something about it that makes you want to move on quickly. Feeling safe, comfortable, and well-provided for by your accommodations is essential.

Checking things out before you check in

The best advice: Check it out before you check in. If you have checked in but are not happy when you see the room, leave everything untouched and go back to the reception desk to ask for a better room (in a hotel in England, I did this three times before I found a room big enough to actually fit my suitcase in it beside the bed).

If you are pre-booking your accommodations, ask your travel agent — or the hotel, if booking direct — to provide all the information you need. Most websites carry this, but if you have questions, don't be afraid to ask.

Unless accommodations are at a premium, book ahead for only the first one or two nights. If your choice is not up to expectations, you can move on.

It's quite acceptable to ask to see a room before committing yourself to take it. If the owner or manager refuses, it's an indication you should move on. Things to look for when inspecting a room:

>> Are the locks sturdy and in good condition? Is there a peephole in the door or a chain on the door?

>> Do the windows open to allow good ventilation?

>> Is the bathroom dirty or damaged?

- >> How accessible to the street is the window?
- >> Is there a fire escape or other escape route?
- >> Is it likely to be noisy, either from other rooms, public areas like the bar, or from the street?
- >> Is there a safe to store your passport or valuables?

Hosteling at Any Age

I once stayed in a YHA (Youth Hostels Association) hostel where I was clearly the oldest person booked in — something I could tell just by looking around. And it mattered not one bit. Hostels today are open to all ages and are a terrific budget choice.

This section gives the lowdown on hostels if you're unfamiliar with them, as well as some resources to find a hostel for your next trip.

What to know about hostels

Youth hostels have been around for more than a century — but wow, have they changed! In fact, many of them have even dropped the "youth" angle they were originally known by and are just hostels that welcome everyone. The first hostels were in Europe, designed to provide affordable basic accommodation for young travelers. Rooms were dormitories, kitchens were communal (and you had to clean up after yourself and do "chores" for the common good), but the price was next to nothing if you were under about the age of 30. Membership to a youth hostel organization was required.

Today, while much of the same ethos applies, the "rules" have been relaxed a lot. While you'll still get a cheaper room if you're a hostel member, people of all ages are welcome to stay, and they're great places for meeting people. But if you want a private room with your own bathroom, you can find that at a hostel too.

Modern hostels are often almost as luxurious as some hotels, with swimming pools, tour desks, libraries, bars and restaurants, free Wi-Fi, co-working spaces, and a host of other extras, depending on where you are. Some also offer discounts to local attractions.

Whether you want a dorm room in a city center, a country escape for peace and quiet, or something a bit different, like a light-house on the California coast or a converted train carriage in Sydney's Railway Square, hostels offer something for everyone. Some are housed in unique buildings, such as historic prisons, chateaux, manor houses, glamping tents, and more. Many hostels give travelers a chance to experience the city — and meet others — through free activities such as walking tours, dance classes, karaoke nights, cooking classes, open mic nights, standup comedy, and more.

As a solo traveler, you have the choice of bunking in with others — usually in dorms of four, six, or eight beds — or booking a single room (for which you'll pay a higher price, of course), where you'd barely know you're in a hostel, such as the one in Figure 6-2, where I stayed in Melbourne, Australia. If you're a solo female traveler looking for security but willing to share a room, many hostels have single-sex dorms.

Lee Mylne(Author)

FIGURE 6-2: A private room at Melbourne Central YHA, Australia.

WARNING

If you're a light sleeper, it might be worth paying a bit more to have a private room, rather than risk snoring companions or late-comers waking you up. It may be the best decision of your trip. Book early, as private rooms are usually in hot demand.

How to find hostels

If staying at a hostel sounds appealing to you (or at least to your wallet), here are a few helpful resources to help with your search:

>> **Hostelling International** (hihostels.com) is a global not-for-profit with 61 member organizations operating around 3,000 youth hostels around the world. Under the Youth Hostels Association (YHA) banner, there are 700 hostels in about 600 cities; the larger ones are in England and Wales, Australia, China, and India. Other hostels in the Hostelling International network operate under different names, such as HI USA, HI Canada, Stayokay (the Netherlands), Danhostel (Denmark), Federation Unie des Auberges de Jeunesse (France), and Japan Youth Hostels.

>> Hostelworld.com is a good site for general information about hostels around the world, with entertaining blog posts about just about every aspect of budget travel and solo travel. Another is hostelz.com.

>> While most hostels are welcoming and inclusive to everyone, if you are looking for one that caters to the LGBTQ+ community, check out leading website misterbandb.com. It specialises in hostels, rooms, and rentals for LGBTQ+ travelers, and offers specific recommendations, such as San Francisco's Adelaide Hostel in Union Square, London's Generator Hostel, Madrid's Pizarro Hostel, and Dorm for Men in Bangkok. Some gay hostels offer discounts on local pride events and gay bars.

WARNING

There's no doubt that some privately run hostels can be dodgy. Or they might just not have the vibe you're looking for. How do you know until you get there? The best way to learn what a hostel is *really* like is to read reviews. Of course, the travelers who bother to spend time writing reviews are usually those who are either very disgruntled or very satisfied. The key to deciding if complaints about the hostel's hygiene standards or the rude staff are worth taking notice of is to look for the same complaint coming up consistently. Reviews will give you a pretty accurate idea of what other travelers thought. On Hostelz.com you can compare reviews from booking platforms such as Booking.com, Hostelworld, and Hostelsclub in one easy click.

TIP

You don't need to be a member of a hosteling organization to stay in one, but if you are, the room rates are a few dollars cheaper.

Becoming Part of the Family at a Homestay

If you really want to get to know the locals, choosing a homestay is a great way to do it. In many places, residents are happy to open their homes to travelers, who pay for a room in the home and, sometimes, for home-cooked meals. It's a wonderful way to give back to a community's economy and immerse yourself in local life.

After a homestay visit in Thailand, in the cute cottage in Figure 6-3, I once wrote: "Take a healthy appetite with you and be prepared to eat like you've never eaten before." My hostess was a terrific cook, as well as being a talented ceramic artist, and my memories of that stay at Don Kai Dee Village, about 47 miles (75 km) outside Bangkok are all good.

Lee Mylne(Author)

FIGURE 6-3: A homestay cottage in Thailand.

Of course, not all homestays include such feasts as I was treated to, but most do include meals with the host, often as part of a family. Homestays usually open doors to local experiences that you might otherwise miss and provide a real chance to connect with those who know your destination best.

Cuba has long offered tourists the chance to stay with local families. Since 1997, the Cuban government has allowed citizens to rent out rooms — and all who do so are state licensed to do so. Staying with a family is one of the best and cheapest ways to see Cuba and get to know its people. A private room, house, or apartment in Cuba is called a "casa particular," and there are two useful websites, www.casaparticularcuba.com/en and casaparticularcuba.org, that list hosted rooms and some private apartments.

Knowing where to find homestay options

One way of finding a homestay is through an organization like **Homestay** (homestay.com), which has 63,000 rooms in more than 175 countries, and operates on the philosophy that staying with a local is an important part of exploring a destination. Many Homestay hosts expect stays of more than a week, giving you time to really get to know them.

Homestayin.com is another simple, user-friendly website that lists homestay rooms across more than 1,200 cities in 85 countries. The majority of the hosts come from cities in USA, Canada, the United Kingdom, Australia, New Zealand, and Europe.

HerHouse (herhouse.co), which is exclusively for solo women travelers, offers free homestays for a maximum of three days, after paying a membership fee. It aims to connect female travelers with female hosts who have passed background checks, offering a safe and welcoming place to stay in a new city. Travelers fill out a profile, including emergency contact details, pay the membership fee, and then search hosts' locations, likes and dislikes, and expectations (no smoking, for example), and submit a homestay request. Users are also background checked to ensure only genuine solo female travelers are using the app. With verified hosts in 21 countries, from Angola to the USA, and more in 50 countries pending background checks, there's plenty of choice. (You can also use HerHouse for house sits and home swaps.)

Another option is to look for a company that incorporates home-stays in their tours, although this is like to only be a night or two. **G Adventures** (gadventures.com) runs small group "local living" tours in Ecuador, Italy, and Croatia, with four to six nights with a local family, including meals (you may be invited to help with the cooking sometimes).

G Adventures also includes homestays in other tours. I highly recommend the Back Roads of Japan tour, on which I stayed with a Japanese family in the coastal city of Hagi on the island of Honshu. It was a rare glimpse into a century-old family home with tatami mat floors and bedrooms behind paper screen doors. Helping with the cooking, I learned to make the popular snack Takoyaki under the watchful eye of my hostess, Toshiko-san and her 89-year-old mother Satoko-san. Despite a language barrier with Satoko-san, there was a lot of laughter — and the end result was delicious!

Homestays in Japan are called *minpaku* and are usually cheaper than hotels, but they may not include meals. As *minpaku* are often in residential areas, respect for neighbors is important (no loud parties!) as is — according to the Japan National Tourist Organization — sorting and putting out the garbage. Some *minpaku* are not registered, but to find those that are, look at official websites such as **Stay Japan** (en.stayjapan.com) or Airbnb.

B&Bs — A homestay and hotel hybrid

In the UK, bed-and-breakfast establishments have long been the equivalent of a homestay. Usually run by the homeowner, they are a long-standing tradition and a great way to meet fellow travelers, both from Britain and abroad, either over breakfast or in a communal lounge in the evening. Expect a wide range of styles, from swish city apartments to quaint cottages and ordinary homes all over England, Scotland, Ireland, and Wales. Not all of them are fancy, and you should expect to pay more for anything with a touch of luxury or sophistication.

While it's best to book ahead using a service like bedandbreak fasts.co.uk or bedandbreakfast.eu, it's also still possible to drive around Britain and stop when you see a "Vacancy" sign in a house window. That's all about serendipity, but such homes also usually have window stickers that show their accreditation with reputable B&B organizations. And most are keen to demonstrate their welcome, as the sign in Figure 6-4 shows.

Lee Mylne(Author)

FIGURE 6-4: Welcome sign on a B&B.

REMEMBER

Ask the rates and to see the room before committing yourself to a stay; going inside will usually give you a good indication if this is a place you'd like to stay or be comfortable with as a solo traveler. (American author Bill Bryson got the B&B vibe pretty right in his very funny 1995 book *Notes from a Small Island*.)

On one occasion, having *not* done my research, I found myself in London during Royal Ascot Week, when everything from the cheapest dorm to the ritziest hotel was booked out. I finally found a room in a B&B in Hammersmith and inadvertently found myself with a minor television celebrity as my hostess. It was great fun to hear some celebrity gossip from an "insider" — and her husband even gave me a lift to the train station when I left.

In Japan, family-run bed-and-breakfasts are called *minshuku*, and are a great way of experiencing Japanese traditional life. They're usually found in tourist areas, as well as in quieter towns and seaside locations. Many include a homestyle dinner as well as breakfast (although some may not offer meals at all). Expect quite basic accommodations, including futon bedding. While you might find some *minshuku* on websites like Booking.com, you can also book them through local tourism associations in your chosen destination.

Cheap and Cheerful Budget Stays

While hostels are perhaps the cheapest form of commercial accommodation, there are other ways to tighten your budget and still find a safe, clean, and comfortable place to stay. From a room in a private home — sometimes at no cost — to a serene temple or monastery or a room above the bar in a pub, the alternatives to a cheap hotel or motel are many.

Airbnb and home-swapping

The most common choice for many travelers is **Airbnb** (`airbnb.com`), which gives you the option of a room hosted by the home-owner, or a "whole house" in whatever form that takes, giving you more privacy. For many solo travelers, cost will be a factor, with some Airbnb options being budget-busting, but it's worth searching for bargains, especially if you're staying for more than a few days.

If you own your home, consider house-swapping: You stay in their house, and they stay in yours. You both get to live like a local. As well as saving money on accommodations, you have access to a kitchen to cook in and sometimes even a car to drive. The bonus is that someone else is looking after your home while you're away, watering your plants and providing an element of security. And personally, I love to browse in someone else's bookcase! There are lots of house-swapping websites, and on most you can browse the listing for free but need to pay an annual membership to view the contact details or to list your own home.

There are many good house-swap websites to consider. **Home Exchange** (`homeexchange.com`) is the world's largest home exchange website, with 150,000 properties in 145 countries. It's free to list your house, but once you organize a house-swap, there's a membership fee of US$220 a year for an unlimited number of swaps throughout the year. Home swaps don't need to be simultaneous — you can "pay" for the use of a home with "guest points" that the property's owner can then use to stay somewhere else at another time (you get 500 guest points on joining).

REMEMBER

All house-swaps are at your own risk. Lock up anything private or valuable that you don't want a stranger to have access to.

House-sitting

Don't have a house to swap? Try house-sitting, where you stay in someone else's home for free in return for taking care of it while they're away traveling. Your "duties" might include light gardening (watering and weeding) or looking after a pet.

There are many house-sitting agencies to choose from, all of which operate on similar lines. You pay a membership fee to the site (which varies depending on the site and the tier of membership you choose), and your ID is verified (US applicants also have to do a free background check). Then you provide a couple of character references and create a profile of yourself. When that's done, you're ready to start applying for your first position!

My cousin Urlys is a frequent house-sitter, and she uses the largest worldwide platform, **Trusted Housesitters** (www.trustedhousesitters.com), which she recommends for international travelers. She says the best approach is to contact homeowners using the app and build up a rapport with them before you commit to the "sit" — and to always ask for a photo of the bedroom you'll be using before accepting. Her best advice: Work on your profile, as it can give you the edge over other contenders, especially for a high-end home.

Other reputable sites include **Mind My House** (www.mindmyhouse.com) and **House Carers** (www.housecarers.com). There are also country-specific agencies such as **House Sitters America** (www.housesittersamerica.com), **Aussie House Sitters** (www.aussiehousesitters.com.au) for Australia, and **Kiwi House Sitters** (www.kiwihousesitters.co.nz) for New Zealand.

TIP

When starting out as a house-sitter, it's important to get good references from friends or employers as it can be difficult to get the first sit without previous history on the site. You can use Airbnb reviews for this too.

Couchsurfing

Couchsurfing is another option for free stays in people's homes. And it's not always actually a couch. Some hosts have an actual spare room, if that's more your style (ask about the level of privacy offered when booking). Couchsurfing.com is the biggest platform for this option, claiming a global community of 14 million users in 200,000 cities. Is couchsurfing safe? As with all online platforms like this, there are no guarantees, and you should always take the normal precautions — and trust your gut — when considering offers for free accommodation in private homes. Always have a back-up plan in case you need to leave in a hurry.

TIP

Read references or reviews of hosts to get a sense of other travelers' experiences. In return, leave your own reviews to help others make their booking decisions.

The Y-M-C-A! (and other nonprofit orgs)

Non-profit organizations that provide affordable accommodations include the YWCA and YMCA.

YWCA Hotels are social enterprises that support local communities, working for women's empowerment, and helping those in poverty or escaping violence and abuse. You'll need to seek these out, as each country has its own website and listings, but the destinations you'll find them in include Vancouver, Helsinki, Rome, Hong Kong, Fiji, Beirut, Singapore, Bangkok, and Sydney. Rooms range from hostel-style with shared bathrooms to very swish contemporary hotels, usually in central locations, which sometimes operate under other hotel names.

Likewise, **YMCA** hotels and hostels are scattered around the world, but there is no online directory that lists them. To find one in your chosen destination, go to ymca.int/ymca-worldwide for a list of members. Each country's listing will tell you if there are hotels and direct you to its national website for details.

University rooms

Another terrific value alternative to a cheap hotel is a university room. Around the world, accommodations in university colleges is often available outside semester times. Filling empty rooms during summer, Christmas or Easter holidays is a way for universities to boost income and reduce student rates — and for you to get a great value stay in lovely surroundings. **University Rooms** (universityrooms.com) lists bed and breakfast or self-catering rooms at universities, college and student residences in around 100 cities in the USA, Canada, Australia, the United Kingdom, and throughout Europe. It's open to all ages — you don't have to be a student.

Rooms may not always be luxurious or large, but if you're simply looking for a place to stay that's clean, functional, and convenient, this might be an option for you. Typically, they are single rooms, ideal if you're a solo traveler who wants a room of your own for much less than you'll pay for a hotel room. For example, you can stay at university residences in Loredo, Texas, for around US$20 per person per night. Some colleges also have apartments.

TIP

Some of the more famous or historic universities that offer accommodations to all-comers include Oxford and Cambridge universities in England, the University of Montreal and McGill University in Canada, and Dublin City University's Trinity College in Ireland.

Pubs

In places like the United Kingdom and Australia, staying in a pub is an excellent budget choice. The pub atmosphere is always warm, the prices reasonable, and you don't have to go far to find a bar or a bite to eat! Locals will fill the bars, so there's always someone up for a chat. While not every pub has rooms upstairs, enough of them do to make it a viable option as you travel around. Often there's history attached to the pub, which makes it much more interesting than a bland hotel room.

For UK pubs, check out **Stay In A Pub** (stayinapub.co.uk) or **English Country Inns** (english-inns.co.uk). Some have been very gentrified over the years (and the prices have risen accordingly), but the variety is huge, from haunted hotels to seaside inns and everything in between, and bargains are still to be had. I've stayed in quite a few and always feel comfortable, although a windy night at the 17th-century Feathers Hotel in the lovely medieval town of Ludlow a few years ago had me wondering if I was in a scene from Emily Bronte's classic novel *Wuthering Heights* as the window panes rattled and the shutters banged (the hotel, pictured in Figure 6-5, has since been refurbished, so hopefully it's quieter now).

Australia has a huge pub culture, too, with everything from colonial style architecture to contemporary cool. Rooms can range from very basic to boutique chic, but as with the UK, the idea of just popping upstairs at the end of the night is very appealing. Even in Sydney, where accommodation prices are high, reasonable rates can be found at older hotels in central locations. The website **Pub Rooms** (pubrooms.com.au) has bookable listings of pubs around the country, including some classic Outback pubs if you plan to travel that far.

Lee Mylne(Author)

FIGURE 6-5: The Feathers Hotel in Ludlow, England.

TIP

Check whether your pub room has a private bathroom; often they are shared and down the hallway from your bedroom.

Temple stays

If you're looking for something a bit different, which allows you to immerse yourself in another culture while sticking to a budget, consider a temple stay in Japan or South Korea. I can assure you it will be a truly memorable experience.

In South Korea, **Templestay** is a cultural program that lets you experience Buddhist life at traditional temples. Usually for one night only, a temple stay will typically include chanting, meditation, a tea ceremony, and Buddhist meal rituals (eating rice and vegetables from bowls, with the resident monks and nuns). Expect to rise before the sun to attend morning chanting and 108 prostrations; during my temple stay, only one of the Western tourists staying alongside me managed to last the distance with this. You might also learn to make lotus lanterns or do some other cultural activity.

There are 27 temples open to foreign tourists in the **Templestay** program. The website (eng.templestay.com) lists each temple with an outline of its history and location. Nine temples are UNESCO World Heritage listed; of those, four — Boepjusa, Bulguksa, Magoksa, and Haeinsa — offer English templestay programs for foreigners.

Accommodation at temples is usually on a share-room basis, from two to six people, but an extra fee can usually secure you a single room (yes, that ol' single supplement applies even in temples!). Bookings can be made online; watch for discounts which are offered from time to time.

REMEMBER

Temples are sacred places; alcohol, smoking, and loud noises are banned.

In Japan, temple lodgings are called *shukubo*, which means "sleeping with the monks" (www.japan.travel/en/guide/temple-stays). These are a bit more sophisticated than the South Korean temples and a bit more expensive. There are only a small number of Japanese temples offering overnight stays to foreigners. The most popular area to stay is in Mount Koya, just south of Osaka, where there are a number of *shukubo*. You can book in English through local tourism associations or websites such as Booking.com or **Japanese Guest Houses** (japaneseguesthouses.com).

All *shukubo* are quite similar, with shared bathrooms. Your room rate usually includes breakfast and dinner, but when booking a *shukubo* stay, be aware that some temples only accept cash, so it is best to confirm the payment method in advance.

WARNING

Bathrooms in temples are sometimes communal; if you are modest about showering with others, even of the same sex, this might not be for you. Check with the temple, as some do offer private bathrooms.

Traditional Japanese rooms usually have a light cotton filled mattress called a futon that you lay out on the tatami mat flooring and sleep on. Some temples offer Western-style rooms (which tend to be marginally cheaper). Temple meals adhere to Buddhist principles and guidelines. Meals at Japanese temples are called Shojin ryori, and do not include meat, fish, dairy, or eggs (similar to vegan cuisine).

To get the full experience, you will have the option of participating in early morning devotions known as *gongyo*. Meditation training is another activity that is often available to visitors.

In a temple stay, you will be provided with a set of temple clothes to wear for the duration of your stay. In South Korea, you will wear this all the time; in Japan, it is usually pajamas and robes for the evening, but it is perfectly acceptable to wear these to dinner.

Monastery stays

Monasteries also offer accommodation for travelers. **Monastery Stays** (monasterystays.com) specializes in booking rooms at monasteries and convents in Italy. These operate as bed-and-breakfasts, with simple rather than luxurious accommodations (think three star) and are owned and/or operated by a religious order (not to be confused with those that have been converted to swanky, expensive hotels).

Single rooms are common in these establishments, so they're ideal for solo travelers. But be prepared for a single bed rather than a double in which to luxuriate alone. All rooms booked through Monastery Stays have ensuite or exclusive-use bathrooms (with a separate door, sometimes down the corridor).

Similar stays can be found around the world, including in the USA, France, Spain, Greece, the UK, and Australia. Other good websites are monasteries.com and goodnightandgodbless.com (which also has a range of e-book guides to various countries, including France, Austria, and Germany).

WARNING

Some monasteries and convents may have rules, including no phones, periods of silence, and curfews. Or you may be required to take part in religious ceremonies. Make sure you check the details before booking.

Splashing Out for Some R&R at a Ritzy Resort

Sometimes, all you might want is a complete flop-n-drop holiday. A good book, swaying palm trees, a pool or ocean to cool off in, a cocktail with an umbrella in it, and to do . . . absolutely nothing. Yes, resorts are all about the chance to relax and reset, to do everything or nothing and not feel guilty about it.

If you're traveling for business, make the most of that work trip to extend your stay. Arriving early or staying later to relax or explore the destination in your own time is a great strategy. You're saving on the cost of a flight and have something to look forward to after days of business meetings, conference sessions, frenetic networking, or making presentations.

Resort holidays are in a class of their own. Spa packages, yoga classes, wine tasting, scuba lessons, golf or tennis sessions with a pro, cooking classes, surfing . . . there's usually a host of things to do on a solo resort stay. Did I mention massage? With solo traveler numbers increasing all the time, resorts are ensuring that there's plenty of choice for those who are checking in alone. If you don't want to be surrounded by vacationing families, choose an adults-only resort or do your research to ensure you can get away from it all and enjoy solitude when you want it, perhaps in a beachfront bure like this one where I stayed in Tahiti (see Figure 6-6).

When choosing a resort for a solo holiday, consider the size and style of the resort, distance from the airport and other places you might want to visit, and the transport options.

TIP

Resorts often have terrific deals. Look for "stay four, pay for three" or similar offers. If you are flexible with timing, these can save you thousands of dollars.

If you crave more balance in your life, a wellness retreat might be the solo trip for you. Indulge in daily spa retreats and nourishing food, read, nap, swim, and let the world slip away. Some wellness resorts, such as the award-winning **Escape Haven** on the Indonesian island of Bali are designed for solo women travelers and do not impose single supplements.

Club Med (www.clubmed.com) is a great option for solos. As well as being all-inclusive, so everything is taken care of for you, Club Med resorts have a huge array of activities and programs to partner you with other guests if you need to — tennis, for example. Some resorts have "Zen spaces" reserved for adults only, and there are plenty of opportunities for spa and pampering treatments. There are 65 resorts worldwide, from tropical islands in the Caribbean to ski resorts in Europe.

Lee Mylne(Author)

FIGURE 6-6: A beachfront bure in Tahiti is perfect for a flop-n-drop vacation.

WARNING

My advice is to stay away from honeymoon resorts. I once found myself in a gorgeous over-water bungalow on an island in French Polynesia that was straight off the brochure — but when I turned up for dinner, I found I was the only person there without a partner. That's not unusual for solos, of course, but in this case the maitre d' questioned me loudly about my solo status, and I was clearly a second-class guest because of it. It's a rare occurrence but made me cautious about future bookings.

Package Holidays for One

Packaging your holiday — flights, accommodations, car rental, tours and other transport, insurance, and sometimes meals — can be a great convenience and also result in good savings.

Look for tour companies who offer group tours for solo travelers in which everything is included. You'll save time in organizing your trip and know exactly what you're going to spend, apart from drinks and personal items such as souvenirs. Package holidays will also provide companions, if that's what you are looking for.

Active holidays where you get to hike, scuba dive, cycle, or sail with others is a great way to meet other travelers. Packages are also the way to go if you are considering an African safari or other trip where the logistics are overwhelming. Going with experts who can take care of any necessary permits, who know the best places to go, and are aware of safety issues is the best choice.

TIP

If group travel isn't for you, but you still want someone else to take care of all the details, look for a company that offers independent bespoke touring packages. I traveled to India's Golden Triangle (New Delhi, Agra — for the Taj Mahal — and Jaipur) on a tailor-made tour with **Intrepid Travel** (intrepidtravel.com), where everything was organized from start to finish, including an itinerary, a driver, local guides, excellent three-star hotels, some meals, and some connecting rail trips.

Many tour operators offer this service, and while this is a more expensive way of traveling, as you are paying extra for a custom-made itinerary, it is also the easiest and most stress-free way to plan a big trip. It also means that rather than booking a package deal "off the shelf," you can pick and choose what you do and where you go, and your itinerary will be designed to fit your individual needs.

The other advantage of a package deal is that you have the support of the travel company if anything goes wrong — as it did for many travelers in the heat of the pandemic. They can be working things out while you relax with a cool drink or carry on with the day's activities.

Staying Safe in Your Space

Safety is a number one priority for all solo travelers, and surveys consistently put personal security at the top of concerns for travelers going it alone. Even when you are not on the streets, ensuring your own safety is the key to peace of mind. Your room — especially a room of your own — may seem the safest place to be, but it's still sensible to make sure it's as secure as you need it to be.

If you're winging it and just turn up at a hotel or hostel without booking ahead, remember that it's perfectly acceptable to ask to see the room before you commit to it. This is your chance to ensure that it has workable locks on the door and to see if there are other safety features like security cameras, a chain on the door, or a peephole. You'll also get an idea of its proximity to the street and potential for being broken into. While the chances of this happening are slim, if you are traveling on a tight budget, cheaper hotels are likely to be less secure than those where you are paying more.

Find out if the room has a safe where you can keep your passport, tickets, cash, cards, and other valuables. If they don't, but you still want to stay there, the other option is to have a lockable bag to leave your things in.

Most hostels have lockers but may require you to have your own padlock (if not, most can usually sell or rent you one). The best type of locks have flexible cables which will fit into any configuration of locker you may come across. Invest in a good quality lock. They will not stop a determined thief but will deter casual theft. Hostels which do not have lockers in the room usually have a safe at reception for guests to use. Another option, if there are no lockers or safes, is to wear a money belt even while you sleep or tuck your valuables into bed with you.

TIP

Always carry a business card from your hotel (or get the receptionist to write the address down for you in the local language) so if you get lost, you can easily ask for directions or show a taxi driver.

While many big hotels have 24-hour reception and don't mind what time you come in at night, some hostels, B&Bs and other accommodations (especially monasteries and convents) have curfews. Make sure you find out if there are restrictions on entry after a certain time and that you know how to get back in — and don't forget your key! Having 24-hour reception, or a number to call in an emergency, is a sign of a safety-conscious management.

If you plan to stay in a hostel and a single-sex dorm or private room is important to you, make sure you do your research and book well in advance. Turning up and hoping they have the type of room you want is risky. This is likely to be more important to solo female travelers but does apply to anyone. If you're in a mixed-sex dorm and are uncomfortable, ask hostel staff if it's possible to move, even if it is to another with a more balanced number of each gender. If it's not possible, strongly consider moving on. Make sure you report any inappropriate behavior to hostel staff.

Pack a headlamp or a small flashlight or use your phone torch to navigate your way around an unfamiliar room in the dark if you need to.

Waking in the night in an unfamiliar place with a fire alarm sounding is something that's happened to me with memorable frequency! Make sure you always know where the fire escape is or any other escape route you might need. Most hotels have a diagram on the back of the door, but who has time to study that in the heat of the moment (pardon the pun). In some cases, in a big hotel, it's possible to just follow the crowd if there is one. I've been in hotels where everyone just assumes it's a false alarm (and yes, thankfully it usually is), but I've also been in big hotels where there's smoke in the corridors and people are hurrying out. While your belongings should be left behind, it's always prudent to pop your passport in your pocket as you leave. And if it's cold outside, throw on a warm coat and shoes (I say this from experience, too).

Remember: Safety first. There's nothing that will spoil your holiday more than being a victim of crime, however petty it may be.

Chapter **7**

Table for One

Travelers are made up of two kinds of people: those who relish the prospect of dining alone, their sole focus on the plate in front of them, and those to whom a table for one is the loneliest place in the world. Show me a solo traveler who hasn't at some stage dreaded facing an empty seat across a restaurant table. In my early days of traveling alone, it was the one thing I hated. Breakfast, yes . . . lunch, yes . . . but an evening meal on my own in a restaurant always made me feel like someone with no friends.

Once, in a relatively busy restaurant in Ireland, the waiter indicated to his colleague that the drink waiting to be delivered was mine by shouting across the room: "It's for the lady on her own!" I wanted to crawl under the table, but smiled brightly and sipped my gin and tonic calmly. It was the moment I felt like comedian Steve Martin in the classic scene from the 1984 movie *The Lonely Guy*, where the whole restaurant falls silent as he is led to his table for one, under a tracking spotlight.

The good news is I have learned to cope with dining alone, and you can too. In this chapter, I uncover the fear of eating out alone, offer some strategies for coping with it, and suggest places where you won't feel as if you are standing out in the crowd. Dining alone can be a wonderful experience, once you get over the initial feeling that it's somehow unnatural. It's not, and many solo diners will swear they love nothing better. It's all about attitude and preparation. With good planning and good humor, you too can relish a table for one — or at least approach it with aplomb.

Check out www.dummies.com/go/solotravelfd for links to all the web addresses provided in this chapter, along with additional resources.

Tackling the Fear of Eating Out Alone

Good food and the rituals that surround it are associated with social events, whether they're family gatherings, romantic dates, celebrations of birthdays or anniversaries, or just casual meals with friends. You meet, eat, drink, and be merry. Food is for sharing, as you share time together. Laughter, conversation, debates — even arguments — make these memorable occasions. Take away the element of company, and eating out doesn't always seem so appealing. Like me, you might feel as if everyone else in the restaurant is throwing you looks of pity and wondering where your friends are (or if you have any).

Of course, that's probably not true. Other diners are too busy with their own companions to even notice that you're a solo diner at a table for one.

In my early days of solo travel, I would order room service if that was an option, rather than go alone to a restaurant. Or sometimes, I wouldn't eat at all. But as years went by, I grew bolder and cared less what other people might think. Let them speculate; perhaps there was an aura of mystery about me? So, if you're a newcomer to solo travel and solo dining, take heart — you will get to that point, too!

REMEMBER

You are definitely not alone. Solo dining is a growing trend as more people choose to travel alone or simply want to have a night out in a good restaurant where they don't have to make conversation and can indulge in "me time." Business travelers do it all the time. South Koreans even have a special name for solo dining — *honbap* — which is a combination of the words *honja* (alone) and *bap* (meal). Just check out #solodining on Instagram, and you'll soon see that there are plenty of others out there sitting at tables for one.

Selecting a good spot for a solo meal

Finding a place to eat where you'll feel comfortable, the atmosphere will be welcoming, and the service as good as if you were with the biggest group in the room can be a challenge for solo diners. Not to worry though. This section offers helpful advice and some locations that cater to solo diners specifically.

Easing into solo dining with familiar and comfy spots

If you're new to solo travel, it's a good idea to test your resolve for solo dining by trying it before you leave home. Pick a restaurant you know well in your hometown and head out on your own. In a familiar place, with no language or money difficulties, you can concentrate solely on the experience, and you'll likely find it's not nearly as scary as you thought it might be. From that point, try a restaurant you've never been to before in your hometown — slightly less familiar surroundings, but now you know you can do it alone! After a few outings, you'll be much more equipped to tackle your foreign dining experiences with aplomb.

TIP

Restaurants with outdoor dining are often a good choice. They are usually less formal and are great for people-watching. If the weather is balmy, sit at a sidewalk table and watch the world go by.

REMEMBER

Choose your restaurant carefully so that you are comfortable. Steer clear of romantic, candlelit restaurants or those that are likely to be full of noisy family groups and roaming children (unless you love that kind of distraction).

Seeking out restaurants that cater to solo diners

Restaurants all over the world are starting to acknowledge that solo dining is a growing trend, and some are even taking care to cultivate a reputation as places that take special care of those at a table for one. A little bit of research on your intended destination is likely to bring up some names for you to check out.

For example, **Yunnan Noodle Shack** (www.instagram.com/yunnannoodleshack) opened in 2023 and made news as Toronto's first dining experience catering specifically for solos. Using a concept popular in Japan, the restaurant features private booth-like seats for a complete solo experience. The Baldwin Village restaurant has 25 partitioned stalls, each designed for just one person.

The concept is based on "focus booths" where diners can eat in privacy and can concentrate just on the food in front of them, relaxing and savoring the taste. You can even use an electronic ordering system in the booth — no need to even speak to a waiter. So, if you're in Japan, look for an **ICHIRAN** ramen restaurant (https://en.ichiran.com) in major cities — they are all over the country. There are also branches in New York, Hong Kong, and Taipei.

In Japan, solo diners often outnumber groups, so you are unlikely to feel "alone" at your table for one. But be prepared for what many foreigners may see as an unnatural silence. Wherever you are, Japanese teppanyaki restaurants, where the chef puts on a show as you sit around the open kitchen, or sushi train joints, where you sit alongside other diners, are both a good option for solo travelers.

Heading Down Under? Several top fine dining restaurants in Sydney are making a play for solo diners' business after online reservation systems identified increasing numbers of solo diners. Some offer private tours of the wine cellar or a chat with the chef, while others save their best tables for solo diners.

Three-hatted Sydney restaurant **Oncore** (https://www.crown sydney.com.au/restaurants/oncore-by-clare-smyth), which has spectacular views of the harbor, provides "talking points" on the table — an ornament or toy — as well as books that might interest solo diners. Others that go all-out to please solo diners include **Mimi's** (https://merivale.com/venues/mimis/) at beachside Coogee and **The Rover** (https://www.liquid andlarder.com.au/venues/the-rover/) at Surry Hills. Another that comes highly recommended — despite a romantic setting and large tables — is **Restaurant Hubert**, where bar seating and live jazz make a great atmosphere for solo diners.

If you want to meet the locals and learn more about the city you're in, make a booking with one of the "eat with a local" organizations. The largest is **EatWith** (eatwith.com), which operates in more than 1,100 destinations, everywhere from Austin to Athens or San Francisco to Seville. You can choose your experience; it might be dinner at someone's home, a walking tour of foodie outlets, or a progressive dinner on a motorcycle tour of Ho Chi Minh City in Vietnam.

TIP

If you're planning to travel in Asia, download the Waygo app. It is designed to translate languages like Chinese, Japanese, and Korean which do not use the Roman alphabet. You simply point your smartphone camera at the script for an instant translation — perfect for reading menus (among other things). It will also provide an image of what the dish will look like and can be used offline.

Another easy way to meet locals or other travelers is to seek out restaurants that offer communal tables, an increasingly common way of dining. Hotel concierges can also offer good advice about where you'll be welcome as a solo diner and not feel out of place.

TIP

If the portions being delivered to the tables around you look huge, ask for a smaller portion or order two appetizers instead of a main course.

Of course, if you're really reticent about going out in a strange city at night and you're staying in a hotel, dine in-house. Most hotel restaurants are full of solo diners. Or just order room service for a change.

Enjoying cheap eats and street food

Eating street food is one of the joys of travel. First, you need to get past the fear of dodgy hygiene and the risk of gastric upsets. Some street smarts and care can help you avoid these and open up the taste sensations that await at hawker food stalls and food markets all over the world.

Food markets are hard to go past, wherever you are. The vibrant colors and the very strangeness of some things are irresistible. What *is* this? Make sure you learn to ask that question in the local lingo, because you're sure to want to ask it. From gorgeous pink dragonfruit or pungent durian in Asia to fresh-from-the-ocean seafood, aromatic pastries and bread, and cheese, sausage, and other deli delights, food markets have something for every taste (literally). As well as fresh produce, most markets also have stalls cooking up a storm for hungry sightseers and are great places to grab a casual bite as you browse the wares.

TIP

Here's my "baker's dozen" of favorite food markets — both indoor and outdoor, and in no particular order — that might tempt your taste buds on your travels.

Borough Market, London, England: This historic market is packed with people, but it's worth the crush to explore its labyrinth of stalls. On the same site since 1756, the market is the capital's oldest and has three main areas, all under soaring green archways. For street food, head to the Borough Market Kitchen; otherwise, browse the fresh produce (and, oh, the cheese!) and artisan offerings, or join a guided tour. Seasonal fruit and vegetables are sold alongside pastries, olives, honey, seafood, gelato . . . oh, and cheese to die for! Open daily except Monday. For more formal dining, head upstairs to Roast restaurant, where I had a fabulous meal at a table for one, with attentive service and a view of the market below. I recommend the pork and chorizo Scotch egg! www.borough market.org.uk

Old Market Hall and Market Square, Helsinki, Finland: Helsinki's cobbled waterfront square is known as Kauppatoria or market square, open daily with stalls to tempt you with specialties like smoked salmon, pickled herring, and reindeer meat, alongside fresh fruit like blueberries and cloudberries. There's often live music and surrounding cafes sell pastries. Next door is the Old Market Hall, with 25 traders offering delicacies, such as reindeer meat, cheese, seafood, and even canned bear meat (see Figure 7-1). Built in 1889, the architecture is also worth seeing with lots of wood and Scandi style. https://vanhakauppahalli.fi/en/

Lau Pa Sat, Singapore: Food in Singapore is cheap and delicious, and the hawker food is legendary. This landmark building, known for its clocktower and cast-iron Victorian columns, is a great place to tuck into some Hainanese chicken rice, chili crab, laksa, or noodle dishes. And it's open around the clock, so whenever you are hungry, they are ready for you. At night, the adjoining Boon Tat Street is closed to traffic and becomes "Satay Street." www.laupasat.sg

FIGURE 7-1: Canned bear meat for sale in Helsinki, Finland.

St Lawrence, Toronto, Canada: Think smoked salmon, peach pies, blueberry jam, peameal bacon sandwiches, lobster rolls, Canadian mustard, and maple syrup. Along with a sprinkling of international goodies, they draw in the locals to this weekly farmers' market. The North Market has hosted its Saturday farmers' market since 1803. Many stalls are family run and you can also pick up fresh fruit and vegetables if you're cooking for yourself. www.stlawrencemarket.com

Amphawa Floating Market, Samut Songkhram, Thailand: About 90 minutes' drive (31 miles/50 km) from Bangkok, this market is worth the effort. Thailand has many floating markets, but Amphawa is my favorite. Wander the river banks, gazing down into small boats laden with fragrant lemongrass, seafood, vegetables, and noodles. The traders will cook you something on the spot, and you can sit on the steps leading down to the water and eat it while village life goes on around you, with the spectacle of boats plying the river and their trade, as in Figure 7-2. In Bangkok itself, Or Tor Kor market has fresh fruit and vegetables and Thai spices. www.tourism thailand.org/Attraction/amphawa-floating-market

FIGURE 7-2: Fragrant food at Amphawa Floating Market, Thailand.

Kowloon City Market, Hong Kong: Get lost among the nearly 600 stalls that make up this bustling market. As a small island, most of the fruit and vegetables are imported from nearby Southeast Asian countries, but that doesn't affect the quality or the huge range. If you're brave, try the durian — a fruit this market is renowned for, but which is definitely not everyone's favorite (hint: it helps if you have no sense of smell). Come early for breakfast or brunch, or late afternoon for bargain-priced seafood or meat. The wet market takes up the first two levels, and the top level is crammed with food outlets, where you are assured of great cheap Chinese food, cooked while you wait and served before you know it. www.discoverhongkong.com/in/interactive-map/kowloon-city-market.html

La Boqueria, Barcelona, Spain: Just off Las Ramblas, La Boqueria market is surrounded by little tapas bars, wonderful respite when the crowd gets too much. Salivate over the jambon, the cheese, the piles of octopus, or huge dishes of steaming paella, rich with mussels and other seafood. Before dining, browse the market stalls selling fruit, vegetables, fresh seafood, meat, and offal (not always for the squeamish). Pick up some olives and jamon for later. One of the oldest food markets in the world, La Boqueria dates back to 1217. Open every day except Sunday. www.boqueria.barcelona

Tsukiji Fish Market, Tokyo, Japan: With the move of its wholesale fish auctions and commercial operations to another location, this famous market is now known as the Tsukiji Outer Market, and continues to attract large crowds for its seafood, vegetables and traditional Japanese ingredients and cooking utensils. One thing not to miss is the sushi — you're in the right place, after all. The best time to visit is after 9am when the professionals have finished their buying; many shops are closed on Sundays. www.tsukiji.or.jp/english

Ferry Plaza, San Francisco, USA: I can still taste the strawberries I bought at this wonderful farmers' market. Everything here is local and organic, and you can taste the difference. Open three days a week, the Ferry Plaza market is a must-visit. Thursdays are the best for street food (think tacos, pizza, sandwiches, and barbecues) while Saturday is the busiest. Crowds — up to 40,000 shoppers each week — come for fresh fruit, rich jams, handmade chocolates, and breads. www.ferrybuildingmarketplace.com

Mercado Central, Santiago, Chile: It may be a bit touristy, but this seafood market is still worth your time for its vast array of bounty from the ocean. And although the tourist hordes are here, so too are plenty of locals. Open every day, there's an eye-popping array of fish (and the smell that comes with the territory). Grab a snack for lunch — try the seafood empanadas — but avoid the restaurants in the center of the market, which will be much more expensive than the takeaway stalls or eateries on the outer edge. https://www.santiago turismo.cl/en/mercado-central-de-santiago-2/

Queen Victoria Market, Melbourne, Australia: Affectionately known as the "Queen Vic" or "Vic Markets," this sprawling undercover market has been a favorite of Melbourne residents for more than 145 years. Unless you've got a kitchen, head straight to the Deli Hall for cheese and charcuterie, and consider taking one of the excellent guided walking tours of the market, which includes plenty of tastings. Food trucks offer everything from Greek baklava to North African merguez sausage and Tibetan momo dumplings, with plenty of vegan options, too. Open Tuesday and Thursday to Sunday, it can be crowded on the weekends when the locals do their shopping. Night markets operate in winter and summer months. Don't forget to take reusable shopping bags — plastic is banned. www.qvm.com.au

Jemaa el-Fna, Marrakesh, Morocco: Dodge the snake charmers and touts selling cheap knock-off goods in Marrakesh's vibrant square and head for the center of the plaza in the evening to find a table and dine on cheap snacks from the barbecue stalls surrounding you. Some of it is not for the faint-hearted, but you'll find grilled sausage, fried fish, spiced lamb, kebabs, and the ubiquitous chicken tagine. Ask your hotel to recommend a stall, and make sure you determine the price before you order. It's chaotic, but fascinating. https://jemaa-elfnaa.com/

Bauernmarkt Kaiser-Josef-Platz, Graz, Austria: This lovely traditional outdoor market takes place at Kaiser-Josef-Platz square, in the heart of the city every day except Sunday. It's lively and fun, with friendly locals selling Styrian specialities, including delectable mountain cheese, Styrian ham and the "black gold" pumpkinseed oil for which this region of Austria is famous. Stalls brim with local and mostly organic produce; try Grazer Krauthauptel lettuce, with its distinctive red leaf edge (also perfect with a pumpkin oil dressing), scarlet runner beans, home-baked bread, and cakes, apples, bacon, and smoked sausages. https://www.graztourismus.at/en/sightseeing-culture/sights/kaiser-josef-market_shg_1458

Tips for Coping with Dining Alone

When you're traveling solo and aren't thrilled by the idea of dining alone, it's mighty tempting to order room service or grab something from a street vendor — and there's nothing wrong with doing either of these things. I certainly have. But then I think about what I would be missing. There's something wonderful about a sit-down dinner at a lovely restaurant, and you deserve that kind of experience. While you're sitting at your table fretting over the maître d's "Just *one*?" comment, think about the amazing food you're about to savor.

If you're absolutely new to solo dining, test yourself by eating alone in a restaurant in your own neighborhood or city. It's a great way to ease yourself into the experience. There are no language or menu difficulties, and you can concentrate entirely on the novelty of being on your own. Chat to the waiter, ask about the menu, discuss the wine choices. You're in your comfort zone and will soon feel the freedom that dining alone can give you. Practice makes perfect; do it again until you are at ease and ready to tackle unfamiliar realms.

Start with confidence. Don't sound apologetic as you front up for a table for one. If you don't like the suggested table — near the kitchen or the toilets, or maybe right in the center of the room — point to one you'd prefer and ask to be moved.

Here are some handy tips, from my own experience and those of my solo traveler friends, to help you ease into the idea of dining alone and embrace it for the wonderful experience it can be.

>> **Do some research into the city or area you're staying in before heading out.** Ask other travelers or your hotel for recommendations or look for places near your accommodations while you're out and about during the day. As a solo traveler, wandering around a strange city at night looking for a likely place to eat is not always the best idea.

>> **Have your main meal of the day at lunchtime.** If you're self-conscious about solo dining in the evening, practice during the day. Lunch is a more casual affair, and there are likely to be more solo diners around. You may also find that some lunchtime menus — including the set menus on offer in Europe — offer great deals, especially on weekdays. From a safety aspect for solo women travelers, this can also be a strategy for staying close to your hotel at night.

>> **Reserve a table.** It avoids the simple, but daunting, act of asking for a table for one when you arrive at the restaurant. If you have booked online or by phone, you already know they are not going to turn you away (yes, it happens). And it's only sensible at popular, busy restaurants.

>> **Eat out early in the evening.** If you beat the rush, you're more likely to find a table, get a warmer welcome, and receive more attentive service. Of course, if you are in Spain

or other countries where dining is traditionally late, you may need to adjust your appetite and timing to fit with restaurant expectations as well.

>> **Dine at the bar.** There's a greater chance of striking up conversation with another solo diner, or the bar staff, and, in some places, the menu may be slightly cheaper than if you took a table. And you never know who you might meet — a friend of mine ate at the bar in a New York restaurant and struck up a conversation with an older man also dining alone. To her great surprise, he turned out to be musician David Crosby of Crosby, Stills, Nash & Young!

>> **Ask for a table beside the window.** It's the best place for people-watching.

>> **Put your phone on silent.** Don't make or answer calls during your meal. Your fellow diners will thank you; haven't most people listened in as someone pours out their troubles loudly to someone on the end of the phone in a restaurant or café? And you'll enjoy the dining experience much more if you focus on it, rather than chatting to a distant friend.

>> **Talk to the people at the table next to you.** Ask what they're eating and if it's good; this is a great ice breaker. They may have stories to tell, and if they are locals, they may have great tips on what to see and do.

>> **Take a book along.** Not only will it help you pass the time while waiting for your meal to arrive, as I did at a restaurant in Figure 7-3, it may spark conversation with another diner. I've had great conversations in cafes — and other places while traveling — with other book lovers. An intriguing title or a well-known author may be enough to start you talking. Just don't give in to the temptation to bury your nose in a book (or your phone) for the whole time you're there. Instead, try to embrace the atmosphere, take it all in, engage with the waitstaff, and enjoy the hospitality.

>> **Take your iPad, phone, camera, or a notebook to write in.** These are good props to keep you occupied, especially if the restaurant is not busy and there's not much people-watching to be done. Scroll through the day's photos, write notes or postcards to friends, or keep up with texts and social media posts.

FIGURE 7-3: Taking a book can be a handy prop.

>> **Keep your belongings safe.** In a busy London pub, my friend waved away a woman begging for money; in a flash, her phone was gone from the table along with the beggar. Keep your phone tucked away in busy or outdoor places, and keep your bag well secured or out of sight (and reach). I learned the hard way not to sling my bag over the back of a chair. Of course, it's inconvenient (and hard to explain you're not doing a runner without paying) for a solo traveler to drag all your belongings with you when you're in need of the bathroom — another reason to carry only essentials.

>> **Carry some cash with you.** Be prepared for the worst to happen when the bill for your meal arrives. Your card is declined by the bank, the restaurant card machine is faulty, or they forgot to mention they only accept cash. And as a solo diner, you have no one else's card to fall back on. Always be ready for the unexpected by carrying at least some cash with you — just in case!

- >> **Drink alcohol in moderation.** This should always be your plan when traveling solo, but it is worth mentioning again here. It's great to have a pre-dinner cocktail or a glass of wine with dinner (or lunch), but don't take any chances; limit your intake to a glass or two. You still have to get back to your accommodations safely at the end of the night. And remember never to leave your drink unattended.

- >> **Don't yield to the temptation to rush your meal.** Dining alone should not be about eating as fast as possible and getting out of there and back to solitude of your room. Savor the experience of a great meal in an interesting place, of seeing the world go by as other diners enjoy their meals — and enjoy every morsel of your own.

- >> **Tip well for good service.** Let's face it, tipping can be a minefield. In some countries, it is insulting to tip, in others it is not expected but appreciated, and then there are the places where it is absolutely expected (if not quite demanded). If in doubt, ask your hotel or a local about what's appropriate and at what percentage. Sometimes a "service charge" is included in your bill, and nothing more is expected. While you don't owe anything extra simply because you're dining alone, it shows your appreciation and may make it easier for the next solo diner to be warmly welcomed.

Finally, if you really can't face going out alone and you're staying in a guesthouse or hostel, look for other solo guests who might like to join you. They may be as reluctant to dine alone as you are and welcome the invitation.

Dining alone means there's no one to steal your dessert!

How to Avoid Unwanted Company

Dining alone can sometime attract unwanted attention. This is particularly the case for solo women travelers; you might need to politely field offers from men who see you as an easy target. Oh yes, if you're alone you must be lonely and need company. Being prepared and having a strategy to deal with this is the best protection.

This problem will be more or less likely to crop up, depending on where you are traveling. Sadly, even being in your home country, where you are aware of customs and "fit in" well, is not necessarily going to mean you avoid unwanted attention by simply being on your own, especially if you are a woman.

Whether you are male or female, if you're not in the mood to make new friends, you don't have to. If the waiter tries to put someone else at your table, firmly but politely say you'd rather eat alone. If another solo diner asks to join you, trust your judgment; if you feel uneasy, politely refuse, but if you're open to new people and conversation, it could be the making of your evening.

WARNING

Keep an eye on your drink, even if it's only water. Don't leave it unattended when you go to the bathroom or ask for a fresh one when you get back to the table.

Have a strategy for ending the evening. Taking a taxi back to your accommodation might be a better idea than walking, to avoid the chance of being followed. During conversation, be vague about where you are staying and don't give more information than you need to. If necessary, lie about having a companion who's not well enough to come to dinner but is waiting for you at your accommodation. It's not necessary or advisable for a stranger to know you are traveling alone or where you are staying.

Enjoying Culinary Experiences as Entertainment

Dining out doesn't need to be a traditional restaurant experience, and if you love food, you may also enjoy food tours and cooking classes as a way of immersing yourself in unfamiliar cuisines. As a solo traveler, joining a group of like-minded foodies can be a very enjoyable way to kill a few hours — and you usually get to sample morsels along the way or eat what you have cooked (that's one less meal you have to worry about).

If combining your loves of travel and food seems like the dream vacation, rest assured that you can do so with ease. There is a plethora of food tours just waiting to be discovered, from short walking tours to weeks-long adventures designed around showcasing regional cuisine. The world is your oyster!

By joining a food tour, you'll learn all about local cuisine, try out various eateries, taste new flavors and ingredients, learn to cook new dishes, and meet new people.

Some cooking classes begin with sourcing the ingredients for the dish, often with a trip to local markets to learn about produce that's grown in the region. Having a guide to the unfamiliar produce is a bonus! Make the most of this to ask plenty of questions and really get into the local culture.

Food experiences can also incorporate other adventures, such as sailing the Greek islands while you feast on dolmades, olives, octopus, and moussaka. Fishing trips in the Caribbean or Pacific islands can end with dining on your catch that night.

Some tours require you to get your hands dirty; but who's going to complain if that means dipping them in chocolate as you learn to handcraft your own goodies?

Truffle-hunting anyone? Parts of Europe — think Italy or France — are prime spots for this outdoor activity, teaching you everything you need to know about these earthy delights. Join the hunters and their specially trained dogs to snuffle for truffles and end with a meal that uses the bounty.

Indigenous food tours are also worth seeking out. In Peru, look for meals prepared in a *pachamanca* or earth oven. In New Zealand, a similar style of earth cooking is the Māori *hangi*. Both cook meat and vegetables on heated stones under the soil; the result is a smoky flavor like no other.

TIP

Search for food tours online. One good booking site is the Berlin-based **Get Your Guide** (www.getyourguide.com).

Along with good food, wine and spirit tasting fit the bill for culinary experiences. Scottish distilleries specialize in whiskey tasting, and sometimes you can learn to blend your own gin, rum, or wine (complete with personalized label). Look for distilleries or wineries that offer special tours incorporating these options. And of course, there's always harvest season at vineyards when you can help stomp the crop.

Chapter **8**

Meeting People and Making New Friends

Throughout your travels, you'll meet many different types of people, from locals to expats, digital nomads to business travelers, and short-term tourists having the time of their lives on vacation.

One of the great joys of travel is the amazing people you'll meet, the stories they'll tell of their lives and their own travels. If you're lucky, they'll be people of all ages and backgrounds and they'll be open, friendly, and willing to be a memorable part of your travels. Sure, you'll be likely to meet some stinkers, too — people who are creepy or boring (or both). But the reality is that those people are few and far between and you'll be savvy enough to spot them, avoid them, or get away from them quickly.

In this chapter, I look at all the different ways you can meet those people who'll become part of the tapestry of your traveling life, how to negotiate new social norms in strange countries, and how to stay safe while doing it.

FIND ONLINE

To find a handy list of all the web addresses mentioned in this chapter, as well as other links you may find useful, go to www. dummies.com/go/solotravelfd.

Doing Your Cultural Homework

With any travel adventure to a country where the culture is fundamentally different to your own, it's essential to do your homework. There might be many factors that impact your ability to make friends and be accepted — even as a visitor passing through — by a local community. This can be as basic as learning the dress code to the more delicate nuances of the dating scene (more on that later!).

Cultural mores are as tricky to navigate as some of the backstreets you'll find yourself lost in during your travels (it's inevitable). But despite that, immersing yourself in a different culture to learn how other people live is one of the richest experiences that traveling can give you.

Knowing the best ways to interact with people you meet in other cultures will ensure that doors continue to open for you, ensuring you a warm welcome and a privileged insight into the lives of others.

Respecting local laws and traditions

The most important thing to remember when you're traveling in a foreign country and an unfamiliar culture is that things may be *very* different to what you're used to. You're no longer on home territory, and very different customs and laws may apply. Take things slowly and cautiously, and treat everything and everyone with respect. Not only will it make your travel experience more pleasant, but it also could save you from unwanted interaction with the law — which in a worst-case scenario could land you in jail.

TIP

Do some research before you leave home. Every country will have its own customs and standards of polite behavior. It's important to educate yourself about topics that matter in the place you're visiting as well as anything that might compromise your safety.

In some cultures, it is rude to look someone in the eye, to shake hands, or to point with your index finger. How should you behave when you're invited to someone's home? Should you take your shoes off before entering a home? Is smoking acceptable? What pitfalls are there to avoid when meeting someone for the first time? Guide books and official tourism websites for the country you are visiting can be good sources of advice and information. So too can websites such as the **Cultural Atlas** (www.culturalatlas. sbs.com.au) of Australia's multi-cultural Special Broadcasting Service (SBS), which lists information about cross-cultural attitudes, behaviors, norms, and practices by country and religion. Google searches can also help you find information on cultural norms in your chosen destination.

It is vital that you understand the laws pertaining to alcohol and drug use in the country you're visiting as these are areas that could potentially land you in the slammer. The governments of the USA, Canada, United Kingdom, and Australia, among others, provide online advice for their traveling citizens (find links to those countries' pages at www.dummies.com/go/solotravelfd) that includes information on local laws. These websites can also tell you what to do if things go wrong and where you can seek help from your embassy or consulate.

WARNING

In some countries, including Thailand, it's against the law to criticize the royal family. In Brunei, it's offensive to criticize the royal family and illegal to criticize Islam.

Respect for other cultures is often based around religious customs and traditions. Often, this is most clearly shown in what you wear and how you behave. Make sure you know what is appropriate and what is not.

If you're visiting a conservative or religious place, such as a temple in Asia or any place in the Middle East, dress appropriately. No matter how hot it is, women should always cover shoulders, arms, cleavage/chest, legs, and sometimes heads.

TIP

I always carry a sarong or shawl that can fit into a day bag in case it is needed. Loose clothing is not only cooler in many places but also does not show the shape of your body.

Men should also be aware that in some places, bare legs and torsos are not acceptable, so pack some light long trousers just in case you need them and keep your shirt on, no matter how hot it gets, unless you are at the beach or pool.

In some Buddhist countries, the penalties for disrespectful behavior can be harsh. In 2014, a British woman was deported from Sri Lanka because of a Buddha tattoo on her arm, and in Thailand, huge billboards such as the one pictured in Figure 8-1, urge visitors to respect Buddhism — the country's largest religion — by not getting tattoos of Buddha or wearing jewelry or clothing with Buddha's image on them, or otherwise using the sacred image as decoration. "Buddha is not for decoration," the billboards read. So if you already have a Buddha tattoo, keep it covered at all times.

Lee Mylne(Author)

FIGURE 8-1: Billboards in Thailand ask for respect for Buddhism.

The island of Bali in Indonesia has introduced similar billboards in respect of Hinduism, urging tourists to dress well and neatly and behave in an orderly way. A "Do's and Don'ts" card is given to visitors on arrival, spelling out what is not acceptable in Balinese culture. Binge drinking and out-of-control behavior can result in fines, jail, or deportation for those who overstep the mark.

In many countries, alcohol and meat are not available on religious holidays. If you are traveling to a Muslim country, check the calendar for religious holidays, including Ramadan, which runs for a month and is a time when followers of Islam fast during daylight hours. The exact dates of Ramadan vary from year to year, so always check. During this time there may be restrictions on the availability of food and drink (although sometimes there are exceptions for non-Muslim visitors). Drinking, eating, or smoking in public on these days is culturally insensitive. Make sure you check on what is acceptable or not.

Find out if it is acceptable to tip, or if it is expected that small gifts will be exchanged with hosts. A small token gift that represents your home country in some way will usually be accepted warmly.

If you are looking for romance on your travels, be sensitive to customs around public displays of affection and laws regarding interaction between unmarried men and women. In some places, even the act of holding hands or being alone together is not acceptable. This especially applies to the LGBTQIA+ community, as around 70 countries criminalize homosexuality. There's more information in the section, "Issues for LGBTQIA+ travelers," on this later in this chapter.

Dress to impress

Apart from being aware about local dress conventions when spending time in cultures that are different from your own, there are other ways to approach a travel wardrobe that will keep you comfortable and carry you through any potential situation.

As a solo traveler, it's a good idea to pack clothes that allow you to fit in. Of course, you want to dress for whatever style of travel you are embarking on — and that will vary depending on if you are on a one-week vacation, a business trip, a long overland journey, or anything in between.

The ideal travel wardrobe is all about comfort. Layers are always the way to go, so you are flexible if the weather changes. Keep in mind that the colder your destination is, the more layers your outfit should have. I once had to invest in a puffer jacket in Finland, when my wool coat (which had been perfectly adequate until I arrived in Helsinki) failed to keep me warm! That's one of the best purchases I've made and still travels with me to anywhere that's going to be remotely cold. It's bulky, but worth it!

Think not too casual but not too dressy. The goal is to pack outfits that can adapt to any situation. Choose items that can be mixed and matched; it will help you to travel lighter, too! Ideally, stay away from anything that might need ironing (unless you plan to carry a travel iron — and who wants to do that?).

If you're planning to blow the budget and dine at that three-Michelin-star restaurant, make sure you can dress appropriately. Always pack at least one outfit — no matter what gender you are — that will carry you across the doorstep of a fancy restaurant.

But in doing so, still avoid wearing expensive or flashy jewelry that may attract unwanted attention while you're on the street.

Comfortable flat shoes with good traction for lots of walking are essential, too. If you care about such things, throw in some wraps or scarves to add some pops of color to your outfits and vary the way you wear them.

For more tips on packing, head to Chapter 4.

Learning the local lingo

Knowing a few words of the local language is a great start to breaking down those cultural barriers. It shows your interest in the destination and a willingness to go out on a limb to communicate with local people. Sure, you'll have a funny accent and will probably mispronounce words or confuse them with others that have a different meaning — but those mistakes might just open up another form of communication — laughter! And be sure, the locals will be laughing *with* you, still happy that you have made the effort.

TIP

Take time to learn basic words: "hello"; "how are you?"; "thank you"; "no"; "excuse me"; "how much is that?"; "what is that?"; "my name is . . ."; and "may I take a photo?" These phrases will get you far.

If you're planning to be in a country for a reasonable amount of time, consider taking a short course in conversational language before you go. You might go along to a class in your hometown, but if that's not possible, there are plenty of options available online and as apps or podcasts. While there are loads of translation apps available, which are undoubtedly useful for travelers, they do not provide the kind of connection with others that learning the language does.

Duolingo (duolingo.com) is one of the most popular language apps, with more than 200 million active users — and even better, it's free. Choose from French, Spanish, German, Italian, Russian, Portuguese, Turkish, Dutch, Danish, Swedish, Ukrainian, Polish, Greek, Hungarian, Norwegian, Hebrew, Romanian, Swahili, and more. Others to consider include italki.com and pimsleur.com (but for both of these you will pay for lessons).

Tandem (tandem.net) is another free app. This is a great choice because it pairs you with a native speaker of the language you want to learn with the idea that you teach each other. It's a more casual approach that is likely to let you pick up popular slang terms and could have the benefit of giving you a new friend who can also give you travel tips or put you in touch with people in the destination you're planning to visit. There are more than 150 languages to choose from and a community of more than a million members. You can communicate by text, audio, or video — whatever works best.

While learning a few basic words and phrases may get you by if you are on a short holiday or just passing through a country, if you are planning to stay for a while and want to achieve reasonable fluency, signing up to a language school is the answer — and you'll get to meet others doing the same and maybe even some locals. Whether you want to learn German, Hindi, Arabic, Japanese, Mandarin, Turkish, or Urdu — you'll find a language school to help you.

TIP

Many language schools will also help you organize accommodation for the duration of your stay, often with the option of a homestay so you can more fully immerse yourself in the language and get to know the locals.

Spanish is the second most widely used language globally, spoken by more than 548 million people. According to online language school **Berlitz** (www.berlitz.com), there are 21 Spanish-speaking countries in the world, with many more that have large Spanish-speaking populations. Mexico has the largest population of Spanish speakers in the world, followed by Colombia and Argentina, with Spain in fourth place.

The number of Spanish language schools in Spain are overwhelming, but you should look for one that is accredited by the **Instituto Cervantes** (www.cervantes.es) or is a member of the **Federation of Associations of Spanish Schools for Foreigners** (www.fedele.org/en). If Mexico seems a little easier, there are as many choices! One to consider is **Instituto Cultural Oaxaca** (www.icomexico.com), which offers a range of programs year-round, and includes an *intercambio* or language exchange with a local who is studying English.

The world's leading French language teaching organization, **Alliance Francaise** (www.af-france.fr/en) has more than 800 schools in 133 countries — but there's nowhere better to learn French than in France, where there are 30 schools. You can learn everything from conversational language to grammar and choose from two- or four-week courses. If you want to start before you get to France, there are 1,016 schools in 135 countries. The United States has 110 branches in 45 states, including in New York, Chicago, Washington, San Francisco, San Diego, and Silicon Valley.

There are Italian language schools all over Italy. One of the best is **Il Sasso** (www.ilsasso.com), in Montepulciano, in the heart of Tuscany (about mid-way between Rome and Florence). Certified and recognized by the Italian Ministry of Education, it has been running for more than 30 years and is open all year round. Classes run in the morning, with afternoons free to take extra one-on-one classes (for an additional fee), to explore on your own, or to join other students on optional activities such as cooking classes.

Of course, there are many other languages you can learn, depending on your level of interest, time to prepare for your trip, how long you're going for, and the difficulty of the language itself. An online search will help you find other language schools.

REMEMBER

Learning the language, even if it is just a few basic words and phrases, is a true sign of respect for another culture and it will be appreciated.

Socializing When You're Out and About

Even though you might enjoy the freedom of traveling solo, it's always great to have a social life. Being open to new people and new experiences is all part of the joy of travel, and there are many ways to connect with other travelers and local people that will make your travels even more memorable. It's not all about sightseeing and solitude!

TIP

Smiling is one of the best ways to meet people. Offer to help a stranger with something — maybe taking a photo of them or offering directions if they look lost. Asking questions of locals about where you are or what you are seeing can be a way of striking up a conversation that can lead to more.

Whether you're looking for someone to enlighten you about the local culture, a new friend to go hiking with, or a potential date, getting out and about is the first step to a social life on the road.

Where to meet fellow travelers

I met one of my oldest and dearest friends on my first visit to Europe as a rookie traveler. I'd signed up for one of those six-countries-in-seven-days coach tours — it was a last-minute cheap deal to fill up the bus —and we shared a room for most of the trip, establishing a long-lasting friendship that endures even though we've never lived in the same city.

Tours that cater to solo travelers and accommodations where you're likely to be among other solo travelers are great ways of meeting people. Hostels are renowned for their ready-made social life, with many offering organized events where outings are taken together, stories are swapped, and good times are to be had.

TIP

Making friends at your hostel also adds a layer of security. If you're friendly with the other people in your dorm, they're more likely to look out for you and your possessions.

Read reviews on **Hostelworld** (www.hostelworld.com) and other sites to get an impression of which hostels are the most sociable. Some websites have chat rooms for solo travelers to connect with others before they arrive in a destination or at a hostel.

REMEMBER

It's great to make new friends, but exercise normal caution when going out with people you just met. Go with a group, stay in public places, and drink alcohol in moderation.

My best advice is to join a free walking tour when you first arrive. That might be at your hostel or through a local tourism organization. You'll find other travelers doing the same thing, and after a few hours wandering around together in a group, you're bound to find something in common with someone else. **Free Tours by Foot** (www.freetoursbyfoot.com) is a good source, offering tours in 50 cities around the world on a "pay what you think it's worth" basis.

Walking tours often end with drinks in a bar or pub — either spontaneously suggested by someone in the group (you, perhaps?) or by the tour guide — so that's a great chance to have a chat to someone you didn't talk to on the tour or continue one with someone you've connected with already.

Pub or microbrewery tours are also great to join, as their very nature is all about being social over a drink. You can even make it a soda if you want to, and no one will care!

There are plenty of websites designed to help you meet up with others who love travel. Try these:

>> **A Small World** (www.asmallworld.com) is a website, app, and global network for travelers, whether you're looking for a companion, romance, or business connection. There are more than 1,000 events in eighty cities each year, from wine tasting and art exhibitions to gourmet dinners, shopping excursions, or tours of local attractions.

>> **Meetup** (www.meetup.com) brings together like-minded people for many reasons — and they may be locals as well as travelers. Join a class, a social group, an outdoor activity, or find a group that shares your hobby or interest.

>> **Tourlina** (www.tourlina.com) is a women-only network designed to help solo women travelers find a travel companion. Every user is verified as a "real" person. You might want to meet up with someone for dinner in Barcelona or travel for a few days or more together in a place you might feel safer with a friend.

Signing up for an adventure day tour is a great way to meet fellow travelers with similar interests. There's nothing like a bit of teamwork to get the conversation flowing. Think about horse riding, whitewater rafting, or a kayaking tour.

If adventure's not your style, taking a cooking class is a popular thing to do and also involves a lot of conversation, sometimes a bit of teamwork — and the finale of sitting down to eat what you've all cooked. Doesn't everyone love to talk about food?

Cafes often have communal tables or armchairs arranged around a coffee table, where solos are often taking time out. Ask about the Wi-Fi password, what that book is they're reading, or something else to start a conversation. You never know where it will lead, whether they are a local or a fellow traveler.

How to meet the locals

Getting to know the locals might require a bit more effort than meeting other travelers. There's a language difference, for a start, and locals are likely to be busy leading their everyday lives. But there are still opportunities to talk to locals and get an insight into their world.

It's important to know what you want from interaction with locals. A tour guide? A dinner companion? A language teacher? A romance? Many locals are delighted to show off their hometowns and do so as tour guides. It may not result in the kind of meaningful interaction or friendship you are looking for, but it's always a great first step toward discovering a place through the eyes of someone who lives there.

Global Greeters (www.globalgreeternetwork.info) are volunteer tour guides who offer free walking tours (usually around two or three hours) of their cities to new arrivals. While you might not necessarily strike up a friendship, you will get useful insider tips from someone who knows the city well and find places you may not discover on your own. It's a great introduction to any city. While many "greeters" are older people — often retired — my friend Tiana highly recommends the greeter service in Florence, Italy, for its younger guides, with an average age of around 30. These tours are sometimes in a group, but private tours are also possible.

Among the other options for finding a local to show you around are:

>> **Show Around** (www.showaround.com) helps you find a local tour guide (usually with an hourly rate, but sometimes free) who can tailor a tour to suit your interests. There's a limited number of destinations in which it operates but still a lot of guides to choose from in each city.

>> **Tours By Locals** (www.toursbylocals.com) is a Canadian-based website that can help you find a local tour guide in 190 countries. Guides are background-checked, and your money is held in trust until the tour is successfully completed.

>> **Airbnb** (www.airbnb.com) is great for suggesting things to do and places to see, often in the company of a local tour guide or as a community event.

>> **Couchsurfing** (www.couchsurfing.com) also offers more than accommodations; it also lists local events that you can head out to — and your host is likely to be a great source of info, too!

>> **Homestays** (see Chapter 6) are another great way of making friends with locals. If your hosts are older people, they may feel protective towards younger guests and have more time to spend with you, going above and beyond to make you feel welcome. If you do experience genuine hospitality like this, remember to reciprocate with a small thoughtful gift, or perhaps offer to help with anything you can (tech advice, perhaps?) or be helpful around the house.

TIP

Of course, you can meet plenty of locals who are not tour guides! Go to local events — big and small, from the local markets or concerts in the park to the huge fiestas that will draw locals as well as other tourists. Check Facebook Events, tourism board websites, and Instagram for places to go and things to do. Look at "What's On" brochures and English-language newspapers or magazines produced locally.

Or just head to that café or bar and strike up a conversation with someone who looks interesting.

WARNING

Sometimes you'll be approached by someone who offers to guide you to local attractions or generally "show you around." This may be a genuine offer, with nothing expected in return except a chance to practice their English, but it may also be a ploy to get you to craft or souvenir shops from which they gain a commission for anything you buy. These people can be persistent — and sometimes it's hard to tell the genuine from the dodgy. Trust your instincts and be prepared to extract yourself from a situation if you start to feel uneasy.

WARNING

Don't overindulge in alcohol or drugs. They will hamper your judgment and make you vulnerable to sexual assault, robbery, and worse. Don't accept drinks from strangers, and never leave your drink (alcoholic or not) unattended. (See more in Chapter 9.)

Sex and the Single Traveler

Travel gives you many opportunities to meet people — and if romance (or casual sex) is what you're looking for, you can probably find it. But there are pros and cons to dating as a traveler. For a start, what if you meet the love of your life, but you're heading in opposite directions. Or one of you is about to leave for home the next day! It's the stuff that movies are made of . . . think *Before Sunrise* and its sequels.

But before I start offering advice on this topic, first a confession: Despite doing a lot of solo traveling, I've never been on the lookout for romance during my sojourns abroad. Most times, there's been a patient partner waiting back home while I scratched my travel itch. So much of the advice in this section comes from my single friends who have ridden the rollercoaster of the cross-cultural and or nomadic dating scene while exploring the world.

Dating in a new country

As if dating isn't complicated enough in your own city or country, there are definitely traps for the unwary when dipping your toe in the romance pool while traveling.

While you should apply the same safety tips for dating while traveling as you would at home, there are some extra layers of danger involved, especially for solo travelers and even more so for solo women travelers. For a start, you're on unfamiliar ground, perhaps in a very different culture and with only a rudimentary grasp of the language (if at all). And there's no easy call to a friend to come and rescue you if necessary.

If you are hoping to date a local, language might be the most difficult barrier to overcome. Communication will be vital to ensuring there are no misunderstandings, as well as making it a meaningful connection on any level. Try to learn at least some basic words and phrases in their language before you meet up for your first date.

Relationship or dating protocols may vary depending on the country's culture, religion, and customs. Some countries will have much more conservative "rules" around relationships — even in the early stages — that your own. For example, in many Muslim countries unmarried couples cannot share a room (a large hotel may not question your marital status, but a small, family-run one might).

WARNING

Be careful how you flirt. Different cultures and individuals will interpret your behavior in different ways. Behavior you think perfectly appropriate may be offensive to someone else, or you might send the wrong signals about your willingness to take things a step further.

Look up the dating "customs" in your destination before you set out. Is it expected that you'll split the bill on a first date — or should the man offer to pay? In some parts of Europe, for instance, it's accepted that on most dates you'll share the cost. In other places, such as Portugal, it's considered rude if the man doesn't offer to pay, even on the first date.

That said, splitting the bill can help keep any expectations in check. However, if someone has put real effort into showing you around their town, offering to pay for a meal or a round of drinks is a nice gesture.

Find out anything else you should know about dating in your destination. A good resource is www.datingacrosscultures.com. Use similar safety strategies as you would at home:

REMEMBER

>> On a first date, meet in a busy, public place during the daytime (or well-lit at night), not too far away from your accommodations. Suggest you check out a local café or even a museum or other attraction together. Make sure it has easy access to public transport, stores, hotels, and restaurants in case you need to leave quickly or seek help.

>> Avoid going to a place where there's no phone signal or that's far away from the city center, which may be hard for you to get away from.

>> If you drink alcohol, know your limits and keep a close eye on your drink.

>> Carry enough money to pay your own way and get back to your accommodations.

>> Always make sure someone knows where you are. Leave a note in your room stating where you're headed and who you're with. Or send a text with your date's contact details, profile, and message screenshots, or your live geolocation to a friend back home.

>> If you find yourself in a dodgy nightclub where your date knows everyone, be wary. In some countries, it's not unknown for dating app matches to be sex workers in pursuit of clients.

>> Make it clear that you have something booked for later so you can leave after a set amount of time if you want to. Even if you don't have to be anywhere, pretend you do. If the date goes well, you can amend your plans and extend it.

>> Find out about public transport before you head out for the evening. What time is the last train, bus, or other form of transport that will get you back to your accommodations? Even in major cities, they don't run all night, and you don't want to be stranded or need to pay for an expensive taxi ride.

Many solo travelers use dating apps as an opportunity to meet interesting people, connect with the locals, share a meal with someone, practice a language, or explore a city in the company of a local. You're likely to find that most people are curious about you, this foreigner from across the world, with your cute accent, and are keen to meet you.

If you're using dating apps, search online for local platforms. Some international platforms such as Bumble and Tinder might be the same as you use at home. Pick the platform that best suits you, and install it ahead of your trip so you can hit the ground running when you arrive.

Tinder offers the ability to change your location so you can browse in any city with its "Passport" feature, available with a "Tinder Plus" subscription. This feature allows you to get a head start with swiping so you can start conversations with matches and tee up plans before you've even packed your bags.

Bumble is the preferred app for many women, because the initial contact must come from the female. The app is used mainly for dating, but it can also be used for business networking or to make new friends online.

OKCupid, Hinge, Badoo, and **Happn** are other popular apps. **Grindr** has long been the app of choice for gay men and its "XTRA" service has an "Explore" feature to search for matches in any location and organize dates in advance. **HER** is the go-to app for lesbian, bisexual, and queer women.

WARNING

Gay travelers should be very aware of the customs and laws surrounding homosexuality in the country you're visiting. In some countries, authorities have used Grindr to target, track, and arrest gay men.

Keep in mind that sex outside marriage is illegal in some countries, and the punishment can be harsh. Whether your partner is another Western traveler or a local, being reported can result in a visit from the police or religious police.

For example, a new morality law in Indonesia banning sex outside marriage will come into effect in 2026. The penalty is up to one year in prison. While authorities have said that the marital status of foreign visitors will not be checked, and that only parents, spouses, or children of suspected offenders will be able to report them, the effect is likely to put a dampener on casual sex, especially if you're hooking up with a local.

REMEMBER

Consent is vital in any sexual relationship. Clear and direct communication about both parties' intentions or expectations is essential if your date is not to end in tears or embarrassment. This is even more important if there's a language barrier.

WARNING

Another trap: Your new friend might present themselves on a dating app as single and fancy-free, conveniently forgetting about the spouse and children waiting at home while they are wining and dining you. If your liaison is discovered, in some cultures you can be seen as the guilty party — sometimes with violent retribution from other family members.

Of course, there are plenty of ways to meet people you may want to date without using dating apps! Pub crawls, walking and adventure tours, and meetups are all great examples.

While you might find true and lasting love while traveling — plenty of people have — if you concentrate on making great friends, meaningful connections, and having fun while getting an insider look at how other people live. In the end, it won't matter if you don't make a romantic connection! You'll go home with great memories and new friends.

Staying safe: STDs and other pitfalls

One in three travelers will have sex with a new partner while away from home, according to the U.S. Centers for Disease Control and Prevention. Being caught up in the excitement of an exotic new place and meeting fascinating new people may just cause you to throw caution to the wind — with sometimes unhappy consequences. One of those is sexually transmitted infections (STIs).

STIs (sometimes also called STDs) include HIV, gonorrhea, chlamydia, and syphilis — all serious infections that can have long-term health risks, especially if left untreated.

Get vaccinated for hepatitis A and hepatitis B before you travel as both viruses can be spread through sex.

Remember that even if you use other contraceptive methods to avoid a pregnancy, you can still catch an STI if you don't use a condom. Always be prepared for anything that could happen and don't rely on others for your own protection.

Reduce your risk of being infected by taking and using your own condoms. They are likely to be of better quality than those you buy overseas, especially in developing nations.

Symptoms of an STI may include pain when urinating or having sex, discharge from the vagina, penis, or anus, unexplained rashes, sores, or ulcers on your skin, genitals, or throat, or jaundice (yellowing of skin and eyes). However, sometimes there are no symptoms, so prevention is the best measure.

If you believe you may have been exposed to an STI, see a doctor or sexual health clinic for advice. Western countries are generally going to have easily accessed sexual health clinics, but you may find language is a problem; if so, find a doctor who speaks English. The best defense against needing one is to be careful about your own sexual health while you are traveling.

Sex work is legal in some countries, but for tourists this can be a trap. Sex trafficking, sex with a minor, and child pornography are criminal activities and are often punishable in your own country, even if the crime has occurred in another country. For example, under US federal law it is a crime for US residents to engage in sexual or pornographic activities with a person under 18, anywhere in the world. It's also illegal to travel abroad for the purpose of having sex with a minor. This is also the case in many other countries that have laws that can be used to prosecute their citizens for crimes committed on child sex tourism trips or while living abroad.

Take a good supply of contraceptives with you as they may be difficult to obtain outside major cities in Asia, Africa, and other remote or undeveloped areas.

Even if you're not looking for anything more than a fun evening and a conversation, carry your own condoms in case the situation changes. Take charge of protecting yourself from sexually transmitted infection or unwanted pregnancy.

Date rape drugs are another risk when dating someone you haven't met before. Never leave your drink unattended and only accept a drink that you have seen poured by the bar staff. If your date suggests getting the next round, go along to help carry them back. If you need to go to the bathroom, finish your drink first, and if another has been ordered before you return, say you've had enough for now. If a date pressures you to drink or take drugs, it's time to leave. Smokers should also be wary of taking cigarettes from strangers, too, as these could also be a conduit for drugs.

Research the destination you are visiting to find out if there are "codewords" to use if you find yourself in a bad situation. For example, in London, **Safer Sounds** (www.safersounds.org.uk) has initiated a campaign where people who feel unsafe or threatened in bars or restaurants could "ask for Angela." This is a sign to staff that you need help to get out of the situation.

Other venues around the world may have similar codewords in place. You can usually find out about this in the female bathroom. If you are somewhere where no codeword exists and you need to get out of the date but can't see how, just ask for help from a member of the staff.

If you're a victim of sexual assault, seek medical assistance as soon as you can.

In Chapter 2, you'll find a list of free apps you can download to call for help if you find yourself in dangerous circumstances.

Issues for LGBTQ+ travelers

If you're a member of the LGBTQ+ community, think carefully about where you are traveling. While most Western countries have long accepted same-sex relationships, it's unfortunately not a universal state of affairs. According to **Human Dignity Trust** (www.humandignitytrust.org), there are still 66 places in the world where consensual same-sex sexual activity is a crime. The laws of 12 countries can impose the death penalty — and half of those have done so.

In 14 countries, transgender people can be charged for cross-dressing, impersonation, and disguise. In even more countries, transgender people are likely to be targeted by other laws such as public order offences. Most of these countries are in Africa or the

Middle East, but there are others, including Indonesia, Malaysia, Papua New Guinea, Myanmar, Sri Lanka, and Guyana.

REMEMBER

To know more about the laws in countries you are thinking of visiting, take a look at this **International Lesbian, Gay, Bisexual, Trans and Intersex Association** online map that details them: `https://ilga.org/ilga-world-maps`

Tinder and Grindr issue warnings to users if they are searching for countries that will be dangerous for them. On Tinder, a travel alert pops up when the app is opened in a country where LGBTQ+ status is a crime, and you must opt in to be shown in these locations. The Grindr app is banned in Turkey, Indonesia, Lebanon, Saudi Arabia, and the United Arab Emirates.

Using your intuition

Trust your instincts. That feeling in your gut that says something here is not quite right, I'm not comfortable here, or I need to get out of here. Those feelings will usually be right, and not acting on them may be one of the worst mistakes you make while traveling.

On my very first overseas trip, young and green, when things didn't quite work out the way I'd planned, I accepted the offer of a room in a stranger's house. I was alone, jet-lagged, confused, on the other side of the world from everyone I knew, and unsure of what my next step would be . . . so it seemed like a gift and I didn't hesitate to accept. Of course, it was fine, the woman was lovely, and she looked after me for several days while I sorted out my situation.

Looking back years later, I wondered if I had been foolish. Could I have ended up in the basement chained to a bed, or worse, buried under the floorboards? Although nobody knew it at the time, that very scenario was playing out for young women traveling alone in a city not too far from where I was, preyed upon by a serial killer couple. But I don't believe it was foolish of me — I believe that my instincts worked. My intuition told me that I would be safe, and I was.

REMEMBER

As a solo traveler, listening to your intuition is vital. If a place, a person, or a situation makes you feel uneasy, follow your gut instinct and extricate yourself from the situation as fast as you can. This is especially important when dating, visiting a stranger's home, or accepting a lift from someone.

Learn some key phrases in the local language — "no" and "go away" (or something similar but more offensive) can be very effective if delivered forcefully. You can see the shock of the unexpected on the face of the recipient!

If you are using a dating app, make sure you message each other for a while before meeting up to get a sense of what the person is like. Keep the conversation inside the dating app, at least until you have met in person. Tell them politely that you don't use Whatsapp or that you don't exchange numbers with anyone before a first date. If they get angry or annoyed, ditch them. If you remain on the app, you can report a user who has broken the rules or has done anything inappropriate and warn others.

Check out their social media profile, and use Google Images to reverse search for their photo. Are they really who they say they are? Suggest having a quick video call before meeting up.

"Catfishing" is a worry for anyone who is dating when traveling. This is where someone — a man or a woman — creates a fake online profile with pictures from other people and a fictional life story. Only when you arrive for your date do you realize they are not the person they said they were. Sometimes it is simply a way to conceal their identity (for example, if they are married), but it can also be the beginning of a dangerous situation if you are a likely target for a scam, robbery, or physical attack.

If you do meet someone who is clearly not who they pretend to be — maybe it's an age thing or something else that doesn't add up — don't waste your time with them. You do not owe anything to anyone and should expect to be treated with honesty and respect.

Some red flags to watch for include a date who immediately talks about plans to visit you in your country, talks about the possibility of marriage (even jokingly), or starts to tell you about their financial problems.

An advantage of dating apps is that they can act as a filter to get to know someone before meeting them in real life. Trust your instincts and block someone if things start to turn nasty or you are uncomfortable talking to them or at the prospect of meeting them. Move on. There are millions of people using dating apps, and not all of them have good intentions. To put it bluntly, some of them are scammers or con artists.

Make sure you don't share any information or images that can be used to extort you for money such as nudes, private details of your work, or any confidential information.

Never accept an offer to be picked up or dropped off by your date. If someone wants to walk you home, tell them you're staying at a hotel near where you met, say goodbye outside the hotel or in the lobby, then wait for them to go and head back out. If necessary, tell reception what you're doing. If you're out at night, order a taxi or ride-share vehicle and stay inside the hotel, bar, or restaurant until it arrives. Using a ride-share app will avoid the need to deal with language barriers, as the driver knows exactly where you're going.

TIP

Always make sure your phone is fully charged before you go out on a date. Never leave your bag at the table when you go to the bathroom — take it everywhere with you and always have it within reach. And always have a little bit of cash with you just in case you need it to get out of a tricky situation.

At the end of the day, trust your gut. If something feels off, leave. Don't worry about offending the other person — better safe than sorry!

Little white lies to keep you safe

While honesty is always the best policy in life, sometimes it's forgivable to tell a little white lie to keep yourself safe.

In some countries, sadly, married women are treated with more respect than single women traveling on their own. A cheap gold band on your ring finger may help deter amorous suitors, along with a few mentions of your "husband."

My friend Chris employs the tactic of "choosing" someone she knows well to talk about as her imaginary husband, if necessary, on her travels. That way, she says, it's easy to keep the story straight and adds a touch of authenticity to what you're saying. You have a name, an occupation, and other details you can impart with confidence so it doesn't sound like a lie (apart from the marriage, of course).

If you think that's a step too far, just say you have a friend (or even better, a couple of friends) waiting for you at the hotel.

Perhaps they had other plans for the day, or weren't interested in coming out tonight. It's never a good idea to tell a stranger that you're traveling alone or where you're staying.

Until you know someone well, stay vague about your job, who you work for or where you live.

REMEMBER None of this is foolproof, of course, but taking sensible precautions will go a long way to keeping your travel memories all good ones. Despite the things that can go wrong, mostly they don't — so enjoy your foreign affair!

IN THIS CHAPTER

» Maintaining your health while traveling

» Beating the dreaded jet-lag

» Coping with COVID

» Remembering to care for your mental
   health

Chapter 9

Keeping Healthy

G ood health is essential on the road. At the very least, getting ill will spoil your vacation. At its worst, it may find
you alone and seeking medical treatment in an unfamiliar
health system, possibly in a country where you don't speak or
understand the language.

The cost of healthcare while traveling internationally may also be
horrendously high (*always* take out travel insurance with medical
coverage!) and signal the end of your travels in the short term.
I found this out early in my traveling life, having an emergency
appendectomy in the early days of an around-the-world trip, and
I have never traveled anywhere without insurance from that day
to this! Without it, I would have been forced to turn tail for home
immediately.

This chapter looks at preventive steps you can take before you set
out, what to do if you do get sick while away from home, and how
to stay healthy along the way.

**FIND
ONLINE**

You can find handy links to all the web addresses mentioned in
this chapter, as well as other helpful online resources, at www.
dummies.com/go/solotravelfd.

Preparing to Travel in Good Health

Changes of diet and climate can drastically alter your constitution when you're traveling. Researching your destination and any health issues that might arise there is essential. Is altitude sickness likely to be a problem? Are there venomous snakes or spiders lurking? What about mosquitoes?

Prevention is the best approach. Take care of the following before heading off on your trip:

REMEMBER

>> Start a fitness program if you don't already have one to ensure you set out in the best shape possible. Walking is always going to be part of any travel, but if you're planning an active vacation, make sure you prepare well by getting fit for whatever it will entail, whether it's cycling, hiking, swimming, or any other form of exercise you're not normally used to. Being physically under-prepared won't enhance your experience.

>> Make appointments with your doctor, dentist, and optometrist before you go, so there are no unpleasant surprises that could have been attended to before you leave home.

>> Make sure you have a spare pair of spectacles in case you lose or break the ones you normally wear.

>> Visit your pharmacists before leaving home to ensure you have enough medication for the trip, and get copies of any prescriptions you might need while away, using the generic drug name rather than the brand name, which may be different in your destination. Keep copies of the original prescriptions to show to border officials if you need to.

>> Check on the vaccinations you might need for certain counties (apart from COVID) well ahead of time. These might include yellow fever, rabies, cholera, hepatitis A and B, Japanese encephalitis, measles, meningococcal disease, tetanus, typhoid, and tuberculosis.

Some of these come in the form of several booster shots over a period of time, so make sure you allow time to schedule them. This also applies to anti-malaria tablets, which need to be taken *before* you arrive at your destination (and continued afterwards). And ensure you have all the documentation you'll need to prove you've had them, such as vaccination certificates.

>> Put together a small first-aid kit with basic needs for minor ailment and injuries. Include bandages, cotton wool, headache tablets, antiseptic cream, mosquito repellent, antihistamine cream (for insect bites), sunscreen, nail scissors, tweezers, motion sickness pills, oral rehydration sachets, anti-diarrhea medication, and any prescription medicines you are taking. Pack condoms, too (just in case!).

>> Make health insurance coverage a priority. It's simple: Don't travel without it! There are many types and levels of coverage, so do some comparisons on cost and coverage before you buy. There are online comparison sites that make it easier. Remember, if you have a serious accident or illness while abroad, you will need to cover the cost of repatriation — and that can potentially run into the tens of thousands of dollars. The cost of insurance will vary, depending on your age and any pre-existing conditions you have.

Staying Healthy While You're Away

While prep work before your trip is key, there are some steps you can and should take during your travels to help ensure you remain healthy and fully enjoy your time away.

Avoiding "economy class syndrome"

Deep vein thrombosis, also known as DVT or "economy-class syndrome," is a blood clot that develops in a deep vein. Caused by lack of movement, such as sitting for too long in a cramped airline seat, DVT is potentially deadly. Part of the clot may break off and travel to the lungs, causing a sudden blockage of arteries known as a pulmonary embolism.

REMEMBER

During a long-haul flight (longer than four hours), make sure you get up, walk up and down the aisle, and stretch your legs every 60 to 90 minutes to keep your blood flowing. Ask for an aisle seat to make this easier for you and those around you. Many in-flight magazines have suggested in-seat exercises you can do to keep your circulation going.

Other preventative measures include drinking lots of water, and avoiding alcohol and sleeping pills while flying.

TIP

Compression stockings or "flight socks" can be purchased from most pharmacies and usually at airport terminal stores. They look like normal stockings, but cling tightly to your legs and keep the blood circulating. As well as helping to prevent DVT, they also help with swollen feet.

Anyone with a history of heart disease, previous thrombosis, or any other medical condition that heightens the risk of DVT should consult a doctor about the best preventive measures to take before a long flight. Taking anticoagulants may be one recommendation.

Risk factors include previous or family history of blood clots, recent surgery or hospitalization, pregnancy, obesity, and cancer or treatment such as chemotherapy.

Symptoms of deep vein thrombosis include leg pain, swelling or tenderness, skin that is red or warm to the touch, or shortness of breath, chest pain, lightheadedness, and an elevated heartbeat.

WARNING

While usually associated with flying, DVT can also be an issue for any time you are not moving around, including long-distance train travel or driving. Make sure you take any opportunity to stretch your legs at rest stops.

Beating the dreaded jetlag

If you're traveling across time zones, the last thing you want is to lose the first day or two to jetlag, as you try to recover enough to start enjoying yourself. How severely it might strike depends a lot in the direction you've traveled. Flying east-west or vice-versa will confuse your body clock and everything is knocked out of kilter. Flying north-south (or the opposite) is easier, and if you feel tired on arrival it is more likely to be because you are dehydrated or generally stressed by the journey.

Staying hydrated is one of the keys to feeling good on a long plane trip. Try to avoid alcohol and drink as much water as you can — before, during, and after your flight. Get enough sleep before your trip and exercise well.

Jetlag symptoms are usually worse if you're flying east and crossing at least two time zones. It usually takes a day to recover for each time zone crossed — which means if you are flying, for example, from the USA or Europe to Australia or New Zealand via the Middle East or South East Asia, you may take several days to get over it.

TIP

Reset your watch to your destination time before you board the plane. Stay on your new schedule by sticking to local mealtimes and not hitting the sack until your normal bedtime.

Daylight will help reset your body clock. Resist the temptation to hit the pillow the moment you get to your hotel. If it's daylight, head outside for a walk. Keep yourself awake until night comes and you'll sleep well and recover more quickly. I like to try to book a walking tour for my first day in a new city as it's a great way to stay engaged and awake.

Some travelers swear that by using an app like **Timeshifter** (timeshifter.com) or **Jet Lag Rooster** (sleepopolis.com/calculators/jet-lag) you can adjust to a new time zone more easily. You need to start preparing a few days before leaving home, following the app's directions on when to sleep, nap, use or avoid light and more, to gradually shift your body's circadian rhythm and minimize the impact of changing time zones when you arrive at your destination.

TIP

You're awake at 6 a.m., it's daylight outside, the perfect time to get up and about. Leave your hotel for a brisk morning walk. If the city's not quite awake yet, you'll see it in a different way — without the crowds. One of my most memorable experiences of this was in Rome, where I found the Trevi Fountain deserted, unlike later in the day when crowds jostled for the best vantage point for their photos.

If you're traveling for business, try to arrive a few days earlier than your first important meeting or event to give yourself time to recover and for your body to adjust to the new time zone.

Try to sleep on the plane if it's bedtime at your destination. This might be difficult if you're leaving in the morning at your departure point, but earplugs and an eye mask might help. Conversely, if it's daytime where you're going, try to stay awake.

TIP

Melatonin is a supplement of the same sleep hormone that occurs naturally in the body. Taken before retiring to bed, it can help offset the effects of jetlag by ensuring a good night's sleep. Check with your doctor first, especially if you are taking other medication.

If you're able to fly with an airline that offers lie-flat beds, this can be a marvelous, comfortable way to get some sleep. Business

Class flights don't come cheap, but some airlines now offer alternatives and new innovations are happening all the time. Air New Zealand will launch its Economy Skynest on new Dreamliner aircraft in 2024, with six lie-flat sleep pods (a little like bunk beds) that would be perfect for that nearly 18-hour flight from New York to Auckland (which is one of the routes it will be available on, along with Chicago-Auckland). Of course, if you're lucky enough to be on a flight with plenty of empty seats, you can always ask for a row to yourself!

Practicing good hygiene

If there's one thing the COVID-19 pandemic taught us all, it's the importance of good hygiene. Basic rules like washing our hands frequently, covering our mouths and noses when sneezing or coughing, and ensuring that surfaces around us were clean became things we all became hyper-aware of doing. Things our mother taught us once again became second nature. Hand sanitizer became our new essential.

Travel hygiene is all about reducing your exposure to bacteria and germs. No one wants to spoil an expensive vacation (or even a budget one) by catching a virus or bug! By staying conscious of good hygiene practices, you'll avoid potentially spoiling your vacation by spending it in foreign doctors' waiting rooms and hospitals.

Put together a hygiene kit to carry with you. Pack face masks, handwash, sanitizer (look for one that's at least 60 percent alcohol), disinfectant wipes, sunscreen, mouthwash, a thermometer, disposable gloves, and tissues.

Face masks, which became compulsory on most airlines and public transport around the world during the pandemic, are still a good idea in crowded situations. No one looks twice at mask-wearing now and it's a good way to avoid catching COVID or anything else while you're unavoidably up close and personal with strangers.

Washing your hands often and sanitizing hands and everyday objects you might come into contact with — I'm thinking hotel room doorknobs or television remotes — is a good start.

Pack a pair of rubber flip-flops. If you're using a shared bathroom (or one that doesn't look too clean), wear them on the tiles and in the shower to avoid the possibility of catching foot fungus.

Drinking the water (or not)

In most Western countries it is fine to drink the water. In those where it is not, bottled water is the preferred option.

In these days of avoiding plastic, take a reusable water bottle with you and fill it up with water that's safe to drink at your hotel. Boiled water is a good option, as well as water purification tablets. These are particularly useful if you are hiking in remote areas; always be careful about drinking from streams or waterfalls.

WARNING

It's not only water you need to be wary of — it's anything that might have been washed in contaminated water. Take your drinks without ice, and avoid anything that may have been washed, such as salad greens or fruit that you will eat the skin of. If in doubt, ask about the safety of the water or try to find out where it comes from. Illnesses caused by drinking contaminated water can make you extremely sick with diarrhea and/or vomiting. Contaminated water can look clean but still have harmful bacteria, viruses, and parasites.

WARNING

Even brushing your teeth, or opening your mouth in the shower, can result in illness from contaminated water.

Always check the seal on bottled water; it's not unheard of for plastic bottles to be reused and resold. Always look for unopened, factory-sealed bottled water or other drinks.

WARNING

Contact with contaminated water, such as swimming, can also lead to illness. Don't wade in dirty water if you have cuts on your skin.

Doing your best to avoid gastro bugs and other nasties

Diarrhea is the most common travel-related illness. Most travelers have had it. It can happen anywhere, but the most likely places you'll get it will be in some parts of Asia, Africa, Mexico, Central and South America, and the Middle East. Although it's not usually life-threatening, a gastric bug can certainly spoil your trip! And for solo travelers, coping on your own makes it even worse to deal with.

The best ways to avoid stomach bugs is to choose what you eat and drink carefully.

Steer clear of the buffet. Food that has been sitting out for too long or has not been kept hot enough can be harboring nasties you want to avoid.

If you are unlucky enough to get diarrhea, drink lots of fluids to stay hydrated. Carry oral rehydration solutions with you (from your pharmacy) and drugs that will treat the symptoms of gastric bugs, such as Immodium or loperamide, which can be bought without a prescription. This will make it easier to continue with your bus, train, or airline travel until you can get to a doctor.

Pharmacists in some countries may not fill a foreign prescription, so make sure you carry enough medication with you to last the trip. A letter from your doctor or pharmacist may also be needed for authorities.

Coping with COVID

The COVID pandemic kept us all home for too long. Now that borders have opened and we are able to travel freely throughout the world again, solo travel is increasing in popularity. But COVID has not gone away, and all travelers have to learn to live with it and develop a game plan to avoid it if possible and to cope with infection if it strikes.

According to the Centers for Disease Control and Protection (CDC), the more you travel, the more you risk becoming exposed to the virus. This fact has led to a new type of anxiety around travel, as you decide if traveling is worth the risk.

Looking into the infection rates in the destination you'll be traveling to should be considered. Check the warning levels published by your government travel advisories (see Chapter 2) and decide if you want to take the risk. Speak to your doctor about vaccination or booster shots.

Vaccination may not stop you getting COVID, but it will minimize the effects when you do. Almost all countries now require foreign visitors to be fully vaccinated.

To alleviate your fears, do some serious research into the risks and the ways in which you can combat them. Look for reliable, scientific sources like the CDC, World Health Organization, or your government website. But resist going down rabbit holes that will only fuel your anxiety. Stay away from social media horror stories, and focus on the great experiences ahead of you as you plan your trip.

Wear a mask on the plane, train, or bus — and on public transport when you arrive. Don't worry about what people around you are doing, just focus on what you feel personally comfortable doing. People have been wearing face masks in the streets of Asia for years before COVID, to prevent illnesses like influenza and to combat the effects of air pollution. Nobody gives them a second look, and that acceptance is worldwide now.

Check out the local rules before you arrive in a new destination. What are the testing requirements? What are the rules about wearing masks? Is quarantine mandatory if you contract COVID and for how long? This applies to individual cities, states, and provinces. Although rules are relaxing as time goes on, some still have more stringent rules than others.

REMEMBER

Carry proof of vaccination. Print out a physical copy and have the digital proof stored on your phone. A photo of it on your phone is also handy.

Research your destination's rules around what you need to do if you are unlucky enough to contract COVID. Do you need to quarantine? Every country, and some cities, have their own laws, so make sure you are aware of them before you leave home — and be prepared to adhere to them. If that means isolating in a hotel, be conscious of the extra cost that might involve or the potential to disrupt your plans. Will your travel insurance cover it? Take a supply of COVID testing kits with you and if you have symptoms, test as soon as you can.

COVID — and other infectious diseases — spread quickly aboard cruise ships. If an outbreak happens, you may be faced with quarantine on the ship or in a foreign country you didn't expect to spend time in.

Staying away from alcohol and other stimulants

There are many benefits to staying away from alcohol when traveling alone, not least of them safety. As a solo traveler, you need to be aware of your surroundings and — to some extent — always on your guard. While it might be tempting to hit the bars in

Barcelona or New Orleans, or to go wine-tasting in the Napa Valley or South Australia, moderation should always be your friend.

If you are a dedicated teetotaler, there are even travel companies who run tours for sober travelers. One is UK-based **We Love Lucid** (www.welovelucid.com), which promotes active and adventurous holidays including hiking, yoga, foodie experiences, windsurfing, yoga — and alcohol-free drinks gatherings. Another is **HOOKED Alcohol Free Travel Adventure** (www.hooked-on-travel.com), based in Canada.

As the trend toward alcohol-free travel grows, so too is the industry that supports it. Forget the obligatory mocktail, now there are booze-free bars and nightclubs springing up where you least expect it. Like Dublin, Berlin, and Tokyo! An online search of your destination might throw up some surprises worth exploring.

Daybreaker (www.daybreaker.com) runs ticketed sunrise dance parties at 28 cities around the world — most of them in the US, but also in Shanghai, Hong Kong, Paris, London, Amsterdam, Buenos Aires, Montreal, Toronto, and Tokyo. It's substance-free and you'll find plenty of locals there, starting their work day with yoga and a dance workout. Yoga sessions (BYO mat) start around 5:30 a.m. or 6 a.m. in most locations, followed by a two-hour dance party an hour later. And there's breakfast included. It's not cheap, but think of what you're saving on the drinks you'd have bought at the bar! Heading to Germany? Check out **Sober Sensations** (www.sobersensations.com), which has been running alcohol-free dance parties since 2016.

Think laterally about nightlife. The choice isn't between going to bars and pubs or sitting in your hotel room watching old movies. Buy theatre tickets or take a night-walking tour, a ghost tour, or a night-time photography tour. Check out late-night entry to galleries and museums. Some river cities offer night kayaking tours, a step up from staid dinner cruises!

Did someone say thermal baths? Many spa towns around the world, from Vienna in Austria to Rotorua in New Zealand, offer evening openings where you can soak up the warmth of sulfur pools either indoors or under the stars. Bliss.

Many craft breweries are also recognizing the demand for alcohol-free beers, and there's highly likely to be several on offer if you're heading to one of these trendy establishments.

Even cruise lines are in on the sober curious trend. **Carnival Cruise Line** (www.carnival.com) and **Norwegian Cruise Line** (www.ncl.com) are two of the big ones who have ensured a good range of alcohol-free drinks is available to passengers. Carnival's Alchemy Bar, a venue on nearly every Carnival ship sailing from the US, has teamed up with distiller Lyre to serve its non-alcoholic spirits.

REMEMBER

And the best part of all? Waking up clear-headed and ready to tackle whatever the day's travel brings. No hangovers, no dark glasses to ward off the bright light, no reaching for the headache remedy, or reluctance to rise and shine. No more worrying that you've lost your passport and can't remember exactly where you've been. Being sober may just hand you a richer travel experience than you expected. To say nothing of the money you'll save by not buying drinks!

WARNING

As for other stimulants, it's wise to stay away from any illegal drugs including amphetamines, cannabis, heroin, and opioids while traveling. While you may be aware of the laws around these at home, foreign countries are an entirely different matter. In some countries, possession, use, or trafficking of drugs can incur long prison terms or even the death penalty. Being a foreigner will not necessarily save you.

Sexual health

About one in three travelers will have sex with a new partner while away from home, according to the US Centers for Disease Control and Prevention. The freedom and excitement of being abroad and meeting new people may lead to engaging in risky behaviors.

Western countries are generally going to have easily accessed sexual health clinics, but even then, you may find language is a problem. The best defense against needing one is to be careful about your own sexual health while you are traveling.

TIP

Take a good supply of tampons, sanitary pads, and contraceptive supplies with you as they may be difficult to obtain outside major cities in Asia, Africa, and other remote or undeveloped areas.

Sexually transmitted infections (STIs), including HIV, gonorrhea chlamydia, and syphilis can be a real risk. Reduce your risk of being infected by taking and using your own condoms. They're likely to be of better quality than those you buy overseas, especially in developing nations.

TIP

Get vaccinated for hepatitis A and hepatitis B before you travel as both viruses can be spread through sex.

Sexually transmitted infections may not always have symptoms. If you believe you may have been exposed, seek medical advice. The symptoms of STIs are different depending on the infection but may include pain when urinating or having sex; discharge from the vagina, penis, or anus; unexplained rashes, sores, or ulcers on your skin, genitals, or throat; or jaundice (yellowing of skin and eyes).

If you're a victim of sexual assault, seek medical assistance as soon as you can to reduce the risk of infection.

I talk more about this in Chapter 8.

Avoiding accidents

I love a good solo road trip, but there are many hazards attached to driving in unfamiliar places — sometimes with fatal consequences.

For a start, which side of the road should you be on? If you're going to be driving in a foreign country, make sure you find out whether you should be driving on the right-hand side of the road or on the left! Laws vary, with many countries driving on the left, as pictured in Figure 9-1 in outback Australia, including the UK, Ireland, Japan, Indonesia, Singapore, Malaysia, Thailand, and New Zealand. In Australia and New Zealand, the perceived danger of this is high enough that many rental car companies have large warning signs on their car dashboards.

REMEMBER

Always wear a seat belt, as a driver or passenger, in the front seat or the back, even if it is not the law in the country you are in.

It's tempting, sometimes, to throw caution to the wind when you are on vacation. Hiring a motorbike in Bali or a Vespa in Rome has great appeal, but make sure first that your insurance will cover you. This also applies to motorized watersports such as jetskiing and, of course, to skiing and snowboarding. Most times, your insurance coverage will be specific to that activity and excluded unless you pay extra for the coverage.

FIGURE 9-1: Many countries drive on the left side of the road.

For on-road activities (even electric scooters), make sure you have a well-fitting helmet and as much safety gear as you need. Roads can do serious damage to bare arms, legs, and feet if you are not wearing protective gear when you fall off.

Check whether you need an International Driving Permit (IDP) to be on the road, in addition to your own country's license. In some countries, your own driver's license will be enough to rent a car with, but others will require an IDP, which is a United Nations-sanctioned translation of your license in nine different languages. An IDP is valid for a year. If you stay in Europe longer than that, you may need a local license. Some countries require that you get a local translation of your license sooner than that. Find out the details before you leave home.

TIP

Foreigners aren't permitted to rent cars in Vietnam or China, where a local license is required to drive. And given the chaos on the roads in both places, that's something you'll be thankful for! Using public transport or hiring a car with a driver is a good option in these countries.

Getting help when you need it

There is truly nothing worse than being ill when you're away from home and alone — even if you're in your own country! And if you find yourself in need of medical help when you're in a foreign country, with all the attendant language difficulties, it's even worse. The most important thing to do is to seek help when you need it; as a solo traveler, you need to ensure you don't put yourself in danger.

If you have a medical emergency, call your embassy, consulate, or health insurance provider and ask for a list of English-speaking doctors or clinics. They can also help with arranging emergency transport home if necessary. Keep these numbers in your phone and in a hard copy with your travel documents for easy access.

If you have a minor illness or injury, the first place to go is a local pharmacy or medical clinic. Your hotel should be able to give you assistance in finding the closest one (or in recommending a doctor). If you're staying alone in an Airbnb or similar, go online to find the closest option. Some public hospitals won't treat foreigners, but private clinics will — and you can claim the cost on your travel insurance (make sure you get invoices, receipts, and other documentation you may need to make a claim).

How to Beat the Blues

Traveling alone has many advantages, but the downside is undoubtedly the potential for loneliness. Some people don't need much company, but isolation can take its toll on even the most self-reliant and independent people. Homesickness can strike at any time, especially if you're traveling alone for a good length of time. A week or two away is manageable, but for anyone contemplating a long solo journey, it's essential to keep your spirits up and forge ahead.

When things go wrong — which they always do, to some extent, when we're traveling — solo travelers have no instant support system. Whether you've been robbed, lost your passport, taken a wrong turn and got lost, become ill, or just feel bored or homesick, as a solo traveler, things can get on top of you. Traveling has its downside, but the key is remembering that the benefits always outweigh that.

Combating loneliness

Solo travel means that when the blues hit you, there's no buddy to comfort you or jolly you out of a gray mood. The best way to prevent it hitting is to develop some strategies to help cope with things.

Talking to other people is the obvious solution to loneliness, but that's not always easy if you are in a country where you don't speak the language. Actively seeking conversation with other English-speaking travelers is the ideal, and it's likely you have a lot in common, even if it's only to share experiences of the destination you're in or one you have been to. Hostel life is great for striking up friendships with fellow travelers and more social than staying alone in a hotel room.

Many large hotels offer inclusions or add-ons that can put you in contact with other guests. It might be an early morning yoga class or happy hour drinks. Even a visit to the hotel gym might result in striking up a conversation with another exercise junkie.

If you think you might be lonely traveling alone, book yourself on a tour where you are likely to be with like-minded travelers (see Chapter 2), or sign up for some volunteer work that will not only create contact with others, but will also give you a feeling of well-being from doing good for others. In other words, if you're new to solo travel and uncertain about whether you'll like it, ease yourself into it with a short trip to start with. The more solo travel you do, the easier it will become (and it sure beats staying home!).

If homesickness is at the root of your loneliness, try calling your loved ones for a boost. There's nothing like a laugh with a dear friend or family member to lift your spirits and set you on a brighter path again.

Resist the temptation to wallow in your misery alone in your hotel room. Exercise is a sure way of lifting your endorphin levels and your mood. Go for a brisk walk, hire a bike and pedal your way back into optimism, or hit the pool or the beach for some therapy. Joining a free walking tour will combine exercise with the chance to meet other travelers, too.

REMEMBER

If the blues escalate to serious levels, help is always available. Call a local crisis line; ask your hotel to help you find an English-speaking one.

Try to avoid becoming stressed or over-tired. Keep alcohol intake to a reasonable level, as it can help feed paranoia and anxiety. Staying healthy is a good step toward staying happy on the road; there's nothing like illness to make you feel miserable and homesick.

Feeling lonely sometimes is normal. Watching that spectacular sunset or having the best meal of your life is sure to make you want to share the experience with someone, but that feeling will pass and it's better to be alone than to not see the world at all.

Exercising around the world

Active vacations are the best way to ensure you keep up your exercise regime while on the road. Hiking, skiing, cycling, horse-riding, and similar activities can all keep you fit as part of your daily routine. For those holidays that are less active it's still possible to incorporate exercise into your day.

Most big hotels now have a gym and offer activities from yoga to jogging groups, step classes, and more as part of your stay (sometimes, but not always, at an extra cost). And don't forget to hit the lap pool whenever you can. If your hotel doesn't have a swimming pool like the one in Figure 9-2, there's sure to be a public one nearby.

Take the stairs in your hotel (unless you are on the 17th floor, as I was recently). It's often quicker than waiting for the elevator.

Many local running organizations hold regular short events that are open to all-comers. Look for **ParkRun** (www.parkrun.com), a collection of free 3.1-mile (5-km) events for walkers and runners that take place every Saturday morning at more than 2,000 locations in 22 countries across six continents. It's run by volunteers and you're sure to meet up with some fun locals!

Take advantage of city cycle schemes to incorporate exercise into your plan, pedaling your way around the sights. Kayaking or canoeing tours are also a great way to get another perspective on a place by seeing it from the water.

Look out for public fitness stations or exercise parks. These are perfect for everything from core to balance work, cardio and coordination. Often, they come with a great view while you work out.

Take a skipping rope in your luggage — it takes up hardly any room at all — to break out when you have the space.

Lee Mylne(Author)

FIGURE 9-2: Hitting a hotel lap pool helps keep up your exercise regime while traveling.

Best advice of all: walk, walk, walk. And remember to use sunscreen, wear a hat, and stay hydrated.

Chapter 2 has my tips for choosing an outdoor adventure holiday for one.

Mindfulness and other strategies

Solo travel can be transformative. Challenges change you; they empower you, allowing you to realize just how self-sufficient you can be when required.

Taking time for yourself is important, and solo travel gives you time alone to think and clear your mind. But solo travel can also be hectic, and the need for clarity is often lost in the frantic pace of travel.

Practicing mindfulness while you travel will allow you to slow down, savor each moment, and be fully aware of your surroundings. Try not to rush from one sight to another, ticking things to see off your list. A more relaxed pace will also help alleviate any anxiety you might have.

One way of introducing slow travel to your style is to pick one place to go and spend your entire vacation there. Maybe it's a village in France or Italy, where you can rent a small apartment or an Airbnb and stay in one place, savoring the local life, shopping at the market, drinking coffee in the town square, and talking to the neighbors. Sound good? Do it!

TIP

Meditation apps like **Headspace** and **Calm** can help you stay mindful and relaxed while on the go and can help with sleep. Make sure you start using them before you begin your travel, so you are familiar with them and get the most out of them when you need them on the road.

Keeping a journal is an important way of practicing mindfulness. It is a means of noting your observations and impressions of our surroundings and reflecting on what you've seen. It does not need to be a diary of everything you've done, but it will certainly help you to later remember tiny details about your travels that you may have forgotten. Doing this over your evening meal is a nice way to think about the day and also gives you something to do while you're dining alone.

Leaving your expectations at home is a good start to mindful travel. Go with an open mind and see what happens!

Dealing with Decision Fatigue

Many people relish the fact that traveling solo means they don't need to compromise on anything they do. There's no one to please except yourself, and that's a liberating feeling.

The downside is that traveling alone means every decision, big or small, rests with you. There's no one to debate the wisdom of taking a certain path or to share the everyday choices that need to be made. From the germ of your idea on where to travel, through the planning and packing, and on-the-ground realities, every decision must be made alone. For some people, that becomes too much — and decision fatigue sets in, a paralysis that can sometimes seem overwhelming.

This kind of mental exhaustion can ruin your holiday. And decision fatigue doesn't just stop you from *making* decisions — it can also cause you to make bad decisions, something that as a solo traveler can range from regrettable to downright dangerous.

But if solo is your preferred way to travel, there's no way around it. Every day, there are hundreds of small decisions to be made. So how to avoid decision fatigue? Here are my tips for making life on the road as easy as possible, by reducing the number of decisions you need to make.

» **Pre-booking helps limit decision fatigue when you are on the ground in your destination.** But when planning your trip, don't try to do it all at once. Break it down into smaller chunks; book flights one day, accommodations on another, and leave activities for another. Some things don't need to be booked ahead — leave room for spontaneity.

» **Pack as lightly as you can.** This limits the choices you have about what to wear every day. Make sure everything you take is mix-and-match.

» **Have some restaurant recommendations sorted out before you arrive at your destination.** You may decide not to use them, but knowing a few good places to eat will help in the early days, until you've got the lay of the land and have seen what's nearby or heard good reports from locals.

» **Make lists.** What do you want to see? What are your top priorities? How will you fit them into the time you have? Use a map to plot a course, so attractions that are close together can be seen on the same day (as long as you are not cramming things in just to tick them off).

» **Take time out.** Have a day of doing nothing. Leave structure and planning behind. Go for a walk, read a book, write postcards, relax in a park, sit in a café, and indulge in some people-watching. It may just be the best day of your trip.

And remember, if things go wrong . . . breathe.

Chapter **10**

Ten Tips for Successful Solo Travel

Whether you are traveling solo for the first time or it's become your preferred way to exploring the world, there are definitely a few steps you can take to ensure that you have a memorable time — for the right reasons.

Everyone travels differently, but some elements of planning are always a good idea when traveling solo, even if they are the most basic.

In this chapter, I share my top tips for successful solo trave,l and you can find more detail on most of these throughout the book. My best tip of all, of course, is to go out and enjoy yourself!

Research Your Destination

Make sure you do your research before you leave home. This is especially important when it comes to knowing about cultural differences. What are the expectations around dress codes or behavior that might be unwittingly offensive in a foreign country? Is it a country where the laws are based on religion or where conservative dress and behavior is expected?

Check health requirements and ask your doctor about necessary vaccinations or medication. Is it a place where malaria is rife or where rabies from monkey or dog bites could be a risk? Do you need to have proof of your vaccinations?

What's the best time of year to go? Find out about the likely weather and try to avoid seasons where hurricanes, floods, or other events might upset your plans. Think about visiting in the offseason, when the crowds will be less and the prices are likely to be cheaper. Check out what events might be on in your destination that are worth attending (despite the crowds). Look for cultural festivals, music events, or seasonal happenings.

Plan Your Budget

Planning your budget is a key to a successful trip. Breaking the budget can put a real dampener on a trip. As a solo traveler you've got no one else to rely on or borrow from, so you want to make sure you have enough money to ensure you can do all the things you dreamed of. Careful research and planning before you leave home will ensure your funds don't run out before the end of the trip. Make sure you understand the exchange rate and cost of living in your planned destination and how far your currency will stretch.

When budgeting, factor in transport (getting there and on the ground in your destination; don't forget fuel costs if you are road-tripping), accommodations, meals, and activities. Look for free or low-cost events and attractions to make the most of your trip.

TIP

Avoid the budget-busting single supplement, most common on group tours or cruises, if you can. Look for special offers where it is waived — or simply ask the company for a deal to avoid it.

Choose the Right Accommodation

Your style of travel will dictate what kind of accommodation is right for you — and that might vary from trip to trip. There are as many types of accommodation as there are kinds of solo traveler, and your choice may be different for every trip.

If you're on a budget, you'll be looking at the options that will help your funds go as far as they can. I think it's better to scrimp a bit on where you lay your head at night and spend what you save on great experiences. After all, you'll mostly only be using your room to sleep, and the rest of the time you'll be out exploring.

Unless you are couch-surfing, house-sitting, or house swapping, hostels are probably the cheapest accommodation option, with the added benefit of being ideal for meeting fellow travelers. Airbnbs and homestays offer a more local experience, but sometimes all you want is the privacy of your own hotel room.

Whatever you choose, the most important thing is that you are safe and comfortable and in a great central location.

Make an Effort to Meet People

Solo doesn't have to mean solitude. While many people love the head space that solo travel provides, it's a good idea not to become a hermit while you're traveling. The people you meet along the way — fellow travelers, expats, locals — are an important and often memorable part of your travel experience.

Take a guided walking tour with a local to introduce you to a new place. Use travel forums, social media, and meet-up events to connect with others — both locals and other travelers — who share your interests and can provide valuable insights into the place you are visiting. It might seem hard to strike up a conversation with a stranger if you are new to solo travel, but believe me, it does get easier!

Make Safety a Priority

All solo travelers need to have their radar tuned for potential trouble. That doesn't mean being constantly afraid of what might happen, but simply taking sensible precautions to ensure your personal safety. With no companion to watch your back, you need to take extra care of both yourself and your belongings (guard your passport with your life).

WARNING

Don't leave home without travel insurance — it will be worth every cent if something goes wrong. Be aware of safety concerns, such as theft and health issues, and have an emergency plan.

Keep in touch with the folks back home regularly and know how to contact your embassy or consulate if things get serious. Make sure that someone at home has a copy of your itinerary and knows where you are supposed to be. If your plans change, let them know.

Take Public Transport

Did I mention that I *love* public transport? It's the best way to get around and really get a feel for a place. You'll be rubbing shoulders with the locals as they go about their daily life and you'll see a lot more than you would from inside a car. The other advantage, of course, is that it's a very cheap way to get around and that will stretch your budget.

So, whether it's a local bus — and depending where you are, a bus can be a fairly loose description — crammed with people and sometimes livestock or a sleek new train that will whiz you to your next destination. So buy a ticket, like I did for local buses in Laos, pictured in Figure 10-1, and join the locals. Or hire a bike from a local bike-share scheme and see the city on two wheels.

TIP

Buy a transport pass. It will save money, be more convenient, and sometimes include discounted entry to museums, galleries, theme parks, and other attractions.

FIGURE 10-1: Catching a local bus in Laos.

If it's feasible, seek out long-distance trains instead of flying. It's better for the planet and gives you a chance to see more of the country you're visiting. You can also save on hotel rooms by taking an overnight sleeper train to the next place on your itinerary.

Soak Up the Local Culture

Immersing yourself in local culture will be one of the most enriching experiences of your traveling life, no matter which part of the world you are in. Learn a few words (at least) of the language before you arrive and bask in the smiles you get! Respect for local customs and traditions will go a long way toward opening doors and making friends.

Find out about First Nations culture and history; this will deepen your understanding of the destination and give you a new perspective on it. Plan your trip to coincide with a cultural festival like the one pictured in Figure 10-2 that I attended on Australia's Cape York, if you can, and spend your travel dollars in ways that will benefit local communities — book in to a homestay, buy local art and crafts, and take a tour with a local guide.

FIGURE 10-2: Laura Indigenous Dance Festival, Cape York, Australia.

Be Flexible

As the saying goes, "The best laid plans of mice and men sometimes go awry" — and that's never more accurate than when it comes to traveling. The great thing about traveling solo is that you can be flexible because you have only yourself to consider!

TIP

When things don't quite go to plan, think about how you can salvage the situation and adapt. Your plane is delayed . . . head to that spa lounge in the terminal that you wouldn't otherwise have time for. Bad weather has canceled your kayaking tour . . . check out the latest exhibition at a gallery or museum.

Take up offers from other travelers to join them on a tour or for dinner . . . you'll find a new place and new friends at the same time. Be open to changing your plans and to the vagaries that travel often brings.

Do Something You Wouldn't Normally Do

Traveling is all about getting out of your comfort zone, stretching your boundaries, and experiencing something new. You've already done that by deciding to go somewhere you've never been before — and perhaps you're traveling solo for the first time, too. Take it even further by doing something that you've never done before or would not have the chance to do at home.

The bravest thing I've ever done while traveling was ziplining through the jungle in northern Laos. While I knew that ziplining was the only method of transport that would get me between the treehouses in which I was staying, the reality was something quite different. I'm not great with heights, and the treehouses (and ziplines) were between 65 feet to 130 feet (20 m to 40 m) above the ground, as pictured in Figure 10-3. Starting from a position of paralyzing fear, I soon learned to step off the zipline platform with aplomb (most of the time) as I rode 15 of them over three days. (But I still draw the line at bungy-jumping.)

Lee Mylne(Author)

FIGURE 10-3: Treehouse in Laos, reached only by zipline.

So, whether it is learning to scuba dive, trying your hand at pottery, or trekking in the Himalayas, take a deep breath and believe you can do it!

Embrace the Freedom

Solo travel is all about freedom. You have nobody else to consider except yourself. You can go wherever you like, whenever you choose, and do anything you care to. There are no compromises to be made with another person.

The secret to successful solo travel is to embrace that feeling of freedom and relish everything that it brings.

Go on, do it!

Chapter **11**

Avoiding Ten Common Mistakes Solo Travelers Make

Travel is never perfect, and you'll always make mistakes. The good thing is you'll learn from those mistakes and hopefully never make them again. I've made plenty in my traveling life, thankfully without dreadfully serious consequences. There have been missed flights, terrible hotel choices, and some awful purchases along the way. If you make mistakes, don't worry about them too much — but remember them!

In this chapter, I point out common mistakes that most solo travelers make, especially when starting out. I hope this list helps you to avoid them!

Not Doing Your Research

Not doing your research before traveling can be an expensive mistake — and so many issues can be avoided just by spending a little time on it.

Some people like to travel by freewheeling through their destination and changing loose plans when something else appeals — being flexible, which is great — up to a point. However, a certain amount of basic planning is important. Do your research and know the risks of your destination before you arrive by checking your government's travel advisory page. Know what documents you'll need to get into the country, how you'll get there, and where you'll spend the first night.

Checking what the season might bring in terms of weather can mean you avoid being stuck in a hotel room during a hurricane or finding every hotel booked out because of a festival. Not knowing about religious holidays can mean you find restaurants and tourist attractions closed, not to mention those places that routinely close for winter (I'm thinking back to my visit to the Bronte sisters' house in Yorkshire here).

It is especially important to do your research when it comes to knowing about cultural differences and expectations, such as modest dress or appropriate behavior.

REMEMBER

Vital to your planning and research should also include travel insurance. Never leave home without it!

Packing Too Much

Always remember that whatever you pack you have to carry. There's nothing worse than lugging a heavy suitcase up the steps at a London Tube station or trying to wheel it over cobblestone streets in Italy. It won't take long before you realize your mistake!

Pack as lightly as you can, aiming for carry-on luggage only if you are flying. It's not only better for the planet but it may also save you money if your bag is overweight — and that's money you could have spent on more enjoyable aspects of your trip.

Sharing Too Much Personal Information with Strangers

It's great to meet the locals and other travelers, but sharing too much personal information can be dangerous. Never tell someone you've just met that you are traveling solo or where you are staying. A person who wants to know everything about you might have an ulterior motive and could be setting you up for a scam or robbery — or worse.

Of course, they could just be interested in making conversation, but it pays to be on your guard. If it seems intrusive, excuse yourself and move on. If you need to, make up a story that sounds feasible — a husband or friend waiting at the hotel for you is an acceptable white lie. Don't feel that you have to add them on Facebook either — just ignore the request when it comes or delete them when you've moved on. Your privacy and safety are your top concern.

Not Listening to the Locals

Local people are the best source of information about the place they live — and it's wise to listen to them. Not only do they know the best places to eat, where to buy that something you're hunting for, or where the best bands are playing, but they also know the places to steer clear of.

Whether it's the concierge at your hotel, the bartender pouring your pisco sour, or the woman you sat next to on the bus, these are the people who can help you stay safe and get the most out of your visit.

Being Careless or Too Trusting

Carelessness is easy to slip into when you're getting comfortable with traveling or with your new surroundings. But when you're traveling, as well as keeping yourself safe, it's important to keep your belongings safe, too.

It might seem harsh to encourage you to trust no one when much of traveling solo is about putting your trust in others, but taking sensible precautions and being alert to what's happening around you are important. For example:

» **Don't trust strangers to watch your belongings; take your bag to the bathroom with you.** If you're swimming, don't leave anything valuable on the beach.

» **If you are at a bar, keep an eye on your drink at all times.** If you leave it unattended, don't drink it when you come back. Someone could have slipped drugs into it while you were away. Be aware of being distracted if you are in a group.

» **Don't leave your bag, phone, or camera on a chair or an outdoor table, even if you are right there.** It's an easy target for a grab-and-run thief. Keep them on your lap or anchored by your chair or foot. When walking, taking public transport, or waiting in queues, keep your bag to the front of your body and make sure all the zips or flaps are closed. Someone can easily reach into your bag and take your things without you noticing it (yes, it's happened to me and it was a lesson learned the hard way).

» **If you're staying in a hostel, make sure your valuables — money and passport — are locked up safely.**

Letting Fear Take Over

There's a fine line between being wary and alert to potential dangers and letting fear take over. As a solo traveler — especially a beginner — you might already have overcome the fear of setting out on your own, and that's a huge step! Congratulate yourself and carry on as you have started, projecting a confidence that you may not truly feel yet. Letting fear take over at any stage of the journey is a big mistake and will rob you of the joy that solo travel can bring.

Although it's difficult to trust everyone in an unfamiliar place, it's wrong to mistrust everyone. Instead, allow yourself and your newfound friends a chance to get to know each other and trust your instincts. Finding company on a solo trip can sometimes lead to lifelong friendships.

If you are spending a lot of time on your own, you may find loneliness creeping in. Shut the door on it! Get out and about and make connections, however brief and superficial, with other people. Loneliness can be insidious, especially if you are traveling for a long time, and it's a mistake to give in to it. But also relish time that you spend alone, you will learn a lot about yourself and your resilience. Learn to strike a balance between enjoying the company of others and spending time in solitude.

Being Too Polite

Sometimes, you can be too damned polite! In your travels, you're going to meet people who push the boundaries and it's a mistake not to push back. Witness the earrings — which may or may not be jade — in my jewelry box, courtesy of a pushy taxi driver who stopped off at his cousin's shop on my way to the airport, and the gray silk sari that I was badgered into buying by a relentless tour guide in India. Be polite but firm with people like this — it gets easier with practice.

REMEMBER

Solo female travelers also need not be polite to a man who won't be deterred by your lack of interest. If a firm refusal doesn't have the desired effect, raise your voice. Get the attention of others and make it clear to anyone around that you are being bothered. If you think it might be an issue in a country you are visiting, learn some appropriate phrases — even some rude ones — in the local language before you go.

Not Keeping Track of Documents

Keeping track of your passport is the most essential thing to worry about when it comes to paperwork. But not keeping other travel documents in order is also a mistake. That means airline bookings, hotel reservations, car hire papers, and anything else you've booked ahead.

Whether you keep them in a digital wallet on your phone or in paper form, keeping them together so you know where everything is will help you from frantic searching every time you need something. Keep scanned copies of all documents as a backup; put them on a USB stick and keep it with your passport. Remember to also leave a copy of your itinerary, your passport photo page, and any other documents at home as a backup in case of emergency.

Getting Tired and Emotional

Exhaustion or too much alcohol — or a combination of the two is a recipe for disaster. Both can affect your judgment and potentially put you in danger. In many situations when traveling solo, you need to stay alert and aware of your surroundings. If you are under the influence of drink or drugs, you're not going to be in a position to help yourself get out of any sticky situations.

Getting enough sleep is also important. Aside from jetlag, it's a good idea to be as well rested as you can be. Travel is tiring at the best of times, so don't let yourself get run down. It can also lead to illness and that will certainly ruin your plans.

TIP

Don't listen to music through headphones or talk on your phone while walking. You won't be fully aware of what's going on around you and may be a target for thieves.

Not Asking for Help When You Need It

If you're confident enough to travel solo, you might be tempted to think you don't need help and should cope with any eventuality alone. It's not true — everyone needs others from time to time. In fact, you should be starting to ask for help while still planning your trip. Ask for advice from friends and family members who may have visited the place(s) you are going. They'll love to share their tips with you, just as I am doing! Check out social media sites and pick up ideas and tips there too.

TIP

Before you get too deep into planning, look at your government's advisories for your destination. It's the best advice you can get about current conditions — and take note of any do-not-travel advisories as they may affect your travel insurance validity.

REMEMBER

While you're on the road, never hesitate to ask for help if you feel you are being threatened or are in danger. Take refuge in hotels, restaurants, and shops, and ask for assistance. In bars, alert the staff if you are being harassed or need help to get back to your accommodation safely; they are usually trained to help.

Chapter **12**

Ten Great Destinations for Solo Travelers

Choosing a destination as a solo traveler is never too difficult. You'll have your wishlist, just as I have mine. But sometimes all it takes is someone else to spark your interest about a place you've not considered before. And then the question is — is it right for me as a solo traveler?

Most avid travelers need little prompting to name their bucket list destinations, places they've always aspired to get to but haven't quite made it yet. But sometimes, you'll hear someone talking about a place you've never considered, and it can turn that list upside down — or just make it longer! Mine certainly keeps getting longer, currently adding to my long-standing dream of the Galapagos Islands by seriously dreaming about Egypt, Iceland, and a few lesser-known Pacific islands.

In this chapter, I share some of my personal favorite places I've traveled solo, had a wonderful time in, and had few worries about my safety. But I've also applied a few key criteria — safety, affordability, and friendliness of the locals among them — that apply to any destination you might choose. If none of my ideas appeal to you, there's another way of picking your next destination. So, go on — spin the globe and see where your finger lands! Then do some research.

No destination is perfect. What is great for one solo traveler might not work for another. Everywhere offers something different, and it's up to you to find what's a good fit for you and your style of solo travel.

Australia

www.australia.com

Heading down under might seem a long haul if you live in the northern hemisphere, but it's well worth the jetlag! Apart from the weird and wonderful wildlife, there are no language problems (except for the slang, which you'll pick up quickly).

Australia is huge and diverse. Whether you decide to hang out in Sydney and soak up the city life and harbor views, or head to the Outback, Australia has plenty of budget accommodation, reasonable (but sometimes expensive) transport options, and lots of free attractions and activities. Australians are friendly and sociable, so meeting new people will be a breeze. Most travelers will start exploring in Sydney, with its stunning Opera House (Figure 12-1), but don't miss at least one trip to the Outback, and try to include the magnificent monolith of Uluru on your itinerary, along with some First Nations experiences.

Lee Mylne(Author)

FIGURE 12-1: The Sydney Opera House, Australia.

TIP

There are opportunities for extended stays through the **Work and Holiday Visa** and **Working Holiday Visa** schemes (https://immi.homeaffairs.gov.au/visas/getting-a-visa/visa-listing/) that allow you to combine travel with work if you are between 18 and 30 or 35 years old (depending on your citizenship).

Austria

www.austria.info

If I had to pick just one European destination to visit solo, it would be Austria. Not only is it incredibly beautiful, it is rich in culture and very safe. While you might start by exploring the major cities, Vienna, Salzburg, and Innsbruck, it's also worth striking out to places like Graz and Bad Ischl.

There are beautiful hotels to stay in, if your budget allows, but also plenty of hostels where you can meet up with other travelers. Getting around is easy by train and bus, and English is widely spoken.

Music lovers will find concerts, opera, and musical history everywhere, and if you are looking for active adventures, there is skiing, snowboarding, hiking, or cycling.

Did I mention strudel and schnitzel? And good coffee? And *The Sound of Music*? These are a few of my favorite things. . .

Finland

www.visitfinland.com

From the capital Helsinki to the wilds of Finnish Lapland, friendly Finns will make solo travelers feel welcome. Most Finns speak English, making it an easy place to get around and it's easy to meet people — just head to a sauna (there are around three million of them) and you'll be sure to strike up a conversation.

In Helsinki, you'll find wonderful architecture, museums, parks, markets, and more — all easily reached on foot or by public transport — but don't ignore the smaller places like Finland's oldest city Turku, with its medieval castle (an easy train ride from the capital), and Porvoo, with its lovely cobbled streets. While it may be best to go to "The Land of the Midnight Sun" in the summer, visit during the winter to try your luck at seeing the spectacle of the Aurora Borealis (Northern Lights). If, like me, you don't get lucky, it's all the more reason for a return visit sometime! The northern city of Rovaniemi is home to Santa Claus's Village, and there are plenty of activities including dog sledding, skiing, and snowboarding. In Lapland, you can also stay in a glass igloo (Figure 12-2).

Lee Mylne(Author)

FIGURE 12-2: Glass igloos in Lapland provide a unique form of accommodation.

There's a reason why Finland is regularly named the happiest country on Earth by the **World Happiness Report** (www.world happiness.report). Go there and see for yourself.

TIP

Ireland

www.ireland.com

I spent a week road-tripping solo around the south-west corner of Ireland and loved every minute of it. There was never a chance of getting lonely, as the Irish love a chat. In a crowded pub in Limerick, I found myself drawn into a table of friends who couldn't bear to see me alone and the *craic* (news/gossip) was flowing. When I left, I had the name of someone's cousin to look up in Dingle, my next stop.

Ireland is a relatively safe place to travel solo, but of course the same precautions you should take anywhere apply, especially for solo women travelers or if you are in major cities. While drinking in an Irish pub — especially one with live Celtic music — is one experience you definitely don't want to miss, keep things in moderation (and don't forget to offer to buy drinks for new friends).

Best advice: Get out of the big cities and into the countryside for a more laid-back experience and stunning scenery. Even in the most isolated spots along the coastline (I drove the drop-dead-gorgeous Wild Atlantic Way), you'll usually find someone to chat with. One of my most memorable conversations was with a farmer called Jim who was walking his dog near a remote lighthouse in Ireland's southwest. He shook his head in disbelief that I'd traveled across the world to be there. While language is never a problem for English-speakers, sometimes the accent can be bewildering.

Japan

www.japan.travel

So many things about Japan are perfect for solo travelers, because being alone — including eating alone — are accepted as the norm in most places. In Japanese restaurants and bars, solo diners often outnumber groups so you are unlikely to feel out of place at your table for one (and some of them are designed that way).

Japan is known for its hospitality and safety. Add to that a terrifically efficient, affordable, and user-friendly public transport system.

Solo travelers can relax in the knowledge that crime rates are low, even in bustling Tokyo, and if the city is overwhelming there are plenty of options to get away from it all. Kyoto is a calmer option, with temples, shrines, and peaceful gardens to explore. Take part in a tea ceremony, soak in an onsen, and stay in a traditional ryokan. Ski bunnies will find some of the world's best slopes in Japan, and hikers will love the chance for some forest bathing.

Accommodation can be expensive, but there are plenty of budget hotels and hostels. To immerse yourself in Japanese culture, book into a *minpaku* (homestay) which will usually be cheaper than a hotel and will enable you to meet the locals. If you're not claustrophobic, a sleeping pod might be a good budget choice. Looking for something different? Try a Japanese temple stay or *shukubo*.

Language can be an issue, but sign language, lots of smiles, and a willingness to help (or find someone who can) go a long way to making this a good choice of Asian destination for solos.

New Zealand

www.newzealand.com

Renowned as one of the most beautiful and safest countries in the world, Aotearoa New Zealand — the Land of the Long White Cloud — is hard to beat. Okay, you're right down at the bottom of the world, but there are definite advantages in that, once you're over the jetlag. Dazzling scenery, Maori culture, fantastic food, towering ancient kauri trees, fascinating fauna, and plenty of adventure sports are just some of its many attractions.

Queenstown is the adventure capital, with bungee jumping, whitewater rafting, jetboating, skydiving, and more, all activities that you can sign up for solo or join a group. Everywhere you go offers spectacular scenery. From fiords and rainforests to glaciers and glow worm caves, and from whale- and dolphin-watching tours to biking or hiking, there's plenty to see and do. Don't limit yourself to one island (there are three), but explore as much as time (and your visa) allows. Wineries abound, and you can even visit the movie set of *The Hobbit* (by guided tour only), pictured in Figure 12-3, for something completely different. According to the 2022 Global Peace Index, New Zealand is the second most peaceful place in the world (after Iceland), so what better reason to visit?

New Zealand is great for road-tripping. I like the freedom of a rental car but the inter-city buses will take you anywhere you want to go. Don't miss the geothermal region of the North Island, around Rotorua and Taupo, where you can kayak on the lakes and soak in the thermal springs.

Lee Mylne(Author)

FIGURE 12-3: Hobbiton, on New Zealand's North Island, is the movie set village that is now a major attraction.

TIP

Most people start their visit in Auckland and go south, but in doing so miss the stunning region of Northland, home to some of New Zealand's most historic places.

Scotland

www.visitscotland.com

Whether you're from London, Los Angeles, or latitudes south, Scotland is a perfect place to enjoy solitary sojourns. Wild and wonderful landscapes, outdoor adventures, and plenty of history will keep you busy. Head to the Highlands or discover the Lowlands, go "Nessie hunting" on the famous loch, or wander the streets of Edinburgh.

It's a safe and welcoming place to travel solo, even if the accent is sometimes baffling. There's a lively hostel scene, or you can pick up other budget accommodation at B&Bs or budget hotels. Lonely lighthouses, ancient inns, homestays, and converted castles provide varied accommodation, and there is always someone ready for a chat. If you're a golfer, head to the world's oldest golf course,

St. Andrews, or choose from more than 570 courses to tee off from. Whether you are road-tripping or hiking, the scenery is stunning, from the stark islands off the coast to the Cairngorm mountains.

There are excellent rail networks, buses, and ferries, and the major cities of Glasgow and Edinburgh have great public transport. If you want to go beyond them, head to the less-crowded cities of Dundee and Inverness.

Throw in whiskey distilleries, forest bathing, yoga retreats, restaurants, museums, and more, and you'll never be short of something to do.

Singapore

www.visitsingapore.com

Clean and surprisingly green, Singapore packs a punch for such a tiny island city-state. Often seen as only a stopover on the way to somewhere else, Singapore is underrated as a destination in its own right and is a great place for solo travelers on their first trip to Asia. Everyone is used to tourists and most signage is in English. Whether you're looking for good shopping, temples, orchid gardens, or resort life, you'll find it here.

Solo travelers are spoiled for choice when eating out, from night markets to smart restaurants and bars on River Quay and Clarke Quay. It's hard to beat cocktails at the top of Marina Bay Sands Skypark Observation Deck for the view! Don't miss an evening at Gardens by the Bay, where a light and sound show happens twice every night among the Supertree structures.

Singapore is clean and safe and well-ordered, and there's a lot to do and see. Public transport is excellent, with MRT trains serving most of the main attractions, and there's great shopping. Accommodations are easy to find, from Airbnb to hostels or budget hotels — or you could splash out and book at room at Raffles for some colonial grandeur.

Thailand

www.tourismthailand.org

There's a reason why Thailand is called the "land of a thousand smiles," as you'll soon find out. Thais are wonderfully friendly, and nothing is too much trouble for them. As a solo traveler, you'll always find someone keen for a chat or to help you if you need it. There are also lots of tourists in Thailand, so it's easy to meet fellow travelers, too.

Solo travelers might have to fend off a few hawkers and scammers on the streets of Bangkok, but Thailand has a lot going for it. As well as being a truly affordable destination, it has delicious street food, great nightlife (if that's your thing), and culture in spades. Bangkok's public transport is easy to navigate, with plenty of options, from trains, subways, buses, taxis, and tuk-tuks — or just jump aboard a *songthaew* (truck) with the locals. If you're short on time and want to fly, budget carriers operate within the country.

WARNING

You may be dicing with danger if you hire a scooter to get around in Bangkok or other cities. They are cheap, but the traffic is crazy, and you need to be an experienced rider and hold an International Driving Permit.

Backpackers love Thailand, but you don't need to stick to hostels, as it's easy to find good, reasonably priced hotels. Spend some alone time in a Thai spa or head to the beach; try Phuket, Krabi, or the Phi Phi Islands. The northern cities of Chiang Mai and Chiang Rai are also worth visiting for rural life and temples such as the amazing white Wat Rong Khun (see Figure 12-4). Head to Thailand in mid-April for Songkran, the water festival which celebrates the Buddhist New Year with parades and street parties.

WARNING

Cannabis was legalized in Thailand in 2022, but if you plan to indulge, understand that you may not be getting a safe product. Be aware that all vaping is banned in Thailand.

FIGURE 12-4: Wat Rong Khun, the "white temple" near Chiang Rai, northern Thailand.

Vietnam

```
https://vietnam.travel/
```

Vietnam is one of my favorite places in Asia. If you're a first timer, there's a long list of must-see places: Hanoi, Ha Long Bay, Hoi An, Hue, and Ho Chi Minh City (Saigon). To explore further, places to consider are beach resort towns like Nha Trang and Mui Ne or the highlands of Sapa.

Solo travelers have little to worry about in Vietnam, aside from the usual precautions against petty theft, and locals are welcoming and friendly. Tourism is big business here and you'll generally find someone who speaks English. Hawkers might crowd you, but for the most part it's very safe, and with the usual precautions you can dodge opportunistic thieves, just as you would in any big city.

Vietnam is budget-friendly, with incredibly cheap and delicious food and well-priced accommodations. While it's not always easy to get around — the roads outside cities are terrible — there are trains and internal flights to get you from place to place if you don't want to join a tour. Public transport is basic, but you can reach most places by bus or train. In the cities, motorbike taxis are plentiful and cheap. Hiring a local guide is often a good idea, but don't even think of driving yourself anywhere!

TIP

Crossing the street in Hanoi or Ho Chi Minh City can seem an impossible task. The traffic never stops. The best way to cross (apart from at a pedestrian crossing) is to line yourself up with a local and when they step out, go with them. The traffic will part around you.

Be prepared to hear the Vietnam War referred to as the "American War" and take the time to visit the attractions that relate to the war, but also dive deeper into this fascinating country's history and culture.

Index

A

accidents, avoiding, 192–193
accommodations
  about, 119–120
  Airbnb, 130, 169
  budget for, 120–121
  before check-in, 122–123
  choosing, 120–123, 203
  cost of, 9
  couchsurfing, 131–132, 169
  homestays, 126–129, 170
  home-swapping, 130
  hostels, 17, 93, 123–125
  house-sitting, 131
  location for, 121–122
  monasteries, 136
  non-profit organizations, 132
  package holidays, 138–139
  pubs, 133–134
  resorts, 136–138
  safety and, 139–141
  temples, 134–136
  university rooms, 132–133
adapters, 90–92
adventure holidays
  about, 35
  choosing, 35–53
  hiking, 35–38
  horse-riding, 46–48
  running, 51–53
  sailing/cruising, 38–42
  skiing/snowboarding, 44–46
  two-wheeled, 41–44
  volunteering, 48–50

African Horseback Safaris
  (website), 48
Air New Zealand, 186
Airbnb, 130, 169
airlines
  lounges for, 64–65
  maximizing benefits with, 61–63
  reward programs, 60
  ticket scams, 113
airports
  amenities in, 64–65
  hotels in, 65
  size of, 27
alcohol
  health and, 189–191
  safety and, 170
  while dining, 156
All Women's Run (website), 53
Alliance Francaise (website), 166
Amphawa Floating Market
  (Samut Songkhram, Thailand),
  149, 150
Amsterdam, public transport in, 32
Antarctic Ice Marathon (website), 52
apps
  authenticator, 107
  Calm, 198
  cash-back, 28
  dating, 173, 178
  Headspace, 198
  ride-share, 179
  safety, 24
Aspen Gay Ski Week (website), 45
ATMs, 102, 104–105
Aussie House Sitters (website), 131

Australia
  dining in, 146
  as a recommended destination, 216
  travel advisories, 22
Australian Outback Marathon
    (website), 52
Austria, as a recommended
    destination, 217
authenticator app, 107
auto-connecting, to Wi-Fi, 107

B

Badoo, 173
Bangkok marathon (website), 51
bar, dining at the, 154
batteries, 91
Bauernmarkt Kaiser-Josef-Platz (Graz,
    Austria) (website), 152
B&Bs, 128–129
Berkshire Hathaway Travel Protection
    (BHTP), 25
Berlin, public transport in, 31
Berlitz (website), 165
The Big Five Marathon (website), 52
bike-share rentals, 34
bilum, 87
Biosphere Expeditions (website), 50
boarding pass, 110
body clock, 185. *See also* jetlag
bond against charges, in hotels, 101
Booking (website), 28
books, 93, 154, 155
Borough Market (London, England),
    148
Bryson, Bill
  Notes from a Small Island, 129
Buddhism, 161–162
budget
  about, 9–10
  for accommodations, 120–121

checking, 57
dining, 147–152
finding travel deals, 26–29
planning, 202
Bumble, 173
bus passes, 27
business cards, from hotels, 34

C

cafes, for meeting people, 168
Calm app, 198
Camino de Santiago (the Way of St.
    James), 35
Canada, travel advisories in, 22
cannabis, 223
car rentals, 193
card skimming, 116
carelessness, 211–212
cargo ship travel, 41–42
Cargo Ship Voyages (website), 42
Caribbean, 39
Carnival Cruise Line (website), 191
carry-my-bag scams, 114
carry-on luggage, 82
casa particular, in Cuba, 127
cash
  about, 100–101, 103
  for dining, 155
  exchange rates, 103–104
  traveler's checks, 105–106
cash-back apps, 28
catfishing, 178
Changi Airport (website), 65
chargers, 90–92
Chirpey app, 24
city cycle schemes, 196
Classic Safari Company (website), 47
cloud storage, 107
Club Med (website), 46, 137

codewords, for safety, 176
comfort zone, 206–207
communal tables, 147
compression cubes, 87–88
compression stockings, 184
contraceptives, 175
Convention on International Trade in Endangered Species, 98
cooking classes, 14, 158
Copenhagen, public transport in, 32
cost of living
  for destinations, 22
  of travel insurance, 67
couchsurfing, 131–132
Couchsurfing (website), 169
COVID, 188–189
craft breweries, 190
credit cards
  about, 100–101
  debit cards, 102
  prepaid travel money cards, 102
  for travel insurance, 69–71
  for travel rewards, 61
cruises
  alcohol-free, 191
  cruising holidays, 38–42
  deals on, 28
Cuba, 127
culinary experiences, as entertainment, 157–158
Cultural Atlas (website), 161
culture
  about, 205–206
  researching, 160–166
culture shock, 8–9
currency, when booking online, 29
customs
  dating, 171–172
  local, 57–58

Customs checks, 98–100
cycling tours, 42–44

D

data roaming, 107
date rape drugs, 176
dating, 171–174
dating apps, 178
Daybreaker (website), 190
debit cards, 102
decision fatigue, 198–199
deep vein thrombosis (DVT), 183–184
destinations
  choosing, 12–16, 20
  cost of living for, 22
  packing and, 85
  recommended, 215–225
  researching, 201–202
  revisiting favorite, 14–16
devices
  about, 95
  scams, 112–118
  setting up, 106–108
  silencing phones, 154
  staying in touch with home, 106–112
  while eating, 154
diarrhea, 187–188
dining
  about, 143–144
  avoiding unwanted company, 156–157
  budget, 147–152
  choosing a location for, 145–147
  cost of, 9
  culinary experiences as entertainment, 157–158
  fear of eating alone, 144–152
  street food, 147–152
  tips for, 152–156

documents, tracking, 213–214

Domino Volunteers (website), 50

dress
  conservative, 24
  importance of, 163–164
  religious, 24

drugs
  cannabis, 223
  date rape, 176
  safety and, 170

Dude Ranchers Association (website), 47

Duolingo (website), 164

E

earplugs, 121

Earth Watch (website), 50

EatWith (website), 146–147

"economy class syndrome," 183–184

electric scooters, 34, 193

emergency plans, creating, 71–72

emotion, 214

English Country Inns (website), 133

entertainment, culinary experiences as, 157–158

equipment, insurance for, 68–69

eSIM, 108

essentials, packing, 84–87

Estancia Los Potreros (website), 47

The European Nature Trust (website), 50

Everest Base Camp Marathon (website), 52

exchange rates, 57, 103–104

exercise, to combat loneliness, 195–197

Expedia (website), 61

expedition ships, 39–40

eye mask, 121

F

face masks, 186, 189

Facebook, 109–111

fake ticket scams, 116–117

family and friends
  reassuring, 78–79
  staying in touch with, 106–112

fear, mistakes with, 212–213

Federation of Association of Spanish Schools for Foreigners (website), 165

Ferry Plaza (San Francisco, USA), 151

Find Online icon, 3

find-my-device feature, 106

Finland, as a recommended destination, 217–218

First Nations culture, 205

first-aid kit, 183

flexibility, 27, 206

flight socks, 184

flip-flops, 186

FlyerTalk (website), 62

focus booths, 146

food tours, 14, 157–158

Free Tours by Foot (website), 167

freedom, embracing, 207

Freighter Trips (website), 42

friend-in need scams, 117

G

G Adventures (website), 128

gastrointestinal bugs, 187–188

Get Your Guide (website), 158

Global Greeters (website), 169

Gojek (website), 34

Google Authenticator, 107

Google Flights (website), 61

Google Maps, 33

Grasshopper Adventures (website), 43

Great Divide Trail (website), 36
Great Wall Marathon (website), 51
Grindr, 173, 177
group tours, 10, 25
Grumeti Fund, 52

H

hand-washing, 186
Happu, 173
Headspace app, 198
health. *See also* travel insurance
  about, 181
  accidents, 192–193
  alcohol and stimulants, 189–191
  checking requirements, 59
  COVID, 188–189
  decision fatigue, 198–199
  drinking water, 187
  "economy class syndrome," 183–184
  exercise, 196–197
  gastrointestinal bugs, 187–188
  getting help, 193–194
  hygiene, 186
  jetlag, 184–186
  loneliness, 194–196
  maintaining, 183–194
  managing emergencies, 72–73
  mindfulness, 197–198
  preparing to travel in good,
    182–183
  sexual, 191–192
health insurance, 68, 183
help, getting, 193–194, 214
HerHouse (website), 127
hiking holidays, 35–38
Hinduism, 162
Hinge, 173
Home Exchange (website), 130
Homestayin (website), 127

homestays
  about, 126–127
  B&Bs, 128–129
  finding, 127–128
Homestays (website), 127, 170
home-swapping, 130
Hong Kong, public transport in, 32
HOOKED Alcohol Free Travel
    Adventure (website), 190
Hopper (website), 62
horse-riding holidays, 46–48
Hosteling International (website), 125
hostels, 17, 93, 123–124, 125
Hostelworld (website), 125, 167
hotels
  airport, 65
  bond against charges, 101
House Carers (website), 131
House Sitters America (website), 131
house-sitting, 131
Human Dignity Trust (website), 176
hydration
  drinking water, 187
  jetlag and, 184
  oral rehydration solutions, 188
hygiene, 186

I

Iceland, 48
ICHIRAN ramen restaurant (website),
    146
icons, explained, 3
ID
  about, 95
  passports, 96–97
  scams, 112–118
  visas, 96, 97
Il Sasso (website), 166
Inca Trail, 36

Instagram, 111

Instituto Cervantes (website), 165

Instituto Cultural Oaxaca (website), 165

insurance. *See also* travel insurance

for equipment and tech gadgets, 68–69

health, 68, 183

warnings about, 69

InsureMyTrip (website), 67

International Certificate, 59

International Driving Permit (IDP), 193

International Electrotechnical Commission (website), 91

International Lesbian, Gay, Bisexual, Trans and Intersex Association (website), 177

Internet access, finding, 108–109

Intrepid Travel (website), 139

intuition, sex and, 177–179

Ireland, as a recommended destination, 218–219

italki, 164

J

Japan

dining in, 145–146

as a recommended destination, 219–220

Japan National Tourist Organization, 128

Jemaa el-Fna (Marrakesh, Morocco), 152

Jet Lag Rooster (website), 185

jetlag, 184–186

journaling, 198

K

Kayak (website), 61

Kiwi House Sitters (website), 131

Kowloon City Market (Hong Kong), 150

Kumano Kodo trail (website), 37–38

L

La Boqueria (Barcelona, Spain), 150–151

Land's End to John O'Groats (website), 36–37

language, learning, 17, 24, 58, 164–166

language barriers, 8–9

LastPass Authenticator, 107

Lau Pa Sat (Singapore), 148

laws, respecting local, 160–163

layovers, 63–66

Leading Ladies Marathon (website), 53

LGBTQIA+

Aspen Gay Ski Week, 45

customs and laws, 173

Grindr, 173

local laws and traditions, 163

misterbandb.com, 125

sex and, 176–177

light packing, 82–83

local customs, 57–58

local language, 58

local SIM card, 108

locals, listening to, 211

locations

choosing for accommodations, 121–122

choosing for dining, 145–147

logistics

about, 55–56

airlines, 61–63

checking health requirements, 59

creating an emergency plan, 71–72

lost luggage, 74–76

managing health emergencies, 72–73

maximizing travel rewards programs, 60–61

Mother Nature, 73–74

purchasing travel insurance, 66–69

reassuring loved ones, 78–79

research, 56–58

self-defense and street smarts, 76–78

transit time, 63–66

using credit card for insurance coverage, 69–71

loneliness, combating, 194–196

lost luggage, 74–76

Luang Prabang Half Marathon (website), 51

luggage

carry-on, 82

choosing, 83–84

lost, 74–76

secondary wallet/purse, 25

theft-proof bag, 25

traveling light, 28

luggage scale, 92

lunch, main meal for, 153

M

maps.me (website), 108

Mapway, 33

marathons, 51–52

MayDay app, 24

medications, 99

Mediterranean, 39

Meetup (website), 168

melatonin, 185

Mercado Central (Santiago, Chile), 151

Milford Track (website), 37

Mimi's (website), 146

Mind My House (website), 131

mindfulness, 197–198

minpaku, 128

minshuku, 129

mistakes to avoid, 209–214

misterbandb (website), 125

monasteries, for accommodations, 136

Monastery Stays (website), 136

money

about, 95

choosing credit or cash, 100–106

customs and taxes, 98–100

scams, 112–118

Montral Convention (1999), 75, 76

Moovit, 33

morality laws, 173–174

Mother Nature, insurance and, 73–74

motion sickness, 41

multi-day transport passes, for public transport, 33

Muslim countries, 162

N

Nakasendo Way (website), 37

Narita Airport, 65

natural disasters, 73–74

Navitime, 33

neck pillow, 93

New Zealand, as a recommended destination, 220–221

nightlife, 190

Nine Hours, 65

noise-canceling headphones, 92–93

non-profit organizations, 132

Noonlight app, 24

Norwegian Cruise Line (website), 191

Notes from a Small Island (Bryson), 129

O

OANDA (website), 104
Okavango Horse Safaris
    (website), 48
OKCupid, 173
Old Market Hall and Market Square
    (Helsinki, Finland), 148, 149
Oncore (website), 146
oneworld (website), 60
online booking, currency for, 29
open-top buses, 34
orphanage tourism, 50
Osaka International Women's
    Marathon (website), 53
overcharging scams, 116
Overland Track (website), 37
overpacking, 85–87
Overseas Adventure Travel (OAT)
    (website), 30

P

Pacific Northwest Trail (website), 36
package holidays, 138–139
packing
    about, 81–82
    benefits of light, 82–83
    choosing luggage, 83–84
    essentials, 84–87
    mistakes with, 210
    recommended items and gadgets,
        90–93
    saving space, 87–90
packing cubes/cells, 87–88
padlock, 93
Paradise Guest Ranch (website), 47
ParkRun (website), 196
passports, 96–97
Patagonia, 83–84
PayPal, 28

peak season, 21
people, meeting
    about, 17, 159, 195, 203
    dating, 171–174
    doing cultural homework, 160–166
    dress, 163–164
    LGBTQIA+ travelers, 176–177
    local language, 164–166
    respecting local laws/traditions,
        160–163
    safety and, 174–176
    sex, 170–180
    socializing, 166–170
    using your intuition, 177–179
    white lies, 179–180
personal information, sharing too
    much, 211
pharmacists, 182
phone
    setting up, 106–108
    silencing, 154
pimsleur, 164
Polar Circle Marathon (website), 52
politeness, 213
portable charger, 91
Prague, public transport in, 31
prepaid travel money cards, 102
preparation
    about, 19–20
    budget, 26–29
    choosing adventure holidays, 35–53
    choosing destinations, 20
    choosing time to travel, 21–22
    finding travel deals, 26–34
    safety, 23–26
    single supplement, 29–31
    travel advisories, 22–23
    using public transport, 31–34
product disclosure statement (PDS), 70

prostitution, 175

Pub Rooms (website), 133

public transport, 14, 31–34, 204–205

pubs

  for accommodation, 133–134

  for socializing, 168

Q

Queen Victoria Market (Melbourne, Australia), 151–152

R

Race for Life Marathon (website), 53

Ramadan, 162

The Ramblers, 38

RedZone app, 24

Registration of Canadians Abroad (website), 23, 79

relative-in-need scams, 117

Relief Riders International (website), 48

religious dress, 161

religious holidays, 58

Remember icon, 3

research

  about, 56–58

  culture, 160–166

  destinations, 201–202

  importance of, 210

Research and Innovation in the Serengeti Ecosystem (RISE), 52

reservations, at restaurants, 153

resort holidays, 136–138

Restaurant Hubert, 146

rewards programs, maximizing, 60–61

RFID-blocking wallet, 93

ride-share apps, 179

river cruising, 28

road rules, 26

Rome2Rio (website), 27

The Rover (website), 146

Rubicon 3 Adventure (website), 39

running holidays, 51–53

S

Safer Sounds (website), 176

safety

  about, 11, 23–26

  in accommodations, 139–141

  alcohol and drugs, 170

  apps for, 24

  of belongings while eating, 155

  making a priority, 204

  sex and, 174–176

sailing holidays, 38–42

sarong, 93, 161

Save the Children, 50

scalpers, 117

scams, 112–118

Scotland, as a recommended destination, 221–222

seasickness, 41

seasonal events, 21

Seat Guru (website), 63

secondary wallet/purse, 25

self-defense, 25, 76–78

Serengeti Girls Run (website), 52

service charge, 156

sex

  about, 170–171

  dating, 171–174

  intuition and, 177–179

  LGBTI+ and, 176–177

  safety and, 174–176

  white lies and, 179–180

sex work, 175

sexual health, 191–192

sexually transmitted diseases (STDs), 174–176

sexually transmitted infections (STIs), 174–176, 191–192

Shanghai, public transport in, 32

shawl, 161

shoes, 24, 164

Show Around (website), 169

shukubo, 135

SIM card, 108

Singapore
  public transport in, 32
  as a recommended destination, 222

Singita (website), 52

single supplement, 29–31

skiing holidays, 44–46

Skyscanner (website), 26–27, 61

SkyTeam (website), 60

Skytrax (website), 62

Sleep Lounges (website), 65

SlowTravel (website), 42

A Small World (website), 168

Smart Traveler Enrollment Program (STEP) (website), 23, 78–79

Smart Traveller (website), 79

SmartTraveller (website), 23

smiling, 166

sniffer dogs, 98

snowboarding holidays, 44–46

Sober Sensations (website), 190

social media, 109–112

socializing, 166–170

Solo Female Travelers, 25, 111

solo travel
  about, 5
  choosing destinations for, 12–16
  encountering others during, 17
  pros and cons of, 6–11

The Solo Female Traveler Network, 25, 111

souvenirs, shipping back home, 89

space-saving, when packing, 87–90

Special Broadcasting Service (SBS), 161

St. Lawrence (Toronto, Canada), 149

Star Alliance (website), 60

Stay In A Pub (website), 133

Stay Japan (website), 128

stimulants, health and, 189–191

Stockholm, public transport in, 32

stopover options, 27

street food, 147–152

street smarts, 76–78

supermarkets, 14

T

table reservations, at restaurants, 153

Taipei, public transport in, 32

tall ship voyages, 39

Tandem (website), 165

taxes, 98–100

taxi scams, 114–115

tech gadgets, 68–69, 90–92

temples, for accommodations, 134–136

Templestay (website), 134–135

Thailand, as a recommended destination, 223–224

theft-proof bag, 25

Thelma and Louise Marathon (website), 53

thermal baths, 190

3 Marathons in 3 Days (website), 51–52

time, for dining, 153–154

Time Out (magazine), 31

times to travel, choosing, 21–22

Timeshifter (website), 185

Tinder, 173, 177

Tip icon, 3

tipping, 156, 163
tiredness, 214
Tokyo, public transport in, 32
The Tongariro Crossing (website), 38
tour companies, 28, 29–30
Tourlina (website), 25, 168
Tours by Locals (website), 169
traditions, respecting local, 160–163
train passes, 27
Trans Dinarica (website), 43–44
transgender people, 176–177
transit time, 63–66
transit tour, 65
travel advisories, 22–23
travel dates, flexibility with, 27
travel deals, finding, 26–34
travel insurance. *See also* health
  about, 204
  creating an emergency plan, 71–72
  lost luggage, 74–76
  managing health emergencies,
    72–73
  Mother Nature and, 73–74
  purchasing, 66–69
  self-defense and street smarts,
    76–78
  using credit card for, 69–71
travel money cards, 102
travel rewards programs, maximizing,
  60–61
traveler's checks, 105–106
Travelling Fit (website), 51
TripAdvisor (website), 62
Tripwhistle app, 24
truffle-hunting, 158
Trusted Housesitters (website), 131
trustworthiness, 211–212
Tsukiki Fish Market (Tokyo, Japan), 151
Two's a Crowd (website), 30

two-step verification, 107
two-wheeled holidays, 41–44
Tzu, Lao, 38

U

Uber, 33, 34
UK, travel advisories in, 22
universal adapter, 91
University Rooms (website), 132–133
unwanted company, while dining,
  156–157
U.S. Centers for Disease Control and
  Prevention (CDC), 174, 188, 191
U.S. State Department (website), 97
USA, travel advisories in, 22
USB charging stations, 109

V

vaccination records, 99–100, 189
vaccinations, 175, 182, 188, 192
vehicle hire scams, 115
victim, of scams, 118
Vietnam, 14–16, 224–225
virtual private network (VPN), 107
visas
  about, 96
  choosing, 97
  regulations for, 56–57
  scams with, 113–114
volunteering holidays, 48–50
voluntourism, 49

W

walking tours, 13, 167
Warning icon, 3
Warsaw Convention (1929), 75, 76
water, drinking, 187

water bottle, 93

We Love Lucid (website), 190

websites

African Horseback Safaris, 48

Airbnb, 169

airport facilities and sleeping options, 65

alcohol and drug use, 161

All Women's Run, 53

Alliance Francaise, 166

Amphawa Floating Market (Samut Songkhram, Thailand), 149, 150

Antarctic Ice Marathon, 52

Aspen Gay Ski Week, 45

Aussie House Sitters, 131

Australia, 216

Australian Outback Marathon, 52

Austria, 217

Bangkok marathon, 51

Bauernmarkt Kaiser-Josef-Platz (Graz, Austria), 152

B&Bs, 128

Berlitz, 165

The Big Five Marathon, 52

Biosphere Expeditions, 50

Booking, 28

Borough Market (London, England), 148

Cargo Ship Voyages, 42

Carnival Cruise Line, 191

casa particular, in Cuba, 127

Changi Airport, 65

Classic Safari Company, 47

Club Med, 46, 137

couchsurfing, 131, 169

Cultural Atlas, 161

Daybreaker, 190

Domino Volunteers, 50

Dude Ranchers Association, 47

Duolingo, 164

Earth Watch, 50

EatWith, 146–147

English Country Inns, 133

Estancia Los Potreros, 47

The European Nature Trust, 50

Everest Base Camp Marathon, 52

Expedia, 61

Federation of Association of Spanish Schools for Foreigners, 165

female-focused, 25

Ferry Plaza (San Francisco, USA), 151

Finland, 217

FlyerTalk, 62

Free Tours by Foot, 167

Freighter Trips, 42

G Adventures, 128

Get Your Guide, 158

Global Greeters, 169

Gojek, 34

Google Flights, 61

Grasshopper Adventures, 43

Great Divide Trail, 36

Great Wall Marathon, 51

HerHouse, 127

Homestayin, 127

Homestays, 127, 170

HOOKED Alcohol Free Travel Adventure, 190

Hopper, 62

Hosteling International, 125

Hostelworld, 125, 167

House Carers, 131

House Sitters America, 131

Human Dignity Trust, 176

Iceland, 48

ICHIRAN ramen restaurant, 146

Il Sasso, 166

Instituto Cervantes, 165

Instituto Cultural Oaxaca, 165

InsureMyTrip, 67

International Electrotechnical Commission, 91

International Lesbian, Gay, Bisexual, Trans and Intersex Association, 177

Intrepid Travel, 139

Ireland, 218–219

italki, 164

Japan, 219

Jemaa el-Fna (Marrakesh, Morocco), 152

Jet Lag Rooster, 185

Kayak, 61

Kiwi House Sitters, 131

Kowloon City Market (Hong Kong), 150

Kumano Kodo trail, 37–38

La Boqueria (Barcelona, Spain), 150–151

Land's End to John O'Groats, 36–37

Lau Pa Sat (Singapore), 148

Leading Ladies Marathon, 53

Luang Prabang Half Marathon, 51

maps.me, 108

Meetup, 168

Mercado Central (Santiago, Chile), 151

Milford Track, 37

Mimi's, 146

Mind My House, 131

misterbandb, 125

Monastery Stays, 136

Nakasendo Way, 37

New Zealand, 220

Norwegian Cruise Line, 191

OANDA, 104

Okavango Horse Safaris, 48

Old Market Hall and Market Square (Helsinki, Finland), 148, 149

Oncore, 146

oneworld, 60

Osaka International Women's Marathon, 53

Overland Track, 37

Overseas Adventure Travel (OAT), 30

Pacific Northwest Trail, 36

Paradise Guest Ranch, 47

ParkRun, 196

pimsleur, 164

Polar Circle Marathon, 52

Pub Rooms, 133

Queen Victoria Market (Melbourne, Australia), 151–152

Race for Life Marathon, 53

Registration of Canadians Abroad, 23, 79

Relief Riders International, 48

Rome2Rio, 27

The Rover, 146

Rubicon 3 Adventure, 39

Safer Sounds, 176

Scotland, 221

Seat Guru, 63

Serengeti Girls Run, 52

Show Around, 169

shukubo, 135

Singapore, 222

Singita, 52

Skyscanner, 26, 61

SkyTeam, 60

Skytrax, 62

Sleep Lounges, 65

SlowTravel, 42

A Small World, 168

Smart Traveler Enrollment Program (STEP), 23, 78–79

Smart Traveller, 79

SmartTraveller, 23

websites *(continued)*

Sober Sensations, 190

St. Lawrence (Toronto, Canada), 149

Star Alliance, 60

Stay In A Pub, 133

Stay Japan, 128

Tandem, 165

Templestay, 134

Thailand, 223

Thelma and Louise Marathon, 53

3 Marathons in 3 Days, 51–52

Timeshifter, 185

The Tongariro Crossing, 38

Tourlina, 168

Tours by Locals, 169

Trans Dinarica, 43–44

Travelling Fit, 51

TripAdvisor, 62

Trusted Housesitters, 131

Tsukiki Fish Market (Tokyo, Japan), 151

Two's a Crowd, 30

University Rooms, 132

U.S. State Department, 97

Vietnam, 224

We Love Lucid, 190

West Highland Way, 37

WiFi Map, 109

Winter Rendezvous, 46

Work and Holiday Visa and Working Holiday Visa schemes, 217

World Expeditions, 48–49

World Happiness Report, 218

Worn Wear, 83–84

Xe, 104

YMCA, 132

Yunnan Noodle Shack, 145–146

wedding ring, 24

West Highland Way (website), 37

white lies, sex and, 179–180

Whitsunday region, 39

Wi-Fi

auto-connecting to, 107

finding, 108–109

WiFi Map (website), 109

wildfires, 74

window tables, at restaurants, 154

Winter Rendezvous (website), 46

Work and Holiday Visa and Working Holiday Visa schemes (website), 217

World Expeditions (website), 48–49

World Happiness Report (website), 218

Worn Wear (website), 83–84

wrong change scams, 116

X

Xe (website), 104

Y

Yellow Card, 59

YMCA (website), 132

Yunnan Noodle Shack (website), 145–146

YWCA Hotels, 132

About the Author

Lee Mylne is a passionate traveler who loves sharing her experiences with others. Born in New Zealand and a long-time resident of Australia, she's been traveling the world for most of her adult life and never tires of it. She's lived in six countries on four continents but now calls Brisbane, Australia, home. She's spent the past 30-something years specializing in travel and tourism, writing for magazines, newspapers, digital, and online publications, and is the author or co-author of around a dozen guide books, including *Australia For Dummies* (2008).

Lee is a Life Member of the Australian Society of Travel Writers, and served three terms as the society's president. She holds a Doctor of Creative Industries degree from Queensland University of Technology in Brisbane. Learn more at www. leemylne.com and on her blog A Glass Half Full. Yep, you got it . . . she's a born optimist!

Dedication

This book is dedicated to my dear friend Julie Hampson, who was my roommate on a tour of Europe that I undertook as a young solo traveler many years ago. Our enduring friendship speaks to one of the richest rewards that solo travel can bring, sometimes when you least expect it.

Author's Acknowledgments

Many people help to make a book like this come to fruition. First, I would like to thank Kelly Regan for putting forward my name for this project (and for keeping in touch remotely for all these years). And thank you, too, to Myka Carroll and Vicki Adang for guiding me through the early stages of getting back into the swing of writing a Dummies book!

The entire team at Wiley were helpful and supportive every step of the way — thank you in particular to Jennifer Yee and Chrissy Guthrie for your trust, confidence, and encouragement as

I worked on the other side of the world, and to Jennifer Connolly for her meticulous editing.

Many thanks to Keren Lavelle, who was not only the first editor to commission me to write a travel book, many years ago, but who lent her own knowledge and experience as a solo traveler to the role of technical editor on this book.

Several other solo travelers helped me with ideas and inspiration for sections of this book. My thanks to ski expert Flip Byrnes, the very fit Fiona Harper for her tips on great destinations for runners, and to Julie Miller for ideas for those looking for horse-riding experiences. Christine Retschlag offered some sage advice on dating as a solo traveler, and Urlys Mitchell shared her experiences as a house-sitter.

On my solo travels, I have met many fascinating people who have shared their stories with me, made me think, and encouraged me to step outside my comfort zone — again and again. They are too numerous to name (and in some cases I don't remember — or never knew — their names), but they all had an impact and I thank them all.

Heartfelt thanks, too, to my personal support team: Glen Cameron, Angelika Larcher, and Julie McGlone, who have kept me buoyant even when the going got tough during the writing of this book. And to my daughters, Sophie and Jess, who provided the reason to leave my desk for family time.

Publisher's Acknowledgments

Senior Acquisitions Editor: Jennifer Yee

Project Manager and Development Editor: Christina Guthrie

Copy Editor: Jennifer Connolly

Technical Editor: Keren Lavelle

Managing Editor: Kristie Pyles

Production Editor: Saikarthick Kumarasamy

Cover Image: Text: © procurator/ Getty Images

Jet: © Anatolii Frolov/Getty Images

Luggage Tag: © RLT_Images/Getty Images

PERSONAL ENRICHMENT

Staying Sharp	**Facebook**	**Guitar**	**Investing**	**Beekeeping**	**Digital Photography**
9781119187790	9781119179030	9781119293354	9781119293347	9781119310068	9781119235606
USA $26.00	USA $21.99	USA $24.99	USA $22.99	USA $22.99	USA $24.99
CAN $31.99	CAN $25.99	CAN $29.99	CAN $27.99	CAN $27.99	CAN $29.99
UK £19.99	UK £16.99	UK £17.99	UK £16.99	UK £16.99	UK £17.99

Meditation	**Pregnancy**	**Samsung Galaxy S7**	**iPhone**	**Crocheting**	**Nutrition**
9781119251163	9781119235491	9781119279952	9781119283133	9781119287117	9781119130246
USA $24.99	USA $26.99	USA $24.99	USA $24.99	USA $24.99	USA $22.99
CAN $29.99	CAN $31.99	CAN $29.99	CAN $29.99	CAN $29.99	CAN $27.99
UK £17.99	UK £19.99	UK £17.99	UK £17.99	UK £16.99	UK £16.99

PROFESSIONAL DEVELOPMENT

Windows 10	**AutoCAD**	**Excel 2016**	**QuickBooks 2017**	**macOS Sierra**	**LinkedIn**	**Windows 10**
9781119311041	9781119255796	9781119293439	9781119281467	9781119280651	9781119251132	9781119310562
USA $24.99	USA $39.99	USA $26.99	USA $26.99	USA $29.99	USA $24.99	USA $34.00
CAN $29.99	CAN $47.99	CAN $31.99	CAN $31.99	CAN $35.99	CAN $29.99	CAN $41.99
UK £17.99	UK £27.99	UK £19.99	UK £19.99	UK £21.99	UK £17.99	UK £24.99

SharePoint 2016	**Fundamental Analysis**	**Networking**	**Office 2016**	**Office 365**	**Salesforce.com**	**Coding**
9781119181705	9781119263593	9781119257769	9781119293477	9781119265313	9781119239314	9781119293332
USA $29.99	USA $26.99	USA $29.99	USA $26.99	USA $24.99	USA $29.99	USA $29.99
CAN $35.99	CAN $31.99	CAN $35.99	CAN $31.99	CAN $29.99	CAN $35.99	CAN $35.99
UK £21.99	UK £19.99	UK £21.99	UK £19.99	UK £17.99	UK £21.99	UK £21.99